One Barrel At A Time

Mapping A Route Across

The Prison Recidivism Desert

JACK CARMICHAEL

DIAMOND MEDIA PRESS CO.
1-304-273-6157
https://www.diamondmediapressco.com/

ISBN Paperback: 9781951302580

Contents

The following individuals were supportive of my efforts as a chaplain and an author:

Harold Green, Colby Smith,

Way McKibbin, Len Santos,

Tony Warnakula, M. Mullin, K.

Prosper, W. and L. Loucks, B.

Steele, G. Palmer, P. Schlepy, CJ

Williams IV, Ciharles Turner,

Todd Bouey, Mike Stillman,

Matt Haff, Gene Beer,

Frank Katanic, R. Barnes, and Jim Papen.

I have also had the undying support of my bride, Judy Carmichael.

.

An Introduction

In late 2002 I embarked on a journey of thousands of barrels that led to the mapping of a road to reduce the recidivism rate at a California state prison. I started this adventure after more than fifty years of ministry.

My professional ministry began when I graduated from seminary in May 19 52. Within two months after graduating, I was sworn into the army chaplaincy by the Sixth Army chaplain at the Presidio of San Francisco. Three days later, I reported to Camp Stoneman, California, one of the embarkation centers for troops going to Korea. I served there for approximately eight months when I received orders to go to Korea. My service in Korea covered the transition from fighting to peacekeeping.

After completing my tour I was assigned to the 82nd Airborne Division at Fort Bragg, North Carolina. After completing my jump training, I was assigned to the division headquarters chapel to serve with the division chaplain. I subsequently was assigned to different infantry regiments as a regimental chaplain. During that time I earned my Master Jump wings, with a total of sixty-six jumps. After five years, I was released from the army to the army reserve.

Upon release from the army, my wife and I decided to plant a church in eastern Carolina, approximately a hundred miles north of Fort Bragg. I served there for three years, during which time I earned a master of science degree in rehabilitation counseling from North Carolina State University.

During my time there, a graduate of Ohio University got acquainted with me and wrote his senior professor, telling him that I would be a great candidate for the PhD program in counseling. After receiving my credentials, they offered me a teaching graduate assistantship. I moved with my wife and two girls to embark on an unforeseen adventure.

I studied for two years and was completing my dissertation when the Peace

Corps, in its second year of existence, awarded Ohio University a Peace Corps project in West Cameroon, West Africa. Since it was a jointly administered project at that time, the university had a field position for an overseas university representative. I was selected and departed for West Cameroon in September 1962, as supervisor of forty Peace Corps secondary school teachers.

Upon returning to the States after a tour of the Near East, Western Europe, and Scandinavia, I took a position in a midwestern church college as their first dean of students. After two years I discovered that I had grown beyond the lifestyle restrictions of my childhood's denomination and felt I was more suited for a public university.

In 1966, I was employed at Central Missouri State University in Warrensburg, Missouri, which is fifty miles east of Kansas City, as their first director of admissions. There were approximately ten thousand students enrolled, and I was privileged to develop new admission standards and practices for more than five thousand applicants received each year.

After two years, I felt I was not having an opportunity to be as creative as I wanted to be, and one of my friends recommended me to an independent midwestern church college. They were looking for someone to organize the student personnel functions of the college as a single unit. I took a leave of absence for a year from Central Missouri and went there to organize that student personnel program.

After a year, I returned to Central Missouri as a licensed psychologist in the University Counseling Center. In the summer of 1970, two student leaders, who had been expelled by the university for leading a sit-in regarding university policies connected with Vietnam, filed a stay of reinstatement with the Sixth District Court. The court ordered the university to reinstate the students in their leadership roles. The previous assistant to the president had advised the university to take this road and he resigned and moved to a public school administrative position.

I was offered the position of Student Ombudsman and Assistant to the President. In addition to my ombudsman responsibilities, I was responsible for the government grant program of the university. Fortunately, I negotiated the traps of working with student leaders and was successful in organizing the grants program. Over the years I was also appointed the first director of development for the university. With the assistance of the university attorney, we developed the Central Missouri University Foundation} a 401c3 charitable foundation} which could accept charitable gifts to the university. Ultimately, we developed a superb planned giving program. After twenty-three years the president retired, and a new president came. He was not happy with me, so I decided to move on.

During my time as assistant to the president, I also served as senior pastor of a United Methodist church, located one mile outside the North Gate of Whiteman Air Force Base. It was a missile base. It was a rewarding weekend experience to have a ministry weekend after the workweek at the university. The weekend ministry provided me with emotional and spiritual energy that improved my work performance at the university.

Northern Colorado State University at Greeley, Colorado, hir,ed me as their first director of development. During my first year, I developed an extensive alumni phone-athon program, where we enlisted hundreds of new donors for the university. We used different social and academic organizations as phone volunteers. During this year, I also served as the pastor of a United Methodist church in the bedroom community of Greeley, with a population of approximately 5,500.

One of my friends called me and told me that there was a Congregational church in Paradise, California, that was open. The mother of my children and I decided that this was an ultimate dream for us to be able to pastor a church. We applied, and I served as their pastor for seventeen years. I retired in 2001. During my tenure at the church, the mother of my children died of breast cancer. I married my Judy in August 2000.

One of the programs we developed in the church was a five-nights-a-week offering of twelve-step rehabilitation programming. It was ,conducted by different traditional twelve-step programs. We were known as the "twelve-step church."

I had long recognized that upon my retirement from the church, I would need to move to a new community; I would have been a pain the neck for the new pastor. Since Judy's childhood home was at Honey Lake Valley in the greater Susanville area in California, we moved to nearby Janesville.

After several months in retirement, I realized I need to volunteer somewhere. I knew that California Correctional Center was nearby. I tried to contact the Protestant chaplain but never got a reply. I didn't know that he was suffering from an incurable cancer. I discovered that High Desert Prison also existed, and someone put me in contact with the Catholic chaplain, who put me to work. These activities at High Desert Prison are a part of the book that help me identify "barrels", opportunities, difficulties and lessons, which might help me in my trek to cross the prison recidivism desert.

All of these career changes and work responsibilities helped me map my path through the desert.

The book's title and the image of barrels are a result of a story told by Brian Tracy, a world-renowned motivational speaker. When he was in his late teens or early twenties, he made a pilgrimage across Africa with a friend. When they were in North Africa, they decide to cross the Sahara Desert in a roadster. When they got to the desert and looked for a map, they were told there wasn't one. The only way across the Sahara Desert was by following a long and tried course.

They were taken to the edge of the desert and told to look out on the horizon. He said the only thing they saw was an oil barrel. They were directed to drive to the first oil barrel, and when they arrived, they would see the next oil barrel. They could only cross the Sahara Desert one barrel at a time.

This my chosen image of my journey of mapping a road through the prison recidivism desert. I hope you enjoy the ride as I tell you about my incredible journey with prison inmates.

I'm using the story method of telling about my mapping. Eugene Peterson created a contemporary English translation of the Bible called *The Message*. He writes without chapters and verses because that was the way the writers first wrote it. It was divided into chapters and verses after it became what we know as the Bible. It's a story. So is my mapping of the prison recidivism desert.

Author Janet Litherland says, "Stories have power. They delight, enchant, touch, teach, recall, inspire, motivate, and challenge." Stories help us understand. They print a picture on our minds. Want to make a point or raise an issue? Tell a story. Jesus did it. He called his stories 'parables.'

My stories, or "barrels," are good and bad, naïve and profound, dull and exciting, but they are the mapping of my path across the prison recidivism desert. They may seem aimless and without purpose, but they all mark my trip across the desert. None is meaningless or purposeless. They all moved me in the direction of helping "Men in Blue" stay out of prison.

One Prison Chaplain's Journey Across the Prison Recidivism Desert

Reason for Book

The reason you are reading this book is because I have spent five years as a prison chaplain and have observed firsthand the failure of the American prisonsystem. The failures are in all areas of the system, from the failure of governance to the shortcomings of how inmates are treated. Change is resisted at all levels of responsibility, regardless of how small the change is and how reasonable it is.

First, let's look at governance at both the federal and state levels. It is observable that both federal and state elected officials are easily swayed by an unexpected violence event, as well as the lobbying of special interests. They often pass laws that make the problem worse rather than solving the problem. The three-strikes law is an example. It has put people who use or sell drugs into prison, when their crimes were not equivalent to the punishment. Such actions are an impairment to society, not to say what it does to the inmate.

The second issue is correctional systems' lack of ability to change, as well as their need to sustain the status quo. The status quo protects their livelihood as well as their vested efforts to do their jobs to the best of their abilities. This is true for all levels, from top state administration to the individual custody officer on a prison yard.

A part of their inability to change is engendered by their unions, which are mandated to work for the benefits of Custody or Prison Guards, regardless of their impact on society, state government budgets, or inmates' welfare. At the state level, elected officials are lobbied to raise wages and initiate laws that negate rather than improve recidivism of inmates. At the local level, the elected union representatives of custody intimidate and force wardens to disregard or discontinue programs that are beneficial to inmates' recidivism.

The prison industrial complex adds to the problem as they push for the privatization of prisons and in doing so push up the costs of incarceration and also carry on the warehousing of inmates. Their contracts with correctional institutions usually have a clause that requires the institution to keep their beds occupied or pay a penalty for those beds that are empty. Their lobbying of Washington and state elected government officials is insistent and unrelenting to get them to privatize more and more prisons to meet their greed and profit margins. Their promotion of the building of new prisons as a job creator and their exploitation of the inmates to provide labor and support in running the prisons is unconscionable. Their educational opportunity for inmates and programs that give the inmates the opportunity for social interactions are also lacking.

Incarceration is the main way people are punished for breaking the law. The United States has more of its citizens incarcerated in prisons than any other country in the world. At year end 2009, there were 743 adults in prisons and jails per 100,000 population. The US Bureau of Justice Statistics certified that there were 1,266,800 adults incarcerated in US federal prisons, state prisons and county jails, which is approximately 0.7 percent of adults in America. When you add the 4,814,200 adults who are on probation or parole, there are a total of 6,9 77,700 adults under correctional supervision. This is about 2.9 percent of the adult population in the United States. No other county in the world treats their citizens like this.

By comparison, the incarceration rate in England and Wales in 2011 was 155 persons per 100,000 residents. The rate in Norway was 71 people per 100,000.Australia was 133 per 100,000. Netherlands was 94 per 100,000. New Zealand was 203 per 100,000. These statistics speak for themselves.

The length of sentences is also more stringent in US prisons. American prison stays are much longer, so incarceration totals are higher.

Non-Hispanic blacks accounted for 39.4 percent of the total prison and jail population in 2009. In 2010, black males were incarcerated at the rate of 4,337 inmates per 100,000 residents of the same race and gender. White males were imprisoned at the rate of 6 78 inmates per 100,000 US residents.Hispanic males were imprisoned at the rate of 1,755 inmates per 100,000 residents.

Another problem is that the percentage of prisoners aged fifty-five and older increased by 33 percent from 2000 to 2005, while the prison population grew by 8 percent. One out of six prisoners in California is serving a life sentence. It is predicted by the year 2020, 16 percent of the prison population will be elderly, which will skyrocket health care costs.

From what is stated above, one can see the system is broken. This book tells the story of how one prison chaplain worked to bring change to a prison and attempted to reduce a purported recidivism rate of over 75 percent. There were some small victories, in spite of the resistance to change on the part of many custody officers. Read the rest of the book to see how it all worked out.

Looking for Volunteer Work

After retiring and moving to Honey Lake Valley, I realized that I needed to find a volunteer job that would inspire me and help others. Remembering that there was a state prison in Susanville, I called the Protestant chaplain at California Correctional Center. I left a message but received no call back. I called his office multiple times and never received a return call.

I was talking to some friends about this and learned that one of them worked at High Desert Prison, which was a Level IV prison, the highest level of incarceration in California. This particular woman said she knew the Catholic chaplain and that she would get him to call me. A few days later, he called to say that he would like to talk to me about a small group of inmates that needed a sponsor. We made an appointment to meet in the snack bar in the Administration Building to talk about the options.

When I met with the chaplain, he explained that he thought I could sponsor a group of "lifers" who met one afternoon a week to share their journey. I would not lead the group or set the agenda, but by my being present, they would be authorized to meet. He said we would meet with them until he thought I was ready to sponsor them.

I would need to get clearance to go inside the prison, so he took me to the Personnel Office, where I filled out the necessary forms. I received clearance a few days later, so I went to the Personnel Office, where they took my picture, and I was issued an identification card, called a "beige card." I felt like this was going to be an incredible expenence.

I called the chaplain, and he came to the entry gate, where my papers were checked, and then he took me to his office. We walked for about a half mile before we got to the yard where the chaplain's office was located.

As I walked, a deep sense of heaviness settled on me like a weight of sadness, as though things were hopeless. I later learned that this spirit also permeated the officers who attended me. Everything was so serious-no sense of joy or buoyancy.

The chaplain's office was on the Level III yard, the lowest level of incarceration at High Desert. California State Prisons have four levels of prisons, the lowest level on prisoners can work out in the community under supervision. Level IV prisons are for the most dangerous prisoners. As I visited the Chaplain's office I met several clerks who worked for him. They seemed pretty normal to me.

I found out immediately that the chapel was like an oasis in a prison, a place that is different from the rest of the prison. I sensed it might be because there was a higher purpose for the chapel's existence.

The chaplain and I talked about the group I would be sponsoring, and we made an appointment for me to come the next week to meet with them. He told me that there were two prisons in Susanville, and the other prison I had called was the first prison here. He told me to contact the community resource manager there if I wanted to find the California Correctional Center (acronym is CCC) Protestant chaplain.

Serving as a Volunteer at California Correctional Center (CCC)

My volunteer chaplain's service at High Desert Prison and California Correctional Center prepared me to take on the task of mapping a way across the "prison recidivism desert."

My experiences at a Level IV facility and CCC's Level I and Level II facilities provided opportunity to test ideas and a curriculum that helped me build the faith-based rehabilitation program, led by inmates, which consumed my five years as Protestant chaplain at CCC.

Intro to California Correctional Center (CCC)

A few months after I started volunteering at High Desert Prison, I was talking to a neighbor and told him I had wanted to volunteer at CCC but had not been able to contact the Protestant chaplain. When my neighbor later went to the Senior Center, he talked with a retired CCC custody officer. He told him about my wanting to volunteer and gave him my phone number.

Shortly thereafter, the CCC custody officer called me to introduce himself, saying he was a religious volunteer at CCC. He invited him to come to his house to talk, so my wife and I went to visit him.

I was in for a surprise. He said he had started his custody career at Soledad State Prison. I told him that many years earlier, I'd known the Protestant chaplain there, Harry Warwick. He told me he was Chaplain Warwick's son-in-law.

"Chaplain Warwick was finishing a degree at the seminary, and I was starting my first year," I said. "He used my room as a stop-off place when he came to the seminary. When I graduated from seminary, I hitchhiked to LA to try and find a job. I stopped off and visited the chaplain on my way down South."

"My father-in-law served thirty years as a chaplain," he said. "He passed away a few years ago.

He continued,The reason you never heard from CCC Protestant Chaplain was because he is fighting a brain cancer and has been on sick leave for several months."

He then suggested I call the community partnership manager (CPM) and talk to him about volunteer possibilities.

The next day I called the CPM's office and was asked to send my resume. About two weeks after I mailed it to him, he called to make a luncheon appointment with me at the prison snack bar. When I met him, he introduced me to the prerelease teacher. Prerelease is a volunteer program for inmates who will paroled within ninety days.

I was invited to observe a class, and when I met the teacher, I told her I would like to do a goal-setting workshop. The next month, when a new class convened, I began my lecture and continued offering workshops for approximately four years, stopping only when I took a full-time job as the Protestant chaplain.

First Visit to Prerelease Class

After having met with the associate warden and the woman responsible for the prerelease class, I made arrangements to visit. The prerelease class-a two-week, voluntary class-is given to inmates who are on the verge of paroling. They spend about thirty hours each week preparing for and finding ways of dealing with all of the obstacles that are normally a part of getting out of prison. One of the lessons was to learn how they might go about searching for a job.

When I talked with the teacher about visiting the class, we agreed it would be good for me to observe the atmosphere so I would be better alble to make a presentation that could work with the inmates who were interested. On the day of my visit, she met me at the Patio Gate, because I did not have access to the prison on my own- I was allowed to visit the education program while under the supervision of a "free staff" or non custody person. The free staff are the secretaries, food service, property support staff, the teachers, and even the chaplains.

The prerelease class was located on the second floor of one wing of the Education Building. I settled in the back of the room and watched the teacher's presentation.

The teacher was awesome. She was young and cute and had a vibrant personality-one of the best I'd seen in a long, long time. She had the gifts you usually find in elementary teachers- if you are looking the best teachers, more often than not you'll find them in an elementary school.

She had honed her skills in the elementary classroom before coming to work at the prison. On this day, she was teaching about different kinds of attitudes that humans have, and she used powerful illustrations. What a lesson I received in what a good teacher looks like.

A little while later, one of the free staff came in. He was the manager from one of the local banks, and he talked about financial issues-how to set up a bank account and other financial ideas that were very elementary but helpful. Many of the inmates or Men In Blue had never had much exposure to financial matters, as they had come out of the inner city. Often, they did not have the opportunity for the kind of experiences that most other human beings have.

After his lecture was over, the teacher took us to the snack bar for lunch. I made arrangements for when I would come back to make a presentation. It was a very moving experience for me, because it was one of the first times that I'd been in that particular prison.

I observed that the atmosphere at CCC was very different from High Desert. At High Desert, there was an overwhelming sense of hopelessness and depression, almost as if it was in the air. But at California Correctional Center, there was a sense of hope, a sense of possibility, and the inmates were much more open, probably because they knew they were going to get out someday. The men at High Desert, however, were hopeless, because most of them were lifers-they would never get out.

I looked forward to sharing my information about goal-setting and job search plans with the men at CCC.

My First Prerelease Class

The day finally arrived when I would give my talk to the prerelease class. When I got there, another older gentleman was talking. I went to the back of the class to listen as the man gave a presentation regarding legal issues. He talked rather extensively about potential places of hurt and difficulties for parolees. He explained how they might forestall any issues.

During the break, the teacher told me the gentleman was a retired Lassen County district judge. I thought it amazing that he would come and share, because obviously, some of the men in the class might well come from Lassen County, and he might have been the sentencing judge. But there were no issues with the people that I saw that day.

I was there one other time when he talked and there were no issues then either. I found it amazing that he would take the time and energy to work with inmates. Of course, he was interested, as was I, in how recidivism could be reduced, as the recidivism rate at CCC was reported at more than 80 percent.

After the break, I gave my talk, speaking for approximately fifty minutes, until the eleven o'clock break time. The inmates went out into the patio in the education area, where they ate a sack lunch and talked. After thirty minutes, they came back in, and then I did the second section of my talk. It was a very stimulating experience for me. I am not sure about the inmates.

I gave similar talks as many as thirty-six times during my tenure as a volunteer in with prerelease programming. It was a great experience.

I will now share some of what I shared with the inmates, because I thin this information is relevant to one's understanding of how one negotiates the journey of getting out and staying out of prison. It is a difficult task to prepare one's spirit and heart to take care of the issues that will come down the pike in crossing the desert of prison recidivism.

The Steps of Goal Setting

After the instructor introduced me, I told the men something about me. It is my conviction that the way to communicate best is by giving others a sense of who you are and where you're coming from- it will build bridges between you. If you just get up and give a lecture about classic kinds of ideas, it won't have the same relevance and the same power to the person who listens. So I first shared something about my journey.

I talked about my experience with the Mankind Project at New Folsom. I told them what had happened to me at New Folsom and how wonderful it was to be able to find freedom from a fear that had bothered me for many years. Even though I couldn't identify what it was I feared, it was gone and it never bothered me again. I told them how important being free was to me.

That experience was one of the things that stimulated me to share about the way we can get a job and have purpose for our lives as well as set goals.

I then said, "Even though I may be an older person, I need to have a purpose." I shared the following quote from Jack London, who said it when he was thirty-eight years old: "I'd rather be ashes than dust. I rather that my spark would burn out in a brilliant blaze than be stifled by dry rot."

I explained, "Even though I am of retirement age, I still need and want to be useful and not just vegetate."

In my sharing about myself, I quoted George Bernard Shaw's statement: "The true joy of living is to be used up for a cause you consider as a mighty one." It has been my experience that seniors too often focus on their hurts and pains and not on the fact that they are here to serve, not to be served. So far me and my house, we were going to be servants.

In my attempt to explain the importance of purpose in my life, I also shared what Douglas McArthur said at seventy years of age:

"Nobody grows old merely by living a number of years. Years wrinkle the skin, but the giving up of enthusiasm wrinkles the soul."

I have known people who are just living, and I propose to make this statement one of the mantras for my life. I felt some of the men would like to make it one of their guiding principles as well. I wanted them to understand that I was on a journey much like the journey they were on. "We all are similar people," I said. "We all have the same kind of spirit; the same kind of energy." To illustrate this I shared the following musing:

"Don't be fooled by me; don't be fooled by the masks I wear. I wear a mask, a thousand masks. Masks I can't take off even though none of them is me."

What I am learning and I wanted them to learn is that we're all on a journey. We all have hurts and hang-ups that we need to solve. All of us are addicted to something. If our addiction is drugs or alcohol, it may be more debilitating. It does not matter where we hurt or what our addiction is. We all have places that need to be healed. We need to be made well.

I told the men that the attitude we have about life is important. How we perceive life is very important. "The instrument panel of an airplane has a gauge called the attitude gauge. This attitude gauge helps the pilot know whether the airplane is flying with its nose up or nose down. It's the attitude of the plane that keeps an airplane in the air. If the nose is up, you'll be flying up. If the nose is down, you could be crashing. If you are level, of course, you're horizontal-you're flying along like a normal airplane might fly.

18

"This is true for all human beings. We all are the same kind of people. We have attitudes, and our attitudes will determine whether we're going up or down. If we leave the prison with an attitude that's a downer attitude, then we are going to end up having a downer experience. But if we have an attitude that's upbeat and positive, it's possible for us to stay upbeat and able to face the challenges that are part of being on the 'outside.'"

I told the men that one of the main reasons men are in prison is because of the attitude they have about themselves more than anything else. Our self-attitude, our self-concept, is very critical to why we are where we are. If people understood who they were and their value, they likely would not be in prison.

Nelson Mandela, in his inaugural speech as the president of South Africa, quoted a statement by Mary Williamson:"Our deepest fear is not that we are inadequate. Our deepest fear is that we are powerful beyond measure."

I believe that this observation is true for many inmates;in fact, for most humans. It is not that we are inadequate, although, of course, we are all inadequate in many areas of our lives. But an even more important truth for men in prison to understand is that we are also fearful of the good parts of us.

If we've been in prison very long, we've been beaten down by circumstances, by the climate, by custody, and by all that goes on with our peers. Thus, we think very little of ourselves.

"We need to see ourselves differently, as one of the problems is our perception of ourselves and the world around us," I told them. "If we have a certain perception about things, that's the way we're going to see them. How we see ourselves is one of the reasons that we don't do very well. We've got to look at ourselves in a different light, because we are, as Mary Williamson said, something of value. We need to let that value be shown."

One of the inspirational pieces that helped me set goals, have purpose, and keep going in retirement is a classic poem that I first heard in elementary school, Rudyard Kipling's "If." The first line is, "If you can keep your head when all around you are losing theirs and blaming you..."

This poem has helped me often as I have faced difficult decisions, challenges, opportunities, and problems. I wanted the men to take heart and know that it was possible for them to be, do, and become, "if" they would heed Kipling's words.

I closed this section of my presentation with a story that Jack Canfield once told. Jack, a motivational speaker and co-creator of the *Chicken Soup for the Soul* book series, was hosting a "big hitter" charity event. He asked Monty Roberts, better known as "the Horse Whisper," to host the gathering at his ranch in Simi Valley, California.

As Jack opened the meeting, he asked Monty Roberts to say a few words. Monty proceeded to tell the following story:

During his growing up years, Monty's family often moved several times a year, and he was enrolled in a multitude of schools. His father's trade was breaking horses to ride. Thus, the family moved when he finished breaking the horses in that area.

During Monty's senior year in high school. one of his teachers assigned the students the task of describing what they planned to do with their lives. Monty caught fire as he considered his future, and he spent many days developing his dream on paper.

He wanted to have a large horse ranch. He not only described his dream, but he drew a drawing of what the ranch would look like. He gave it his best, turned the paper in, and waited anxiously for the paper to be returned with a grade.

After several days, the teacher finally returned his paper- with a big red F on it and a note for Monty to see the teacher after school.

The teacher explained to Monty that his paper was an impossible dream. There was no chance for him to fulfill it, based on his past and family history. The teacher told Monty to rewrite it, and he would review it for a new grade.

Monty took the paper home and talked to his dad about it. His dad said he could not make the decision for Monty, but that whatever Monty decided was certainly important.

Monty pondered the matter for several days and finally took his paper back to the teacher and said, "You keep your grade, and I'll keep my dream."

As Monty finished telling his story, he walked over to the big fireplace in the room, and there on the mantle was the framed written paper. It was Monty's dream, and it coincided with what the folk were seeing when they looked at Monty Roberts's ranch.

He concluded his remarks by saying that a few months ago, the teacher brought a group of students to Monty's ranch. While he was there, he admitted that he had been a dream-killer, but he was glad that Monty had not let him kill his dream.

I challenged the men in the class to keep their dreams and not let anyone kill them. "Get to work and begin to do what you can to fulfill your dreams."

When the class went to break, I marveled at what I had received by sharing the above ideas with them. I didn't know if it had done them any good, but it had been a dream builder for me.

Strategy for Finding a Career-Type Job

In this section of my lecture, I talked about one of the most difficult things that inmates face, which is finding a job. Most of us on the "outside" are prejudiced regarding folks who have been in prison.

A more important barrier to finding a job, however, may be the preconceived notions that parolees have about the difficulty of getting a job. It is related to one's self-concept- how inadequate the person feels when it comes to job skills and a lack of experience in having and keeping a job.

A major problem is that many inmates have little formal education, so when they go to an employer, the first thing they may say is, "I don't have any education."

That is not true. Every inmate who has ever been to prison has an education. It may not be formal schooling, but it is an education-and what an education!

In my opinion, it is equivalent to a Harvard education, if one applies the lessons learned to living and working on the outside. So I urged them to say, "I don't have much 'formal schooling,' but my education has taught me the value of hard work and giving the best I can to any job I may have."

When we look for a job, we must have a plan. We can't go out helter-skelter and expect to find a job. We need to know what kind of job we really want-not just anything, but what we can invest in when it comes to work. Otherwise, an employer can see our indecision and expect that we aren't a long-term prospect.

I suggested that one of the first steps in our plan is to decide what kind of income we need twenty years from now to have the lifestyle we desire. As a ballpark figure, we agreed that $100,000 a year would be an income that would give most of what we wanted.

They would not have to resort to selling drugs- or even using drugs- because this level of income would make them feel wonderful about themselves. Unfortunately a $100,000 job is not something anybody is going to get when he walks out of prison.

Then we discussed what particular places someone might go to make that kind of money, without having a whole lot of formal education.

We settled on the idea that food service was a place that we could do it. If someone was a master chef in a five-star hotel, he would probably make about $100,000 a year. The easiest path to becoming a master chef would be to go to cooking school. There are many very powerful ones in Europe and in the United States. Unfortunately, they cost too much money for someone just getting out of prison. "Ist there any other way we can become a master chef besides going to a cooking school?" I asked.

We decided that it was possible to rise to such a lofty position in the food industry by on-the-job training. Then we fleshed out what such a climb up the food preparation ladder would look like. If one was willing to start at the bottom, could he rise to be a master chef?

Food service was one of the best places to start because there many entry-level jobs available. Inmates might find it possible to start at a lowly position, because almost anybody can get employment in an entry level position in food service.

We imagined going to a fast-food place. At our interview, we indicate that we are willing to do anything. If someone is needed to go outside and pick up the cigarette butts and take the trash out and do whatever else that needs to be done, we would do it. We could also keep the tables clean inside the facility. That's an entry level job.

"Most people don't want to do such work," I said, "but if we're hungry, and we're looking for a future, we have to start somewhere, so let's imagine starting there." We talked about faithfully doing that over a period of weeks or even months.

This commitment would likely cause the manager of the fast-food place to suggest that maybe we could help in the kitchen. "Suppose he suggested he needed a pots and-pans worker who also would keep the stove and ovens clean," I said. [11]Would you do that?"

Imagine you were faithful in doing that, and one day there was an emergency, and they asked you to help with the cooking or preparing the food. You agree to do it, and over a period of months or a year or so, you move up and become one of the fry cooks. You continue to cook in the fast-food place until you have sufficient experience to begin to build a résumé.

With your résumé and experience, you go looking for food-franchise businesses that serve complete meals-Denny's, for example.

When you interview at Denny's, you tell them that you'll take any job they have, even if it is an entry-level position. You talk about your food service experience, but you tell them you are willing to start at the bottom and take any position they have.

They offer you the pots-and-pans job. As you're faithful in doing what you've been asked to do, it is likely that you will be asked to do more. If you do more, it won't be very long before you could end up being the fast-order cook.

You do the frying, or you work the grill, or possibly you make the salads. As you watch and help prepare the food, you suggest a way of doing it more efficiently or suggest a slightly different way of flavoring a particular dish. You help to make the food preparation process little better. By doing more than expected of you1 you grow yourself. The first thing you know/ you are the primary cook in that franchise establishment.

I said to the men1 "Let's say you do this for a couple of years. Do you think this process is too long to earn the projected $100,000- a-year salary?" Interestingly enough, their overall response was that this process was too slow.

The majority of the class felt my timetable was too long. In their opinion, they should be able to reach the top salary level in two or three years. I attempted to explain to them that their timetable was unrealistic, and that was why we were going through this process. Itwas my attempt to show them how long it takes to be successful. It's not an overnight project.

If you start as a minimum-wage person, you don't get to a $100,000 salary overnight. You have to prove yourself, especially if you don't have formal training, which can help jump-start you and promote you more rapidly.

"Let's stay with the scenario that we started and see how it finally plays out," I suggested. "You are now working at Denny's as one of the lead cooks. At this point, you have been employed for about four and a half years, and you decide it is time to find a new position in a first class restaurant like in a Marriott Hotel. You apply for a job, but the only opening is a pots-and-pans position. Do you say, 'I'm too good for pots and pans. I've been there before, and I can't do it again'? No, you have a plan, so you take the job. Over time, because you were a good pots-and pan man, you work yourself up to another position. One day, a chef says, why don't you help with the salads.' Over time, you become the expert on the salads.

"Or it could be that it happens with the desserts. They have a bakery, and they ask you to help mix the flour. Eventually, they let you start making a simple dessert. You invest and start expanding your gifts.

"You become a dessert expert. It is even possible that you end up as an assistant to the head chef. As you cook with him, you discover he is earning $50,000 or $60,000 a year. You begin to imagine yourself in a similar position, even if you are only making $30,000 to $35,000.

"You've now been in food service about seven and a half years. As you continue to learn and develop your gifts and knowledge, people begin to recognize your expertise. As you get better and better, one of the main cooks gets promoted to a five-star hotel. While working with you, he recognized your gifts, so he suggests that you come over and work with him for three years. During that time, you learn all his gifts and observe his skills.

"At the same time, you are developing your own ingenuity and your own ideas, since you have been working in food service for at least ten years. If you-continue to develop the dream, a $100,000 salary will become a reality. It will only happen, however, if you continue to push yourself and grow.

"You cannot be too good to start over, and keep starting over until you realize your goal. As someone has said, 'Success is a moving target.' Nothing happens in a straight-line sequence. Life is two steps forward and one step back, or three steps forward and two steps back. So it is with reaching your dream for a $100,000 salary."

As we went through this procedure, we also plotted it on the white board at the front of the class, showing how this could be done.

I reminded them that it was a dream about what they could do if they were willing to start at the bottom and work their way up. "What that means if you are being paroled/' I said, "is that you should expect and be willing to start at the bottom. You can't start at the top. It doesn't matter where you are in life; you have to start at the bottom. Sometimes we can jump-start, as I said, through higher education, but most of the time, if we're doing on-the-job training, it's going to take us years to arrive at the boss's position."

It's a good experience to dream because dreams are what make life happen. Kipling said, "If you can dream and not let dreams be your master. If you can think and not let thoughts be your aim.." One has to put legs on his dreams, especially when it comes to finding a job with a $100,000 salary.

I'm excited about the possibilities for people if they get their act together and are willing to grow out of being a felon. As someone has said, 11If it is to be, it's up to me." If this is true anyplace, it is true with a man getting out of prison. He must have a purpose and pay the price to achieve it.

Meeting an Old Acquaintance

I went to the prerelease program about three or four times, and one day when I was coming out of the education facility with the teacher, inmates were going from the vocational training program back to their houses. As one of the inmates went by, he said, 11Hello, Jack," and I turned and recognized that the speaker was a man I had known when I was in Paradise, California. He had come to the church a few times and was a son of one of the members of the church. I was surprised to see him. I knew he had been in prison, but I never dreamed that he would be here.

I thought about it as I left. While waiting at the patio control window for the teacher to turn in her keys, somebody came to the cascade fence. It was my acquaintance again, and he'd said, uJack, I want to tell you-don't report me that you know me, because I don't want to leave CCC. I've got less than sixty days to the house, and I don't want to get transferred." He turned and went away.

I didn't realize until later what he was talking about. There is a rule in the prison that if you know an inmate and you are a free staff or custody officer, you must report it. And in most cases, they will transfer the inmate to another facility. Occasionally, they may transfer the staff person. I recognized that I had some issues I had to deal with.

I recalled a story about a free-staff employee in a cell block at High Desert. She unexpectedly recognized somebody, and she gasped, turned white, and almost passed out- it was her son, whom she had not seen or heard from in more than six years. She did not know where he was. What a trauma for her to see him in prison. I thought about that story, and realized that I had to report my acquaintance.

I went to the community partnership manager and told him about this man. I reminded him that I only came in once or twice a month, and I wouldn't be in touch with him. I hoped, for the inmate's sake, that he would not have to move.

Fortunately, he was paroled without any problems- I'd had to write a report, but I never saw him again. This experience taught me how important it is to recognize people and deal with them in a way that is forthright and open.

Final Observations

I went to the prerelease program once or twice a month for more than a year. I had an appointment for a goal-setting presentation and was ready to go to the prerelease class whe:n I saw the classroom was closed. I couldn't figure out why it was closed. It didn't seem reasonable. I asked the education officer. who said there was some issue with the program.

When I got back outside, I went to see the community partnership manager. He said there was an investigation of the misuse of the prerelease computer. Since it was jointly used by the teacher and the inmate clerk, there was an accountability issue involved. I eventually found out that there were some inappropriate pictures on the computer.

As a result of that, the teacher was suspended and the program was canceled. After about three months, the program resumed with another teacher. In my opinion, losing that teacher was an unbelievable loss to the program.

From this experience I learned how vulnerable we are if we have inmates on computers. Most custody officers hate allowing inmates access to computers. If possible, they will stop it. If you have an inmate computer or are able to get computer access for a clerk, be careful that it isn't misused. If it is, both you and the inmate clerk will be in trouble.

This was a valuable lesson for me when I finally got an inmate computer for Oasis Chapel. I discovered that giving trust to an inmate carries an innate problem of vulnerability. Inmates can easily cost you your job if they are not trustworthy.

The Four Stages of Learning

At the beginning of presentation on the Seven Habits of Highly Effective People by Stephen Covey, I talked about the four stages of learning. We go through these four stages with everything we truly learn. It is a simple concept, but it is very profound.

The first stage is unconscious incompetence. *We_don't_know_that_we_don't know.*

Two-year-olds are wonderful people. They have such confidence. If you watch a two-year-old trying to pour a glass of milk from a pitcher, he thinks that he can do it. But you know that you have to take the pitcher away from him, because he can't lift it, much less hold it over a glass. He doesn't know that he is not competent. He doesn't know that he can't pour a glass of milk from the pitcher. We all have experienced something similar. Often, we don't know that we don't know.

The second stage is conscious incompetence-*we_know_that_we_don't know.*

The little two-year-old grabs a pitcher of orange juice and fills his glass-as well as the kitchen countertop and a large portion of the floor. (By the way, scratch one pitcher. Next time, buy plastic.)

There is an upside to this disastrous experience, as the two-year-old has passed from stage one into stage two. He knows that he is not competent to pour liquids into glasses from heavy containers.

That's a lot like most of us when we want to learn a new task. We have to first understand that we know that we don't know. Then we are willing to learn.

The third stage is called conscious competency. *We_work _at_what_we_ don't know.* We make a concerted effort to learn a new skill. We practice. We drill. We repeat the task.

The two-year-old will someday be pouring his own milk. He'll have help at first, but he will learn. Itis a challenge for a while, but there will come a time when he can get it. He will then learn other things too like throwing a ball, hitting a ball with a bat, roller skating, or riding a bike. Learning is a process, and the third state is that we work at what we don't know.

The fourth stage is called unconscious competency. *We_don't_have_to_ think_about knowing_anymore.*

When the child is ten years old, he throws a ball, swings a bat, roller skates, and rides a bike. When he's sixteen, he's driving without having to think about what he's doing. It's second nature to him. He's acquired these skills because he's acquired a set of habits. Each skill operates automatically at an unconscious level.

Learning is the same kind of process. Wherever we are in the process of-learning. stage four is our goal.

In my presentation, we discussed these principles as related to the work. If we are going to learn to work, take a job, and keep the job, we have to learn how to work. We should start learning to work when we are two or three years old by being assigned some chores to do. Unfortunately, many of us have never learned to work. It is a process that we need to go through.

If someday we earn $100,000 a year, we will do it by following these four stages of learning. We first have to recognize that we don't know. Then we know that we don't know. Eventually, we work at what we don't know, which results in work skills for a given task. These skills are transferable. If we learn to do something in one area, it makes it much easier to do something similar in another area.

The Seven Habits of Highly Effective People

After the discussion of learning, I introduced Steven Covey's *Seven Habits for Highly Effective People.*

Steven Covey says that if we are going to be successful at work, we have to recognize we are dependent beings. We begin life as dependent beings.

Obviously, most inmates are also dependent. They are dependent because the prison system breeds dependency. Too often, the culture on the outside does the same. People are dependent on somebody else. They don't think they have any gifts.

In order to become effective, the first lesson is moving from dependence to independence. We must recognize that we are not governed by circumstances or by people. We have the ability to operate on our own. We can become independent. We can make our own decisions. We can move in the right direction.

If we are going to get a job with six figures, we need to learn to be independent. Unfortunately, we can't do it by ourselves.

The next level of understanding is to recognize we are *interdependent*. We discover we do have responsibility to others and that others have responsibility to us. We become a team.

In order to do that, Covey says we must learn seven habits.

The first habit is called being *proactive*. To be proactive means that we must move on our own. We must take responsibility. We must begin to do something ourselves. We can't wait for somebody else. We must move and and do what needs to be done, because it needs to be done. We are the only one who will get to or can do it.

The second thing we must learn to do is *to begin with the end in mind*. We must know what our goals is.

Obviously, if we want to make $100,000 a year, we must determine that's our goal. In order to truly realize this, we may have to begin by picking up cigarette butts and trash on the prison yard. When we are paroled and get a job at McDonald's we must do whatever is required there, whether it is washing pots and pans or carrying out the trash. If we do whatever is required of us, we can position ourselves so we can become a five-star chef.

This doesn't happen by skipping steps. We must begin with the *end in mind*. If we know what we want to be and what we want to do, we can stand anything in between.

The third stage is *first things first*. We must know what our priorities are.

Most of us operate out of a sense of the immediate. If an issue comes up requiring our attention., we will deal with it. We have not set our priorities, what the steps are, and what we must do first if we are going to be successful. In order to be success and get a job like we have been talking about, we must be willing to put first things first.

The next skill is to *think win/win*. We can't afford to think that we will lose. We must think win/win.

Thinking win/win is a situation where we win and the other person wins as well. We must find a way to do that.

If we are going to move up the occupational ladder, when it comes to food service, we have to think win/win. We have to think that we are going to win ourselves, but we have to believe that we are going help our employer win. It's a win/win situation in which there are no losers.

The fifth habit is that we must *seek first to understand and then to be understood*. We feel we are understood, but if we are going to be able to take all the things that come to us in the world of work, we must understand the other person.

We also must seek to understand where our employer is coming from, what our employer has in mind. Then we can do our best to let our employer understand who we are and where we are. But we must seek to understand, rather than to be understood.

That's a big problem for many inmates because they, like most humans, put themselves first. If we are going to be successful, we must put others first, because that is a critical part of being successful.

Then we must learn what's called *synergy*. We must be able to tie various kinds of experiences together to move us in the direction of our final goal. We must synergize both our work experience and our people experience and all the other parts of our lives if we are going to be successful.

The final step is to *sharpen the saw*. By that, Covey means that we must be willing to be lifelong learners. Do whatever it takes to grow and stay current, even if it means going back to school.

To be $100,000 five-star chef, we must sharpen our saw. We need to learn new skills and learn new ways of doing things. We need to have a better understanding of what work is. In that way, we can grow.

I gave these lectures while I was at High Desert as well, but the question-and-answer sessions at the end of these three lectures were very different from my experiences at CCC. I don't know if I had more experience, or if it was the fact that the CCC inmates seemed more concerned about asking questions. More inmates seemed willing to see finding a job as a lifelong term project.

I suspect that having been in prison for extended sessions may have helped the inmates get a vision that it doesn't get done overnight. It is going to take ten years if you want to move from a beginning position in an occupation to the place where you are making six figures a year.

Seven Habits at Antelope Camp

When I was working with the prerelease program at CCC, the instructor suggested I might want to go into one of the twenty two California fire camps located throughout Northern California and offer a course on Covey's *Seven Habits of Highly Effective People*. She suggested that I go to Antelope Camp, which is adjacent to California Correctional Center. I contacted the sergeant at the camp, and he authorized the class.

When I arrived at the camp, I was told I could use the visiting room one night a week to conduct the *Seven Habits* class. There are usually about 120 fire campers in a camp. Twelve inmates signed up for the class. We worked together for eight weeks. As we went through Covey's book, we discussed each of the seven habits and how they applied to their lives.

They reported that it was highly successful and meaningful to them. I felt privileged to have had such a delightful class. Unfortunately} as my obligations at High Desert Prison increased} I was not able to follow up with other groups at the fire camp.

Assisting the California Correctional Center Chaplain

I got a telephone call from the transient Korean volunteer chaplain} who after volunteering for two months at High Desert was now volunteering for two months at the California Correctional Center.

I would be remiss if I didn1t talk about a religious volunteer who came to High Desert for approximately eight weeks.

He was a transient prison volunteer who traveled from state to state and visited pnsons.

He was a Korean Christian who came to the United States when he was an adult and was ordained as a Presbyterian minister. He lived in New Jersey and while there, he established a leather goods dry cleaning business. It was purported to be the largest one in that area. Other dry cleaning businesses from the region sent leather goods to him to be cleaned.

Some years ago, he decided to work with Korean Christians who were in prison. He bought an old van and began his pilgrimage to prisons throughout the United States. He said he was following what Jesus said when he sent his first disciples out. Jesus instructed his disciples to take minimum stuff with them and not to worry about tomorrow, because tomorrow would take care of itself.

On several occasions, he told me about his experiences as he moved from state to state, in keeping with Jesus's mandate.

His van was his home. He slept there at night and stored his food and all of his belongings in it. While at Susanville, he parked in the McDonald's parking lot.

One day he showed up at High Desert and met the warden, who introduced him to the Protestant chaplain. The Protestant Chaplain invited him to volunteer at the pnson.

He had an awesome message, even though it was difficult to understand his accent. Itwas his spirit and his passion that reached out and touched people.

He went from place to place within the prison and was able to share. He wore a clerical garment, which gave him a sense of austerity as well as authority.

He told me about some of his experiences working with Korean inmates in other prisons. He also shared an experience he had in Montana in the winter, when he didn't have anything to keep him warm, and he actually got frostbite while he was sleeping in his van.

One of his traditions was that whatever he was given when he came to a community, he would give it to the first homeless person he saw when he drove out of town. It didn't matter what it was; he gave it away, even if he needed it.Somehow, he related this to Jesus's sending out his disciples for the first time. He was committed to keep life simple. He depended on the new community's benevolence to take care of him. It takes a man of faith to do that.

The last time I saw him was after he left Susanville and was on his way to Sacramento. He stopped by the house, and I urged to stay overnight with us. After he left, the guest room was impeccable, as though it had never been used. My wife told me she didn't think that the bed had been slept in. He must have slept on the floor.

He stayed at High Desert for eight weeks and left an awesome witness. He went to California Correction Center for another four weeks. He's an amazing man, and I felt very privileged to know somebody who had the passion he has for sharing his faith with his countrymen.

About three weeks into his experience at CCC, I received a call from him. He told me that I should get in touch with the Protestant chaplain at the California Correctional Center. He said the chaplain was suffering from brain cancer and had just returned work after having been on sick leave for several months. His cancer was in remission, but he was very fearful about losing his job.

Many volunteers wanted his position. The Korean chaplain indicated that the chaplain would not be fearful of me because of my age and past experience; he knew that I would not undermine him in any way. He thought that I could serve him and help him keep his position longer than he would be able to do by himself.

After thinking about it for a couple of days, I arranged a meeting with the chaplain. When I went to visit him, I discovered a wonderful human being. He had played the guitar in one of the big bands back in the sixties. Often, the concerts were before fifty thousand people.

Drugs had ultimately become a problem, and in his search for an answer to his addiction, he had become a Christian. He changed his lifestyle, enrolled in seminary, and became a volunteer chaplain at San Quentin.

When the chaplain's position opened at CCC, he applied and received the appointment. He had been the CCC chaplain for four years when he was diagnosed with cancer. As a result of the cancer treatment, he couldn't work full time.

Forming a Drama Club

On one of my visits, the CCC chaplain told me that he often dreamed of forming a drama club. He asked me if I would consider sponsoring one. I said I could do it on Wednesday afternoons. Sixteen inmates signed up.

I got on the Internet and found five minute dramas that churches used in their worship programs. I shared them with the inmates, and they chose several for the program.

The chapel clerk, who played the guitar and led the music at worship, had written a play. The group chose to practice the play. The inmates chose the cast and started to practice. After three months of weekly practices, we scheduled the presentation.

Excitement was high. Unfortunately, the chapel clerk had a big ego, and over a disagreement, he got mad and quit and would not allow the play to be performed. Ultimately, we had to cancel the whole program. What a disaster it was, but as custody officers would say, "That's an inmate."

Chaplain McKibbin's Freedom from Addiction Program

In one of my visits with the CCC Protestant Chaplain McKibbin, who had the brain tumor, he told me about his journey to freedom through meditation. While in seminary, he studied meditation in many different forms, and it had helped him handle his addiction. His dream was to use meditation to help inmates overcome their addiction.

After he became chaplain, he realized that the major issue of inmates was addiction. As a result of this insight, he began to develop his Freedom from Addiction program.

It was an eight-week program, and its purpose was to encourage inmates to discover their spiritual gifts and how their higher power could help them. His method of meditation was biblically based. The psalmist said, "Let the words of my mouth and the meditations of my heart be acceptable in the sight, 0 Lord my strength and my Redeemer."

Doing this saved him, and he believed that inmates might also find release, as he had. We talked extensively about how hard he had been working for three years in developing the curriculum. The warden had approved his project and authorized him to initiate it throughout the prison.

Prior to meeting the chaplain his supervisor, the community partnership manager, had told me about the chaplain's gift of leading inmates in meditation and the use of silence for personal growth. He often would have a hundred inmates in the chapel and would enable them to meditate and focus on their inner selves and the spirit of God for at least one hour.

His supervisor indicated this gift was amazing; he was truly impressed. Thus1 I was already prepared and open to listen to what the chaplain had to share.

All Christians must remember that meditation has always been a part of the Christian tradition. Unfortunately} the New Age movement has stolen the truth of Christian meditation and imposed concepts on the word "meditation" from Eastern religions. As a result many Christians are challenged and spooked by these concerns about meditation. Many conservative Christians see meditation as the I "work of the Evil One."

When I met the chaplain, it was apparent that he was a spiritua] and committed Christian. His understanding of biblical principles and psychological concepts were outstanding. I had the privilege of observing his spiritual inner person and the depth of his perception of what God can do with someone who

38

is open to God's Spirit.

A week after our talk about his addiction program, the chaplain told me he was conducting a Freedom from Addiction workshop at Lassen Chapel on Tuesday and at Main Chapel on Wednesday.

I asked him if I could attend as a participant. I did not want any responsibility in the program, as I didn't know anything about his program. He agreed that I could come.

In Lassen Chapel, there were about fourteen or fifteen participants. Inmates had different closing times for various housing levels. Some inmates had a closing time of 7:30p.m.; others could stay until 8:30p.m. As a result, three inmates left at 7:00p.m.; the rest of them were there until 7:30p.m.

One of the participants who left early had a deep understanding of the meditation process. He was middle-aged and had been in prison for many years. His leaving early truly affected the rest of the participants.

Two inmates had participated in previous workshops. One was an African American who was required to return to his cell early. The other, a white inmate, was in his late twenties. I discovered later that both these men were clerks in the chapel.

After this program was over and the chaplain was on leave, I left the chapel and went back to High Desert. I had done all I could do for chaplain- that was the reason I was there.

Of all the men I've known during my four score years of living, Chaplain McKibbin is unique. If I were to list one of the most influential men in my life, he would be one of them. He was an awesome individual, and it was a great tragedy that the prison lost him and the world lost him. He still had much to give. It was my honor to have known him.

Helping an Inmate Find a Halfway House

As the drama rehearsals continued, I got acquainted with several inmates. One of the actors was getting out of prison within two months. He was concerned about returning to the Bay Area when he was paroled. He wanted to return to Morgan Hill, near San Jose.

Prior to his present incarceration, he had been in a halfway house outside of Morgan Hill. He wanted to go back there again. The halfway house was sponsored by the Morgan Hill Victory Outreach Church.

I made an appointment to visit the church, located in downtown Morgan Hill, in the former United Methodist Church. Victory Outreach Morgan Hill worked primarily with individuals in recovery. After talking with the pastor, he sent me to the halfway house to talk to the director. The facility, located about three miles outside of Morgan Hill, was an extremely attractive two-story home with fourteen or fifteen rooms. The director, who was also a recovering addict, remembered the inmate I was representing.

He told me that if he would abide by the house rules, they would accept him as a member of the house. I took the necessary forms to the inmate to complete and prayed that he would follow through with his opportunity.

Sponsoring Main Chapel Band

In one of my visits with the chaplain, he talked about the band he had organized. Because of his illness, he was having difficulty with rehearsals. He asked me if I would come on Friday and Saturday afternoons and sponsor the band. The band leader was the clerk who had ditched the play. I agreed to do it.

One afternoon the captain of Sierra Yard came to the chapel and asked me to tone down the band. There was a window near the ceiling of the chapel, which was open, and the sound was so loud on the yard that custody officers could not hear an alarm when it sounded.

I was able to change the band practice time by out-counting the band during the evening count, where inmates are counted throughout the prison as one of two official counts of inmates each day.

They practiced from 3:30p.m. until count cleared at 5:00p.m. Thus, the chapel music program survived.

My Participation in a Freedom from Addiction Class

The chaplain gave me instructions on how to turn on the lights in CCC Lassen Chapel-it was an antiquated system and difficult to do. It was important to be able to have access to the staff and inmate restrooms. It turned out to be providential because the chaplain had a relapse after he had been doing the program for three weeks.

One of the issues in Lassen Chapel was that inmates had to use the restroom one at a time, and free staff had to unlock the door for inmate access.

A major problem was that at approximately 8:00p.m., the chapel door would burst open, and a custody officer would let three or four inmates into the chapel with guitars, which they put in the closet.

It was an intolerable distraction. It was as though the chaplain wasn't there. It was incomprehensible how they could do this. It was demeaning to the chaplain. Every week, they continued to interrupt his program.

He was five weeks into the program when his cancer reoccurred. Since there were only a few weeks remaining in the program and the inmates wanted to continue, I asked the chapel clerk if he would conduct the program until it was completed. His success in leading the program was remarkable.

When I took responsibility for that program, I went to the custody officer who was responsible for the guitar program and talked about the interruption caused by storing the guitars in the middle of a chapel program. I suggested we set a specific time for him to store them, and I would ensure that the chapel program would be completed by that time. He agreed. In this way, we no longer had interruptions.

I still don't understand why the chaplain didn't take the initiative to do this himself. He certainly could have. I suspect that the problem had existed for years, and the meditation program helped to make it an issue that needed to be solved.

The inmate clerk continued the program for the remaining weeks. I wanted to continue to sponsor the program, but the inmate clerk told me he didn't think he should do it.

He said there were several religious volunteers who didn't like the idea of meditation, and they would create problems for him. They thought that Chaplain McKibbin was in error in his use of Christian meditation. Once again, one sees how a belief can keep something good from happening.

Since no one else was available at Main Chapel to conduct the program I continued it for the three weeks. When the inmate leading the program at Lassen Chapel told me his concerns about being misrepresented by some of the Protestant Chapel Volunteers, I recognized that I should not continue the program at Main Chapel.

Chaplain McKibbin had developed an excellent program. Unfortunately it was not fully developed, so it was not something another person could duplicate. He had an excellent curriculum; it was biblically based and psychologically sound.

I knew a former inmate who had been at CCC. He had participated in this program, which gave him tools to stay out of prison. He did relapse, but in spite of his failure, he maintained that if he had followed the program, he would still be free.

Lassen Chapel Clerks

The lead clerk at Lassen Chapel was seventeen years old when he received a life sentence for a capital crime. He had been at Lassen Chapel for approximately eight years.

Early in his incarceration, he became a Christian and had made radical shifts in his behavior. He was extremely intelligent and taught himself Spanish and completed at AA through the local community college. He had initiated several self-help programs, including teaching a prerelease program.

He invited me to be a guest speaker at this program. Custody trusted him implicitly. His integrity, ingenuity, and clerical gifts made him a great asset to the chapel program, especially after the chaplain's illness, as he was able to continue programs that otherwise would have been canceled. Inmates recognized his spiritual maturity and followed his leadership in chapel programming.

The black clerk/custodian was a gifted musician. He had formed a choral group that sang in close harmony. They were terrific entertainment. Unfortunately, as a music leader he wanted to entertain rather than lead in worship. These two clerks were not only leaders in meditation but in helping the chapel to be an effective support for the chaplain and the religious volunteers.

My First Prison Volunteering Was Life-Changing

On Wednesday afternoon, I went to the High Desert prison snack bar and waited for the Catholic chaplain to pick me up and take me to the men's group.

We set up chairs in a small circle and waited for the inmates to come. There were six men in the multi-ethnic group two blacks, two whites, and two Hispanics. The group varied over the months.

One of the members was serving three consecutive life terms. Another grew up as a Seventh Day Adventist and got into drugs and was responsible for someone's death. The Hispanics were gang members, as were the blacks.

When they arrived, one of the men set the agenda for the meeting. It was about some personal growth issue in his life. They went around the group, sharing about the issue, and each one said his name before he started talking. The chaplain and I did not talk; we listened. It was an awesome expenence.

I learned that whenever a new member joined the group, each member of the group told his story. Over the months I was with the group, I learned that each time a member of the group told his story, he told more than the previous time.

Over the months, I grew to admire these men and their honesty, forthrightness, willingness to stand up and be counted for their faith.

There was a riot on the yard, and the two black brothers didn't want to participate; they ended up in Administrate Segregation or the "Hole" for a full year. As I visited them in their cell, I could see the stress and the breaking up of their persons. It was psychologically damaging to them. I often wonder what happened, but I can't go back and find out.

New Folsom Workshop Changed My Life Forever

Several months after I began to sponsor the Men's Group by myself, I was talking with the chaplain about how the Men's Group got started. He told me that his friend, the Catholic chaplain at New Folsom Prison, had developed the idea and was doing it on C Yard at New Folsom.

He explained that the chaplain had also developed a weekend seminar for lifers. It was sponsored by the Mankind Project, a worldwide organization that is committed to helping men to learn to be men.

He said that New Folsom had scheduled one of the seminars for the following month. I told him I would like to go to it. Could he help me schedule it? He called his friend and was told that I could come as an observer and visitor. My ID from High Desert would get me in.

I made housing arrangements at a Folsom Motel so I could attend the meeting. New Folsom and Folsom Prison are adjacent to each other.

On Friday morning, I went to the Main Gate of the prison, and they gave me directions on how to get to the program. I wandered through several halls and finally arrived at the meeting room, which was next to the chapel. It was a room with tiered seats and a large meeting area below the seats. Piles of mattresses were in that area.

Twenty-five Mankind volunteers had come from all over the world to participate in the program, at their own expense.

Twelve lifers were to be involved in the training. These inmates were coupled with two of the Mankind volunteers for the weekend.

The volunteers were called "dogs," because dogs are faithful and always there regardless of the circumstances, and so the volunteers would be with the individual lifer for the rest of the weekend, regardless of what they experienced. Several other inmates were part of the support staff for the program.

Just before the program began, a yard alarm sounded. It turned out that there was an incident involving the Hispanic inmates. Immediately, all His panic participants were returned to their cells. It was a real downer. Everybody was discouraged, but they started the meeting anyway.

The first exercise was a meditation about their childhoods. As they prepared to do the exercise, the moderator of the meeting came to me and told me that I should experience the exercise, not just observe it, because I would not be able to receive the value from the exercise unless I went through it.

He said that he would have three inmates be my "dog" for the exercise. I agreed. As we did the guided meditation, the three inmates were beside me. After it was over, I was expected to process it. The inmates said I could either write out my observations, or I could tell it to them, and they would take notes and give them to me.

I decided to talk my reactions and let them record them. The inmates said they would type the notes they had taken. I went back to the permanent seating and prepared to be an observer.

The inmates came out and asked me why I was in an observer's role when I had some work to do. They told me that I was now a participant in the three-day program, and they were going to be my "dogs." I decided it would be better to participate than sit on the sidelines.

Another free-staff person also participated in the program. He was a writer and was going to write a book on his experience. He published books under the title of *Uncle john's Books*.

As the moderator was preparing to continue the program, word came that the Hispanic brothers were being allowed to come back to the program. The warden had made a special dispensation so they could return. He felt this was a special program that helped inmates to change, so he decided to allow the Hispanic inmates to return. What an inspiration for the rest of us.

The moderator divided the inmates and volunteers into three groups to do the work expected for the inmates. After the groups were formed, one inmate was chosen to do his work. The work dealt with the hurts and anger in his life.

47

It was then that I discovered what the mattresses were for. The inmate went to a corner of the room and started his story. When he became emotional, the inmate volunteers immediately took a mattress and put him against the wall, with the mattress to protect them, as he fought his individual demon.

There was screaming and unbelievable emotion. After one inmate finished his journey, they processed the experience with him. This was what the remainder of the sessions were used for. It was unbelievably draining and taxing.

My session with this program took place on Sunday morning. I told my story and got unbelievably emotional. They didn't use mattresses with me, because they knew I didn't have that much strength. My issues were an early childhood memory that I hadn't been able to recall before. We processed it, but I didn't feel full relief.

So my "dogs" took me to the other side of the room and coacihed me into letting go of the hurtful memory. I really emoted. They continued to help me, and I ended up exhausted. It took a couple of hours to recover.

I had always felt that there was something that was bugging me, but I could not uncover it. I have spent thousands of dollars in counseling and seminars, attempting to uncover it, but never could. It was like there was 11a hole in my soul." I couldn't find it and had given up ever being free.

The result of this experience was that since that day, I have not felt " the hole in my soul."It all happened because the inmates took me through the journey. They set me free!

Now you know why I have such a passion for serving inmates and helping them find healing for the hurts, hang-ups, and wounds. Thank God for my "dogs."

The Last Workshop Meeting

On Sunday morning when we arrived at the meeting room, the chairs were arranged in a large circle. When the meeting was called to order, all participants in the program sat on chairs or on the floor in a circle.

The moderator introduced the founder of program, who had worked with the Catholic chaplain to develop the encounter experience. He was a former felon, a heavily tattooed, bearded biker. He looked like a tough dude-a middle-aged hippie. He told how life had turned for him and that he had a passion for doing the same for "Men in Blue" (MIB, or inmates).

He described how they had had several sessions, and he introduced all the assisting MIBs as graduates of the program. He thanked the Mankind volunteers for their support in making this experience possible.

After he talked, several of the Mankind volunteers shared their experiences and feelings about the program. Several of the graduates also shared how life-changing this experience had been for them. Opportunity was given to the staff to also share.

Then the moderator said it was time for sharing of words of wisdom-these words could be from whatever source one might have gleaned them. At the close of the sharing, the moderator said he wanted to share a poem written by a graduate of the program who had moved to another yard in the prison. He shared a poem titled "My Brother." It begins, "Renegade, scoundrel, robber, thief, con man, junky, alcoholic, dope fiend, abuser, prisoner..."

When I heard this poem, I was determined to get a copy of it and memorize it. As one of my friends said, "Most, if not all, of us are unconvicted felons." I have used the poem many times during the last seven years in my talks at prison and on the outside.

The moderator said it was time for closure, and the last exercise was the opportunity for the dogs to name their masters. With that, he turned to the volunteers on his left and asked them to talk about their experience with their masters and to name them. They proceeded around the circle until they finally came to me.

I was one of the last three participants to be introduced. The inmates talked about their experience with me and then said that the name they had chosen for me was "Wise Folsom Fox." Their mandate to me was to go back to Susanville and share the wisdom I had learned at Folsom.

With a mandate like that, is there any wonder that I am passionate about helping MIBs to be healed of their hurts, wounds, and hang-ups?

Additional Learning at Mankind Orientation and Initiation

While at the inner-circle meeting at New Folsom, I talked to some of the Mankind volunteers about the program. They told me that an orientation and initiation weekend was planned for the near future. They gave me an address to contact, and I signed up for the program, which was scheduled for a retreat center in Ben Loman, California.

It was a long trip for me-about seven hours. I was told to bring a potluck-item for the feast, whlch would end the program. I stopped at a Safeway store in Ben Loman and bought four dozen hot wings as my contribution. We were scheduled for a Friday-night-through Sunday-noon program.

When I got to the center I was guided to my dorm bed. I was asked to put my valuables and keys in an envelope and seal it. It would be given back to me at the end of the program.

Early Friday evening, we assembled in a meeting room. About twenty-five others were there for the orientation. About twenty Mankind volunteers were there to support the program.

A questionnaire was given to us to fill out. It was to help us focus on what we wanted from the weekend. After each of us completed the questionnaire, we were oriented about what we could expect for the weekend. They indicated it would be full of surprises and to hang loose. We were informed that at this time, we were beginning a forty-eight-hour fast, which would end with the feast to which we had all contributed.

We were told that a spiritual leader was available and that he would interview each of us. One by one, we were invited into an adjoining room, where we met a Mankind volunteer who was a retired Catholic priest.

He ask us one question: what is your purpose in life? The first thing that popped into my head was Augustine's dictum: "To love God and enjoy him forever!" I quoted that, and the priest's face showed real shock. But he did not respond. I left the room and was directed to another assembly room for the remainder of the evening.

In the assembly room, we were divided into two groups. These groups ended up being much like the inner-circle groups at Folsom Prison. Each participant was given a time to talk about a hurt, hang-up, or wound that was plaguing him.

Three Mankind volunteers were to lead or tease the participant to open up and share. Sometimes it got very emotional. At about 10:30, they called a halt to evening's activities and sent us to our dorms.

Restrooms were several yards from the dorms. I had a fitful night of sleep. We were awakened early in the morning, before the sun was up in the compound.

We were led to an open area, where the spiritual leader led us in a thanksgiving for the new day. He focused on the east, west, north, and south and offered prayers and thanksgivings to the Great Spirit over us all. It seemed to me to be in an American Indian tradition.

We were released to freshen up for the day in the communal restroom-we took turns using the shower and shaving area.

At about 8:30, we m,et for another session, similar to the one in the evening, where new participants were given their turns in the inner circle. This went on for an hour and half or so. There were no timepieces available to the participants.

When this session was over, we went back to our dorms, where Mankind volunteers led us to the sweat lodge.

It took some time to get all the participants into the sweat lodge. After we were all in, the spiritual leader took water and dropped it onto tihe heated rocks, and steam began to fill the room. It took some time to create enough steam to begin the sweat process.

At that point the spiritual leader let us in a ritual that had the traditional elements of worship, adoration, thanksgiving, confession, forgiveness, and praise. I felt it a very significant spiritual experience. I felt released, cleansed, and forgiven.

As the ceremony was concluding, I felt a deep need to get into the open air. Fortunately, I was next to entrance, and I slipped out into the outside air. I sat down on a nearby stump, because I felt overheated and dizzy. All of a sudden,

I passed out. When I woke, I was being attended to by two Mankind volunteers. They sat with me for several minutes, and when I fully recovered, I went back to the dorm to rest for a few minutes.

Following the sweat lodge and recess, the group reassembled for another session of the inner circle. It was my turn in this group. I don't remember what I shared, but it was not as emotional and traumatic as my inner-circle experience at New Folsom.

When this session concluded, we had another recess and were called back together as a full assembly. In this session, one large circle was formed, and we were instructed that now was a time for each of us to have time in the center. We were instructed to share something important to us that we wanted the rest of the group to know.

I talked about my prostate cancer and urged members of the group to see a doctor when signs of difficulty in urinating occurred. Ifl had done it, I might have delayed and possibly escaped the cancer. Three members of the group came out that they were homosexuals.

Over all, it was a moving experience. Mter another extended recess, we gathered together in a room as participants. It was dark by this time. Mankind volunteers picked us one at a time. They blindfolded us and let us into the yard and through bushes, with branches hitting us as: we walked. This went on for what seemed like an eternity. Finally, we were led into a room filled with people.

Men that I had not seen before were there, gathered for the closing ceremony. Several of them spoke about the power of the Mankind concept in their lives and urged us to get training so we could begin local groups to help men find themselves. After this was over, we broke our fast with the feast. It was a powerful time for me.

After this program, we were released to go to our dorms to sleep. We were awakened the next morning for the outside meeting with the Great Spirit. After that, we were released to go home. What a weekend!

Mankind Community Group Workshop

While at the orientation workshop, I learned that local areas had training sessions for the establishment of Mankind community groups, much like Men's Circle at High Desert.

I was directed to one of No. CA Mankind Board Member for a schedule of events. When I got home, I called him. He lived in Grass Valley, Californiia. He told me there was a training workshop scheduled in about three weeks. I signed up. It was to be at his large ranch-style home in Grass Valley.

His home had a large open living area and a beautiful kitchen. The family/ living area accommodated the meeting.

The orientation for the weekend was conducted by the host, who was on the board of directors of the Mankind Project. He told us what we could expect, the eating schedule, and the projected program. He indicated that we would bed down in the main living area.

After a potluck dinner, we gathered, and the host told his story with the Mankind Project. It was a very moving story, which indicated that Mankind had deeply influenced and helped him through some traumatic circumstances.

After his story, he introduced the staff. We were then released to go to bed.

Early on Saturday morning, we were awakened to face the day. Toilet facilities were somewhat limited, so we took turns.

When we gather for the first session, we each were given a partner with whom we would do an exercise that would give us fodder for the inner-circle sessions. I was able to share some of my concerns with my partner, which prepared me for my turn in the center of the circle.

We were divided into two groups for the inner circle, and we had three volunteer facilitators. There were about nine participants in each group. We met for about two hours on Saturday morning.

It usually took a minimum of an hour to process an inner-circle encounter.

In the afternoon, we had sharing from staff: who described the local Mankind group's activities. Without doubt, they were serving a great need in the community.

On Saturday afternoon, I had my turn in the inner circle. As I shared my concern, one of the facilitators told me that I was a phony, and my concern was not a real concern. I informed him that I was a man of integrity, and his judgments were unfair and erroneous. He finally apologized, and I took my place in the outer circle.

The host shared several incidents on how to gain insight into someone's problems. We also continued the inner circle encounters throughout the evening. Sunday morning was spent in processing agendas that had not been completed in the inner circles. We were also told more about how to conduct the weekly meetings.

I found the experience rewarding. I got some ideas for how I might use small groups to help people grow. It is an experience that will help people appreciate the possibilities in the community Mankind groups

Custody Demeaning of Chaplain and Volunteers

A second-watch custody officer, who treated Chaplain McKibbin and religious volunteers with distain, also misused, showed distain, and mistreated me throughout my career at the prison. He was mean and irreligious with inmates as well. He demeaned them at every opportunity. If possible, he would keep them from coming through the gate to the chapel. He was truly a pain.

Chaplain McKibbin had issues with Officer P. throughout his tenure as chaplain. The day the chaplain left the chapel for the last time, Officer P. said to him, 11Good riddance. It's good you are out of here." For an officer to voice such a remark indicates how sick he is regarding life.

After this program was over and the chaplain was there no more, I left the chapel and went back over to High Desert. I had done all I could do for the chaplain.

2004 Celebrate Recovery Summit

In early August 2004, I received a call from the community partnership manager at the California Correctional Center. He said the interim Protestant chaplain was unable to attend a meeting that the warden wished him to attend. He asked ifI would consider representing the California Correctional Center at the meeting.

The meeting was a yearly workshop on Celebrate Recovery, held at Saddleback Church in Lake Forest, California. Rick Warren is the minister of Saddleback Church.

I told the community partnership manager that I would go. WhenI met him at his office, he informed me that the Celebrate Recovery administrator, John Baker, and Rick Warren had requested that each of the state prisons have a representative attend the summit meeting.

There would be many workshops concerning how the Celebrate Recovery program could take place in a prison. He directed me to the travel department to make arrangements to travel to Southern California.

I flew out of Reno to John Wayne Airport and rented a car to drive to Lake Forest. After settling in at the hotel, I drove out to Saddleback Church. The church facility was on about one hundred acres of land.

There was a primary worship center that seated approximately four thousand people. There was another permanent building and many, many temporary buildings that were the inflatable type. The inflatable buildings were where Sunday morning worship was held for various venues.

Sunday worship services had seven different venues. There was a venue for those who belonged to historic churches, a venue for those who liked a charismaticservice, and a venue for those who enjoyed a rock-and-roll type service. Most of the buildings held six to seven hundred people.

My experience there was not only life changing, but it made an impact on the rest of my ministry.

Celebrate Recovery (CR) is a Christ centered twelve-step program that deals with all addictions.

The premise of Celebrate Recovery is that it will help anyone with any addiction and that all people have addictions. The program is to help every person to heal their hurts, hang-ups, and wounds. It doesn't matter who we are; we all have some kind of hang-up. We need to be healed of it, and Celebrate Recovery was created to help human beings change.

The program was created by John Baker. He was in recovery and attending Alcoholic Anonymous (AA) meetings. AA wasn't allowing him to use his faith as a tool to assist him in recovery in the way he wanted AA to help him. He went to Rick Warren with a vision.

His vision was to build a curriculum that would be Christ-centered, and it would meet all the twelve steps that are part of the traditional AA recovery programs. Rick Warren told John he would support his vision, but it was John's vision. John Baker developed the plan while working for a corporation.

After working on the program for many months, John knew his dream was bigger than Saddleback Church. It could meet the needs of many communities throughout the United States and the world.

John Baker was appointed to a staff position at Saddleback Church to develop the Celebrate Recovery program. He attended seminary in the Bay Area, flying back and forth from the church to his semmary courses.

By the time I became involved with the Celebrate Recovery program, John had completed the seminary and was working full time to expand the Celebrate Recovery program throughout the world. One of the areas he was endeavoring to include in the Celebrate Recovery program was the prison population.

The CR seminar included special speakers, various workshops, and small group meetings, where different activities were explained and experienced. It was one of the most intensive seminars I have ever been involved with in my life. It was very tightly woven; there were no wasted minutes.

On the first day, participants were able to choose which events they wanted to attend and how they wanted to be involved in the CR program.

In the morning, John Baker introduced himself and spoke about his personal journey. He also explained his vision for Celebrate Recovery.

After he spoke, a short worship service was held. After worship, keynote speakers, Henry Cloud and Bill Townsend, spoke. They are clinical psychology partners in the Costa Mesa area who have written and published extensively. They were really powerful in sharing their concepts.

Following the speakers, seminar participants attended workshops on the many aspect of the Celebrate Recovery program. Music and Lecture CDs were available for each workshop. I purchased all the CDs to provide the California Correctional Center with the resources to implement the program at the prison.

The first day, I attended an 11:00 a.m. program about CR "inside the walls" of prisons. The national director of the prison CR program was a retired associate warden of a penitentiary in New Mexico.

In his presentation, he described how New Mexico has implemented Celebrate Recovery in all their prisons. New Mexico completed a study that showed statistically that the recidivism rate had been radically diminished as a result of individuals being involved in the CR program. He spoke extensively of how the CR program was used in the women's prisons and the men's prisons.

He then introduced Hector, a custody officer from the Sierra Conservation Center (SCC) in Jamestown, California. At sec, this custody officer, who had a rank equivalent to a captain, was responsible for establishing a faith-based drug rehabilitation program on the Level III yard for approximately 150 participants.

The program was a twenty-four-hour, seven-days-a-week program, funded

59

by a federal grant for drug rehabilitation, for which the CCC warden applied when she was chief deputy officer at sec.

After the custody officer explained how the sec program operated, everyone was invited to have lunch. I was eager to talk with the custody officer, because I wanted to understand clearly how the CR program was related to his program at sec.

I introduced myself and expressed my wish to speak with him, one on one. He invited me to his table for lunch. We sat down together, and as he and I talked, he stated that the drug program at sec was the dream of the CCC warden.

He had worked with her to bring about the funding and implementation of the program. He was a believer, and it was because he was a believer that he was able to get the program implemented and funded.

The custody officer said that Rick Warren had been to sec for a couple of sessions and that it was the only purpose-driven church within the walls of a prison. As we discussed the program, he said he thought that the same program would be feasible at California Correctional Center.

While we talked, it seemed as though I had what I might call an epiphany-a revelation or insight that that there was something special that I could do for the Men in Blue. This program could make a difference at the CCC.

I was overwhelmed with the possibility and especially with the possibility that I could be involved in some small way. It overcame me, and I broke down emotionally and began to cry. After I cried a bit and regained control of myself, he and I prayed that I might be an instrument in making Celebrate Recovery a part of CCC.

It was a high moment in my life that has impacted me ever since and will continue to impact me as long as I live.

After my encounter with Hector, the sec custody officer, I had even a deeper commitment to learn all I could about CR.

That afternoon, we had another general session in which people shared the story of their recoveries. The Celebrate Recovery band from Saddleback Church led an awesome musical program.

They'd made several CDs, and I bought several to take back to High Desert and California Correctional Center. The CDs became a part of the worship experience at both places.

There were two more workshops in the afternoon. We finished early, which enabled us to have free time for our dinner. The evening session began at seven o'clock. There was a special worship experience with a lot of singing and sharing on the part of several individuals, who had found help through Celebrate Recovery.

After being served dessert, we were sent to various groups in which we had a particular interest and had a chance to dialogue with those of the same interests. The evening ended about nine o'clock.

The next morning, there was another general session at eight o'clock. John Baker and his wife shared experiences from their journey. Several other CR staff shared about the work they were doing.

At the prison workshops, we were taught ways that we might implement the program inside the prison. The Associate Warden and Hector, the custody officer, were the leaders of the workshop.

At 10:00 a.m., another general session was held, and one of the keynote speakers gave a very inspirational talk that helped us understand something about the possibilities available to us as we served men and women who had addictions. A bag lunch was held on the grounds.

Another general session was held after lunch, along with several more workshops concerning different topics. We were able to choose which workshop we wished to attend.

When the meetings were concluded about four o'clock, I bought some more 40 Days of Purpose CDs and also all CDs concerning the Celebrate

Recovery program to take back to the prison. The total cost of the CDs was around six hundred dollars. I was glad to make the investment because the experience I had was worth more than six hundred dollars to me as I looked into my future.

On Thursday, a Celebrate Recovery celebration was held. The celebration normally would be held on Fridays, but the leaders wanted everyone to experience the celebration so it was held on Thursday night. There was a lot of singing and a few testimonials of what the Celebration Recovery program had done for them.

Friday morning started with a keynote speaker and workshops to attend.

Lunch was again served out on the grounds. I was looking for a place to eat, when I saw Hector, the custody officer, and reintroduced myself. He once again invited me to join him at his table.

There were people at his table from Texas who were involved in faith-based rehabilitation. I spent the hour talking with them about their program and how it compared with Celebrate Recovery.

The closing ceremony was held that afternoon with John Baker. Rick Warren was not able to be at the closing ceremony because he was on a trip overseas. He had left a short DVD in which he challenged us to take what we had learned at the summit and go out and implement it in our particular world.

John Baker challenged us, asking us to take whatever our dream was-or maybe what our addiction was-and write it on a piece of paper and then nail it to one of the three large crosses in front of the sanctuary. Each person had his or her dream or problem written on a piece of paper and nailed it to a cross.

When I went to the cross, I had the dream of what I wanted to do at the CCC. I did not have an issue of which I wanted to be cured, but I wanted to be able to use my gifts, in some small way, to help inmates not return to prison.

This summit was so important to me because I received a new vision of what I could do. I made the commitment that I would carry out my vision at any cost. No matter how much it would cost me financially or at any other cost, I was willing to undertake the challenge, and I promised that I would not turn away from it. It was one of the greatest decisions I ever made in my life because it impacted how I have lived the last six years and how I will live for whatever years God gives me in the future.

Return to CCC

On Monday morning, I went to see the community partnership manager to report what I had experienced at the summit. I explained the events of each day and that I planned to write a report, which I would complete in seven or eight days. He could turn the report over to the warden.

He asked me to meet with the newly appointed interim chaplain, who had been a custody officer at California Correctional Center. He was appointed interim chaplain because his predecessor was terminally ill from cancer.

He and his wife had been coming to Main Chapel for fifteen years. For much of that time, he had not been a participant, although he was a practicing Christian.

His wife led the Bible Study and he had attended for her sake. He had been in retirement for some time, but he worked in many other venues, such as a law office, for six months at a time.

I found the interim chaplain at Lassen Chapel. He was a really wonderful man, with very few of the characteristics of a typical custody officer. He could be tough when he needed to be, but he was mellow and a caring person. He introduced me to the staff; I already knew several of the clerks.

After I met the chapel clerks, the chaplain and I had lunch together at the snack bar. I told him of my experiences at the summit and explained the program to him. I showed him all the literature, CDs, and audio visuals I had purchased.

I offered to commit myself to having the first 40 Days of Purpose program, along with the Celebrate Recovery program, on C Yard. I wished to start these programs in gratitude and payback for having had the privilege of attending the wonderful summit.

During our conversation, I told the chaplain about the Sierra Conservation Center custody officer's offer to come for several days to orient us to the program. He said he would work with the people on Lassen Yard to implement the 40 Days of Purpose *and* Celebrate Recovery. The Warden agreed that Hector could come in two weeks.

I continued my volunteering at High Desert while waiting for Hector to come and share with us. When Hector arrived, he and I met with the warden. We then met with the chaplain and discussed extensively how the program could benefit CCC.

We decided to meet with the inmates on Lassen Yard that evening. Hector shared with all of us the vision of the programs. He explained how the 40 Days of Purpose program worked at the Sierra Conservation Center.

A purpose-driven church had been established at SCC. Hector showed us a DVD of a church service that Rick Warren had given. It was very inspirational.

Hector also shared that we were worthy as individuals. What the world and our peers said about us was really not how God sees us; God sees us far differently.

He told of their experiences and how the program was designed. It was a 24/7 program. He told of the five principles of the 40 Days program. For example, why in the world are we here on earth? He went over our being a part of the family of God and being in relationship with each other.

"Be someone who is able to learn and grow and share" was his goal.

We would share our experience with those who may not know us. The experience we would share was not a lot of doctrine but our own personal stories. He shared his story and others that occurred at the Sierra Conservation Center. It was a very powerful presentation of all that was involved in having one of these programs. The inmates asked many questions, especially the clerk, as did the leadership members of the chapel.

Hector met with the warden and the administrative staff, and he talked about the program and how effective it was for sec.

The warden had submitted an application for a simHar program at the California Correctional Center. Unfortunately, even though the CCC submission for the grant was in the top of the ten submitted, the grant was awarded to support a reception center in the San Joachim Valley, rather than to support a faith-based rehabilitation program. We were very disappointed, but we still had the inspiration to make what we had work for the program.

Lack of Chapel Budget: The Need for a Video Projector

I quickly recognized that if we were going to run the program, we would need to have a video projector of some sort, not just a television, in order to serve such a large group of participants in the Visitors Center of Lassen Yard. It was a very big room, and we would be able to have as many men as we would like to attend. One of the previous chaplains had held services in the visiting room, and it accommodated 150 to 200 people.

We felt that we would probably have about eighty, but when they broke into small groups of five or six, it meant we would have many small groups. A large space would be needed. The small chapel would not serve our purpose.

In late 2004 and early 2005, when I researched on the Internet and in catalogs about the size and type of video projector we would need, I discovered it would cost three thousand dollars. There was no funding available through the prison, so the funding had to come from private sources.

In grappling with where that money might be raised, I rem,embered that I had a contact with a nonprofit missions program in Southern California. I had a very close relationship with the man who had begun the nonprofit mission. I contacted him, and he connected me with the person in charge of donations. I spoke extensively with the person in charge of donations about our need. He told me he would present my request to the board for the projector.

Within a few weeks, he called me with the good news that the board had approved my request for funding of the audio-video projector.

We discovered we needed something to project the picture from. Normally, the images could be projected onto a wall, but there was no clear wall in the Lassen Yard Visitors Center that we could use as a screen. The screen we would need would cost approximately six hundred to eight hundred dollars.

I had made a decision during my experience at the summit at Saddleback that I was going to set up the program, no matter what the cost. I looked at my personal budget and found that through sacrificial giving, I could donate the money for the screen. I made a personal decision to purchase the screen so that we would be able to use the materials effectively in the visiting room.

By the time we organized the entire program, it was already December. It was now time to bite the bullet and make a decision as to where I was going to get my energy to do the project. I decided that I was going to say good-bye to my High Desert program for a while, in order to get the energy and time I needed to make the 40 Days and Celebrate Recovery programs work on Lassen Yard at the California Correctional Center.

The chaplain was able to get the clearance for us to use the visiting room, and we went through the process of inviting people. About sixty-five signed up for the program. We started the program, and it worked well.

The big problem was that the sound was not very good. The sound system was actually for the chapel, and we would have to set it up in the visiting room. The discrepancy between the sizes of the two rooms made the system much too small, but it worked better than not having a sound system at all. Still, it was not as satisfactory as we would have liked.

We had organized the inmates to run the program. It was my conviction that if the programs were going to work, they had to be run by inmates. Inmate-driven programs are far more effective than programs that are run. by people on the It outside."

The chapel clerk and the chapel custodian were part of the team. Five inmates also were part of the team. Each one had a given responsibility. The chapel clerk was responsible for making the presentation of the program to the group.

One inmate was responsible for publicity of the program, making sure that all inmates were aware of the opportunity to sign up and participate in the programs.

One inmate was responsible for making sure that all of the materials needed were available and ready to be used. Saddleback Church agreed to give 40 Days books for the session. They sent one hundred, and I had already purchased all the video materials that were needed for the program. We were ready to begin the program, and it went well.

I only worked the program for about three weeks. I had a previous commitment to be gone for three weeks, but the chaplain kept the program going, and it was doing really well.

We began teaching the program before we received the projector, so we temporally used a large television that we had to roll about two hundred yards from the chapel to the Lassen YardVisitors Center. Along with the TV, we took a moveable screen on which we could project words to songs, so the inmates could sing along.

We also moved the musical instruments, such as the guitars and keyboard. It provided a very lively program, but having to move all the equipment every Friday and Saturday was very labor intensive. We had very little time to move everything back to the chapel in time for the inmates to be back in their housing by the required time. It required a lot of hardship, but the inmates did a good job of performing the tasks.

The music group of six men who sang in the chapel provided the special music for our program. The group was in such perfect harmony that it was suggested they should make a CD, but unfortunately, we were never able to accomplish that.

The Second Celebrate Recovery at Lassen Chapel

We organized a follow-up program with Celebrate Recovery, and at the same time we did a second *40 Days of Purpose* program. In order to be in the Celebrate Recovery, an inmate had to have completed the 40 Days program. We began the CR program, which were held on Friday nights, with about forty people. The Celebrate Recovery meetings were on Saturday nights.

The visiting room was used for visiting of friends and family on Saturday and Sunday during daylight hours. We had to be observant of what was going on with inmates, because there were a lot of vending machines that held cash money in the visiting room. We had to make sure none of the machines were broken into while we were busy with the programs.

In the course of the programs, we were put in a compromising situation when some of the machines were robbed. We almost lost our privilege of using the visiting room.

On one occasion, the Celebration Recovery staff was accused of taking some of the food in the vending machines, but it was found out that it was actually the inmate custodial staff that was responsible for the misdeed.

The chapel programs were at a real disadvantage with the custody officers. They resented the fact that they had to come down and be responsible for the inmates in the visiting room for the programs. They did not want to change their routine by having to come and pat down any inmate going in to or out of the visiting room.

When I would call for the guards to come to the visiting room to pat down the inmates, the guards were passive/ aggressive. They would not come to the room in a timely manner, which prevented the inmates from being back in their cells on time.

The other problem was that when the guards were patting down an inmate, they would make remarks about the inmate's masculinity. They implied that since the inmates were attending church, they were less masculine. I reported one particular young guard to a lieutenant after having heard him make a derogatory remark to an inmate. The lieutenant called the guard into his office and reprimanded him.

I spoke with the young, bright guard, and he did not seem to act out with me. I did not think his behavior improved, but he seemed to be a little more guarded around me.

There was another officer who let me know that he did not like my having gone to the lieutenant. I told him I had a responsibility to make sure that the inmates were treated fairly, and he mouthed off at me. A few days later, he came to me and apologized for his behavior. I did not report him.

During my orientation with Hector from Sierra Conservation Center, he informed me that after 40 Days program, they would teach a Rick Warren set of videos on the book of James. The book of James in the New Testament is a very practical book, with practical lessons to teach individuals how to live effectively.

We implemented that program after the 40 Days. We continued to teach the book of James during the time that I was a volunteer, I was a volunteer for the Celebrate Recovery and 40 Days programs on Lassen Yard.

After the second 40 Days, a group of inmates came to the interim chaplain and requested that they be baptized. They had found a new beginning for their lives through the 40 Days of Purpose program. The chaplain conducted the baptismal service.

We had to improvise in order to perform the service. We used a canvas laundry cart as the baptismal vessel and filled it with water. The chaplain immersed the inmate in the water. This was performed outside, behind the Chapel Gate, in the area that is restricted from the general population.

Normally, we performed baptisms in the evening, before other inmates were on the yard. We did not want to put the inmates who were going through this Christian ritual on public display. It was a meaningful experience, although it was performed with very primitive materials.

The First Celebration Banquet for Celebrate Recovery

When the first 40 Days program was completed, I suggested that we might have a celebration for the graduates. After talking for a while, it was decided that that when the second 40 Days was completed, we would have a special celebration with food and possibly a musical group. We would invite the officials of CCC and others to celebrate this experience with the inmates of the program.

The chaplain submitted the proposal to the warden for approval. The warden gave her approval and agreed we could bring in an outside musical group. Hector, from Sierra Conservation, had mentioned that he knew of a Celebrate Recovery band from the San Cruz area. He gave me the name of a contact at the church, who went to the leader of the group for me, and they agreed to perform for our celebration. We really had a package put together.

We were going to have administration there, as well as the graduates from the first and second 40 Days of Purpose programs and other special guests. This would take place in the visiting room, because it was the only place to house such a large group. We were unable to use the gymnasium because it was being used for housing.

We decided to serve pizza for the event, which would cost five dollars a person. I was able to procure a five-hundred-dollar donation. It was a tenuous time, because we did not know if the band would be cleared to perform, but it was cleared.

We had invited a local minister from Susanville to be the keynote speaker for the event. He was a very powerful speaker, and we knew he would motivate and celebrate the special group event in a very wonderful way.

We made special arrangements for him to be cleared to get through the gates. When he came, however, he did not bring his driver's license or any identification. He went home to find any ID he could. The only ID he could find was his AAA motor club card. We did not think he would be able to get through the gate, but fortunately, at that particular time, the officer of the day, the associate warden for financial affairs, was present, and he personally escorted the minister into the visiting room. If he had not been there, we would not have had a speaker.

We had a great celebration. The warden and several of the associate wardens were there. We had sent them special invitations, designed especially for this occasion. It was a wonderful, wonderful expenence.

The chapel singing group performed, and they wowed the band. It was a real capstone for the first and second 40 Days programs.

The food was especially appreciated by the inmates. For many of them, it had been years since they had tasted pizza from the outside. It was a well-attended, well planned and well-executed program.

Applying for the CCC Protestant Chaplain Position

Following the meeting, I had an evaluation with the chaplain. In the course of the conversation, he asked me if I would consider being a part-time chaplain.

He did not wish to be a full-time chaplain; he was interested in sharing the job. He said he would go to his supervisor to submit the suggestion to the warden. About ten days later, he told me that the warden had agreed that sharing the job of chaplain would be a possibility.

I was pretty excited about having a position that was only part-time, because that would allow me to do what I wanted to do with my spare time.

Unfortunately, about ten days after that approval, the chaplain told me that he would not be able to apply for the chaplaincy, because if he did, he would lose a significant part of his retirement as a custody officer. What he would make as a chaplain was about 50 percent of what he had been making as a custody officer. This would radically change how much money he would take home on a monthly basis. That meant that the chaplain's position was wide open.

I learned about two or three of the applicants for the position, and as I thought about their qualifications, I recognized my passion for doing something in the faith-based rehabilitation area. I gave long and thoughtful consideration to whether I should apply for the position.

After thinking about it for several days I sat down and wrote an extensive letter to the warden telling her of my qualifications and what I would be willing to do to make the dream of 40 Days of Purpose and Celebrate Recovery programs a reality in both of the chapels. Along with that I would spend much of my energy finding other ways to facilitate inmatesdiscovering ways to never return to prison.

I submitted my letter feeling that I was "blowing my own horn.'1 Even more than that I felt I might have been out of order. When I did not hear anything about the position for two months I thought that I was not going to be considered.

Then one day, the community partnership manager called to inform me of the day and time of my interview.

When I arrived at the prison, I was given a form to fill out, which requested much of the same information I had already submitted. I had to fill the form out on the spot and in my own handwriting.

I have an intentional tremor, which means that when I write, I do not write very effectively. I've never had very neat handwriting, even in my prime, but at this point in my life, it was not very good at all. When I saw what I had written, I recognized that the probability of my getting the position was small- or nil.

As part of my preparation for filling out my application, I had to get an endorsement from my church denomination. When I retired from the church, I did not anticipate ever working again.

I called the Congregational Church headquarters and was told it would take six months for me to get an endorsement. I called the executive secretary and told him what my issues were. I had served seventeen years in the church and had only been retired for two years. The church where I had pastored was the second largest in Northern California. He said he would talk to the committee members. He called me in a couple of days to say that the committee would endorse me.

I discovered that there were five applicants for the position. Three of them were locals, and two had come from some distance. I knew the two local applicants but did not know the others.

I was finally called in for the interview. The community partnership manager and the chief deputy warden were the interviewers. They ask me a series of questions, most of which I felt I answered adequately.

Then they asked me a question about a federal law that had been passed in recent years, and I did not have clue as to what the law was. I told them as much and said I was not going to attempt to snow them with some answer, whlch would probably not be correct anyway. I knew I had not done well in the interview.

I left that afternoon, very discouraged, because I was smart enough to know I could have performed a lot better. Weeks passed without communication from them.

One day, I was walking across the campus, having just finished a volunteer session in Main Chapel. The community partnership manager walked up to me and told me that I was still under consideration. They had submitted the material from the interviews to Sacramento. He said it was possible that I was still a viable candidate for the position.

I explained to him my chagrin at having failed to answer the question that had been posed. He said none of the other applicants could answer the question either, but all of them gave an answer that was erroneous. I was the only applicant who spoke my truth. I felt better about being transparent.

I have discovered over the years that transparency1 although sometimes it may hurt you, in the long run can help you. I continued to anxiously await the result of the interviews, but I didn't receive an answer.

On a Wednesday afternoon, I was visiting in Main Chapel. I was told by the interim chaplain that he would not be able to attend the warden's six-month meeting with the chaplains. The warden was required to have a meeting with the chaplains twice a year, and this would be held the next day, a Thursday.

On Thursday afternoon, I went to the warden's office. The warden, the Catholic chaplain, the chief deputy, the community partnership manager, and I were the only ones in attendance. The Muslim chaplain was half time, and

Thursday was his day off. During the meeting, a lot of discussion occurred.

Toward the end of the meeting, the warden said that she had a special announcement to make. She turned to me and said, "Jack, you are the new Protestant chaplain at the California Correctional Center."

It completely amazed me. I could not believe it was possible. When the meeting was over, she gave me a big hug and said, "I'm grateful you applied for the position. I believe we will be able to do good work together." It was about three weeks before all the paperwork was cleared from Sacramento, and I was given the position.

Reviewing My Goals for My Prison Ministry

One of my first tasks in my prison ministry was to review my goals as a prison chaplain. As I pondered this question, I remember reading a book back in the 19 70s titled *Success Is a Moving Target*. Its premise was that you can't make a definition of what success will look like when you start out on a journey. There may be a definite ultimate goal, but when you get there, it won't look like it did in your early imaginings. The target will change. It may even move, so you must be flexible in defining what your success is.

So I enlarged my target for what I wanted to accomplish. What you see here are my findings. I committed to the warden that she would have a model faith-based rehabilitation program. In determining how best to describe that, I used this mission statement:"Make Disciples; Reduce Recidivism.

Some of my sub-goals were as follows:

1. Change the twenty-five inmates assigned for each chapel volunteer to a flexible number, based on preparation and experience of the volunteer.

2. Create ready access to chapel programs for inmates. This would require a revision oflong-standing, unwritten policies that were practiced on the main patio.

3. Develop an external funding source for audiovisual equipment and curriculum materials for the correctional institutions of Lassen County through a 501c foundation established for that purpose.

4. Discover and use curriculum materials in the chapel programs that help inmates learn coping skills to improve their chances of not returning to prison.

5. Give inmates teaching and leadership opportunities to learn the skills for success on the outside. This will occur by leading their peers in small-group practical-life-skills programs.

Orientation of the New Chaplain

On April 26, 2005, I reported to the camp associate warden's office for duty as the new Protestant chaplain at California Correctional Center. The associate warden for camps was my supervisor. After serving for several years as the community partnership manager, he recently had been promoted to an associate warden. When the California Department of Corrections discontinued that position, the warden of California Correctional Center promoted him to associate warden for camps.

One of the primary missions of California Correctional Center is to provide fire fighters for Northern California. There are eighteen fire camps, each of which houses approximately 110 inmates. The camps are spread out in rural and forest areas from Santa Cruz to the top of Northern California. When the inmates come to California Correctional Center, they are screened, and those who are eligible to go to fire camp to become fire fighters. It usually takes inmates approximately six months to get through the orientation and be assigned to a fire camp.

It is the responsibility of the Protestant chaplain to provide for the two yards in the main division, which are Level I and Level II yards. Only those inmates who are Level I inmates are qualified for fire camp.

There are also a significant number of Level II inmates who are not eligible for fire camp housed on these yards. Many of them are in vocational training or work inside the walls of the prison. Most of the inmates who work in the chapel, are Level II inmates, since they are at the prison long enough to serve the long-term mission of the chapel.

When the camp associate warden was assigned the responsibility for the camps, he volunteered to continue to be responsible for religious programming and self-help groups. All prisons gave these programs to an associate warden. Since Matt, Associate Warden for Camps was acquainted with the programs and had an investment in them, he was willing to take on that extra responsibility as my primary supervisor.

Matt explained to me that my responsibility was for Cascade Yard, Sierra Yard, and Lassen Yard. Sierra and Cascade Yards were Level I and Level II yards, respectively, and Lassen Yard was Level III. These yards housed approximately 3,200 inmates. He informed me that I had no responsibility for fire camp programming, as the camp lieutenants had responsibility for the religious needs of fire camp inmates.

Matt told me that the Catholic chaplain was willing to help and support me. He suggested I use the former interim chaplain to assist me with any questions that I might have. He indicated he was available to me whenever I needed him and that I was to make an appointment, and he would see me that day.

He introduced me to Laurie, his secretary, and told me she would support me with much of the clerical work that I could not do. He directed me to the Personnel Office to obtain my identification card. I completed the paperwork and received my photo. My identification card was good for five years. By the time I completed all the paperwork at the Personnel Office, it was lunchtime.

The interim chaplain came to the snack bar, and we talked about my responsibilities. I had grown to know him well as a result of working with him on Lassen Yard in the 40 Days of Purpose and Celebrate Recovery programs during my days as a religious volunteer.

After lunch, we went to the chapel, and he helped me with the initial orientation to the chapel. After being cleared into the patio, he took me to the correctional captain's office. He asked the captain to authorize chits "prison money", which would be used when I picked my chapel keys. I was told it would take several days before the chits could be issued. Fortunately, I had some chits from my High Desert volunteering, which were identical to those used at California Correctional Center. It is my assumption; similar chits are used throughout the California State Prison system.

Len took me to the Control Office, where I picked up the keys to the chapel. The chaplain's set of keys were different from the volunteer chapel keys, as the chaplain's key set had a key for his office.

When we opened the office, I saw that it was exactly like it was when the previous chaplain worked there. The interim chaplain had left everything exactly the same. After we talked, he introduced me to the chapel clerk, whose name was Frank. He had been clerk in the watch commander's office when I was volunteering for Chaplain McKibbin. On several occasions I had talked with Frank for a few minutes. He was a gregarious and engaging personality. I was shocked to learn that he was my chapel clerk.

The interim chaplain told me that my office computer did not need a password, but as he was computer illiterate, I'd have to learn to use it on my own. I had a minimal acquaintanc,e with the computer- I could use it to type letters- but I had no knowledge of Window programs, such as Excel. I had good typing skills but little knowledge of any computer programmmg.

After our office visit, Len took me into the chapel and oriented me. He showed me the sound system and how it was secured. He took me up on the platform, where musical instruments were stored and locked, and informed me how I was to keep them secure. There were two file cabinets on the stage where music was stored. The chaplain's office only had one file cabinet.

By the time we completed the orientation, it was quitting time. The interim chaplain told me to call him if I had any needs, and he left me to close the chapel. My first day at work had been a taxing one.

Arranging My Work Area

My daily work schedule was from 8:00 in the morning until4:30 in the afternoon. I soon discovered that a chaplain's day is not an eight-hour day or a forty-hour week.

A chaplain is a staff person, which means that he's on call to do whatever needs to be done with whatever time it takes to do it. There is no overtime or compensatory time for any work he does. Each day is a day to itself, and I could not accumulate extra time and take it off later. It didn't seem that this expectation was always appropriate, but that was the procedure at California Correctional Center.

When I got to the chapel the next morning, the clerk was already there. He came to work as early as 7:00a.m. Like the chaplain, he often did not work an eight hour day. Often, he worked ten hours a day. Part of the reason for doing this is because it's easier or better to be at work than to be in their cells, especially during custody's shift changes.

Prisons have three work shifts, and the first shift at the California Correction Center starts at 10:00 p.m. and works until 6:00 in the morning. The second shift is from 6:00a.m. until2:00 p.m. The third shift is from 2:00p.m. untillO:OO p.m. All of the work at the chapel was done during the second and third shift. Evening programs were during third shift, since that was when the inmates were free from their work.

My first task that morning was to rearrange the office. Before I arrived there, the office was traditional-a desk with the chaplain sitting behind it. Anybody visiting the chaplain would sit opposite the desk, so the desk separated a visitor from the chaplain.

In the course of my ministry, I discovered that a desk or any other object can get in the way of communication, so it was best to have open space between people. I wanted to have that kind of arrangement in my office, but I was cautioned by the clerk and by others that I couldn't do that.

They said I needed to have the desk between me and the inmates, so the desk was protecting me. As I thought about it, that the desk held little protection, and if somebody really wanted to get at me they would come across the desk.

I wanted to make the seating arrangement as I traditionally had my office. So I pushed the desk against the wall. I sat facing the wall when I was working at the desk. If somebody came into the office, I might not realize they were there, but I judged that the office was so small, it would be impossible for any movement to take place behind me without my being aware of it.

If somebody came to see me, I would turn my chair around, and they would be sitting across from me, and we would be visiting across an open space. It worked well, because it helped the inmates know that I was open and available. It also provided an excellent setting for counseling, since we could talk with no physical barriers between us.

I quickly realized that I needed a computer desk, and I told my supervisor I would donate one. He informed me I should fill out a donation form, and my request would be submitted through channels to the warden for approval.

It took about ten days before that request was granted. I went to Reno and made the purchase, and the clerk helped me assemble it. It provided me exactly what I needed to store materials that a computer might use. I easily was able to move from one workstation to the other.

I discovered I also needed a coffeemaker and a microwave. My supervisor told me that these items were authorized for offices if I requested them. It would continue to be my private property. [found a table on the stage that could be used for the microwave and the coffeemaker. This was the way I took care of my creature comforts.

Religious Volunteers for Weekend Chapels

Weekend Chapel Schedule

I talked with the clerk about the schedule of events at the chapel. I told him that I'd be working for the foreseeable future at least three nights a week at Lassen Chapel in the 40 Days of Purpose and Celebrate Recovery programs. No programs would be implemented at Main Chapel for a few weeks, until I got my feet on the ground and understood my responsibilities.

The chapel clerk told me that we had a Sunday morning worship service at the Main Chapel and a Bible study on Saturday morning. These two programs were under the direction of religious volunteers. I knew that Lassen Chapel had a Bible study on Saturday afternoon and the Protestant worship service on Sunday afternoon. The only other schedule at the Main Chapel was a Bible study sponsored by Len S.'s wife.

Len also attended that service to support his wife. It was a charismatic study that had been going on for several years on Thursday evening.

I learned there were four different groups of volunteers who covered the four Sunday worship services and Saturday Bible study during the month.

The first weekend sponsors

There were several different sponsors for this first weekend. One of the primary couples came from a hundred miles north of Redding. They traveled over two hundred miles every first Saturday to participate in the service. He had been retired for many years and recently became the pastor of a small rural church. Even with this responsibility, he came to the prison every first Saturday. He had done this for more than twenty years.

He would often bring a video that could be shown to the inmates. He was an unbelievable man.

Elbert H. and Jerry P. spelled them and covered the Sunday programs.

Elbert H. was always present, and if he could not be there, Jerry P. would substitute. Elbert H. retired as a men's clothing traveling salesman. He was the first African American who held this position in Northern California. He had worked as a salesman for more than two decades, and during that time, he developed his own line of clothing. He knew how to make contact with the clothing industry in Los Angeles, where one could get extremely good deals. He is a classy dresser.

He spoke slowly and lucidly. His message was extremely powerful; it was always relevant, fair, and practical. He was popular with inmates and always drew a big crowd.

He had a colleague who lived near him in Madeline, California-a retired free staff person from California Correctional Center, who had served in the food service area before he retired. He supported Elbert and provided companionship on that long trip back and forth to Madeline in the winter time.

The second weekend sponsor

On the second Sunday of the month, a Hispanic couple by the name of Ledesma had the services. Mr. Ledesma was a retired teacher from Redding. He had taught Spanish and several other subjects at one of the Redding high schools.

When he retired, he moved to Reno. He established a weekly Hispanic Christian newspaper that he and his wife published. They distributed 2 5,000 copies throughout the greater Reno area. He had been coming to the chapel for about twenty years when he lived in Redding. His wife was from Argentina, and she had a very heavy accent. She usually shared for a few minutes, and then he would share his faith. He had a unique message and a unique way of presenting.

The third weekend sponsor

The third weekend sponsor was Buck S., who had been coming to the chapel for more than fifteen years. He was from Weaverville, California, which is sixty miles west of Redding. He traveled two hundred miles each time he came to the service.

89

He had been a pastor for a short time. He'd had a significant drug history before he discovered reality and God. He was a metal worker and rebuilt homes in the Weaverville area. Not only did he volunteer at the California Correctional Center, but he was also involved in the county juvenile program for delinquents in Trinity County. He served every week at a youth facility and counseled troubled teenagers. He also volunteered at Trinity Fire Camp each week.

He was an unbelievable storyteller. He would talk about a life experience and relate it to the larger reality of living, in a way that was compelling. He could do it better than anyone I have ever met.

One of my favorite stories was about mission tours to Eastern Europe and smuggling Bibles into the countries that didn't want them. He often shared about somebody he'd met on the street or picked up as a hitchhiker when he was coming to the chapel. His stories always touched home, and they all spoke to the greater reality of how we can live victoriously and how we can live effectively as individuals, so we do not have to be overcome by drugs.

He claimed that his brain did not work as effectively as it once had because of his misuse of drugs in his past. If he had a better mind in the past, it must have been an exquisite one. It was tragic that it was wasted, if what he said was true.

As he closed a service, he would play the mouth organ. He could really make it hum like a harp. He would play old hymns and new hymns. He was as good a talent on that instrument as I've ever seen.

The fourth weekend sponsors

The fourth weekend of the month was covered by a trio of volunteers from Yuba City. Yuba City is approximately 17 5 miles from the California Correctional Center.

The senior member of that group was in his late eighties at the time I met him. His name was Aubrey. He had been coming to California Correctional

Center for more than thirty years. He came faithfully once a month. He could quote Scripture as few men could. He spoke clearly and effectively, and the men really appreciated him.

He had a friend who lived inSusanville, who served as the volunteer chaplain at the Lassen County Jail. This man opened his home to Aubrey and his friends every weekend when they came to CCC. He provided them with housing and a great meal on Saturday evening, between the afternoon service and the evening activity. The man had been opening his home for at least twenty years.

The second volunteer was Henry. He was a Hispanic man who taught at a Christian high school in Yuba City. He had been coming with Aubrey for approximately fifteen years. He conducted Spanish services on Saturday nights in the Main Chapel. His English was superb.

The third volunteer was Frank K. Frank, who had recently retired as a community college teacher in Yuba City. He ran an automotive program that was recognized throughout Northern California as the primary program of all automotive programs in the community college system. He had been coming with Aubrey for about eight years. He was an excellent teacher and ultimately, he became one of the primary volunteers who supported the faith-based program, which was my mission as a chaplain.

All of the weekend volunteers traveled more than two hundred miles each time. They received no financial or personal assistance. They paid their own way, they came faithfully, and without them, during the interim while the chaplain was ill, there would not have been a program.

They told me that when the chaplain was active and able to do the job himself, they normally didn't have anything to do on Sunday morning. On those Sundays mornings, he had the band, which provided the music, and he spoke. When Chaplain got sick and couldn't do it anymore, they stepped in the gap and fulfilled a great need.

Problem Areas forWorship Programs

When the interim chaplain took responsibility for Main Chapel, he extended the hours of the services. They started at 9:00 in the morning and ended at 11:20, at which time the men went back to their houses for noon count.

The extension of the services had some complications. One of the issues was ensuring that the inmates got out of their housing in a timely manner. They didn't always get out,because custody officers did not release them according to any regular time schedule. In some cases, individual custody officers would not allow inmates to go to church. Housing releases were inconsistent, which made the attendance fluctuate a great deal, depending on which custody officer was on duty.

The second issue was that the nearly two and a half hour service created problems about using the restroom. There were no restroom facilities for individuals who came to the chapel. Although there was a facility at the other end of patio, inmates who came to chapel were not allowed to use it.

If an inmate went to medical or any other areas, he had the privilege of using the restroom. If he came to chapel, he had to tough it out. You can imagine what kinds of problem that created. In many cases, individuals would come to chapel and

have an urgent need. They were required to go back to the Patio Gate and to their house so that they could go to the restroom. As a result, they would lose the opportunity of completing the worship service. This had been a problem for many, many years.

Originally, there was a restroom for the chapel, but during somebody's reign, a decision was made to make it the office for the inmate assignment lieutenant. Therefore, there was no facility for inmates who came to chapel. This procedure was rigidly upheld by patio custody.

They would not extend any exception to the rule, except for inmates to go back to their house. Sometimes an inmate would wait at the gate for more than a half hour before custody came.

Another problem was preparing the list of inmates who were eligible to come to the program. It toolk a great deal oftime to make the lists. The chapel only had an ancient electric typewriter. It took a significant part of the clerk's time to make the lists for the Saturday, Sunday, and Thursday evening Bible study programs.

The security/custody culture operating on the patio was a law unto itself and had existed several years. This patio custody culture was a power unto itself. I do not understand how it developed but there was no written policy for what one did on the patio. How second watch custody operated was often radically different from the procedure on the third watch. There was no consistency.

When I requested a copy of the written rules of how the patio operated I was told that they had none. It turned out that several officers had been on the patio for as many as fifteen years. There was a policy for transferring custody to different locations every three years. The exception is you can choose a second tour and that makes a total of six years.

There were five positions on the patio and an officer could work at one position for six years, then get assigned to a second position, work that for six years, and continue this process through all five positions, for a total of thirty years on the patio.

As a result, several of the officers had been on the patio for several years. They had seniority, and they had a certain way of doing things, and that was exactly what everybody else did. If somebody new came on the patio for a short period, they were expected to perform in the manner the senior officer expected.

When I brought this to a lieutenant's attention, he told me it was none of my business. They were running the patio, and I just had to stuff it. I didn't need to worry about it. Being the kind of individual that I am, I was not willing to accept this idea so I challenged it in various ways.

One day when I was talking to the third watch lieutenant, who had been the watch lieutenant for five years, he told me that he didn't like me because I didn't bend to the security officers' desires. I always found a way of getting around them.

I would develop a proposal, or I would work a change. I was changing things, and custody didn't like things to change. They wanted them exactly the way they were.

The lack of consistent procedures was detrimental to chapel programming, and there was no way that a chapel program could run effectively with the lack of consistent procedures that were in place. This wasn't only true for the Protestant program. It was also true for the Catholic, Islamic, and for other special denominational programs. They all suffered from these procedures.

Patio Custody Treatment of Religious Volunteers

Another issue that was problematic on the patio was how the custody treated religious volunteers. They were often not treated with respect, especially by custody that had been on the patio for an extended period. Some of custody had developed a dislike for the chapel and for chapel programs. This attitude stemmed from the way custody officers saw inmates- as criminals, which they were, but custody officers didn't see inmates as redeemable. Thus, custody officers: resented chapel programs where inmates were treated with respect- many of the custody felt that inmates didn't deserve that type of respect.

As a result of that, they categorized volunteers as not worthy of their respect, and they treated volunteers accordingly. Custody did not realize that volunteers were so desirous of being of service in the chapel that they'd undergo any type of indignity. They were mistreated but kept their mouths shut. They didn't complain, because they feared that if they complained, they would not be able to come anymore to give the service that in their hearts they desired so deeply to give.

I found this was also true with Chaplain McKibbin when I attempted to support him during his illness. It was especially true with third-watch patio custody.

Several officers made despicable comments to all the volunteers. After I became the chaplain, I was talking with the interim chaplain, and he told me the custody I had mentioned as having mistreated me had mistreated him also, as well as other volunteers. This seemed unusual to me because, he was a custody officer himself for more than twenty-five years.

When he retired, he decided to come back and support his wife in her service on Thursday night. They treated him the same way that they treated the rest of the volunteers. From my perspective it appeared that this was something ingrained in them.

The Power of a Volunteer to Affect Change

Imagine a scenario where there are fewer than ten religious volunteers working with the Protestant chaplain at California Correctional Center. Obviously, with that limited number, much of the work needed at the prison doesn't get done.

If you were at a Level I and Level II prison in the more populated areas of California, there would be a minimum of a hundred volunteers. Unfortunately, in low population areas, such as Lassen County, there are few who can volunteer, and the prison's high profile in the community creates a climate that does not support religious programming.

Since the local community does not support the chapels, volunteers must come from long distances, and those individuals are not easy to recruit. I was privileged to have experienced being a volunteer and the rewards that come from volunteering at CCC.

Custody and the Chapel Programs

One of the big issues in chapel programming is working with custody officers.

The mission of custody is twofold. It is to provide safety and security for the inmates, employees, and all the others who are connected with the prison. This means that custody has the primary authority and decision-making ability.

I discovered that if I ever had an issue with custody, I always lost. The first thing they would do was claim it was a security issue. There was no argument against it. It was a safety and security issue, and they had the last word.

From my perspective as a Protestant chaplain, custody created the biggest issues for the inmates and for the fulfillment of the mission of the chapel program. Custody saw inmates as not worthy.

The academy teaches that inmates cannot be trusted; that they are manipulative; that they will take advantage of you at every opportunity. The mantra is, ({If their lips are moving, they're lying." Custody is ingrained with this idea, and they carry it into their spirits. When an officer graduates and returns to the prison, this attitude comes with him.

If an officer is effective, he will get promoted. The attitude or baggage he drags behind him regarding inmates is that inmates are all ugly.

Not all administrators have this attitude, but many of them do. This attitude continues even when they are promoted to associate warden, warden, or an administrator in the California Department of Corrections and Rehabilitation in Sacramento. Their attitudes toward inmates are jaded and prejudiced. They see inmates as bad.

Another problem is that when somebody disagrees with Departmental policy and sees inmates with possibility and as possessing a sense of direction or of value, too many custody officers don't like it, and they become that person's enemy.

The very nature of being a chaplain carries with it the possibility that custody officers will not like you because of a built in prejudice that a chaplain is someone who is working *for* the inmate. So chaplains are perceived as fighting against custody on behalf of inmates.

From what I have already written, you have picked up on my prejudices. I would like to enhance my reasons for being that way.

I am sharing my perception of my own experience, which may not be true for other chapel workers- but I sense that it is.

The primary issue is that custody has so much power. They have power, to a large degree, because of their labor union. Their union allows them to continue to behave inappropriately with inmates because of the nature of prisons.

Custody, by nature, wants to protect the status quo. They will fight against change. Custody and their union will do whatever is required to resist change. Over the years, they have negotiated contracts that give them great power.

Over half of all custody positions within the prison are controlled by the union that makes the assignment. They decide which officer will be assigned that position. The prison administration can only make assignments to the other positions.

In my opinion, it is impossible to run a prison effectively with a divided job assignment responsibility. If we want to understand why the California Department of Corrections and Rehabilitation is in trouble-as well as probably all prison systems in the United States-we need to discover why the warden is limited in his areas of decision making.

Someone other than the warden is responsible for staff assignments, and the people in those positions have minimum or no guidelines.

I had to face this challenge many, many times during my experience at the chapels.

At a High Desert housing unit or cell block, the officers on duty were the ones who allowed access. They could hinder a counselor getting access and could give you problems if you wanted to talk to inmates privately. They might tell the counselor they were too busy or they might infer they didn't want to give access they wouldn't do it.

I discovered that having a job that can't be taken away from someone allows that person to do as little as possible.

Too many custody officers will not do any more than necessary. They will not go the second mile, because there is no incentive for them to do it

I'm not against custody officers, but I want it understood that custody's power is a primary issue that plagues prison chapel programmmg.

Administrative personnel are usually promoted out of the ranks of custody. Very seldom do prison administrators come from outside of the system. Since administrators come from custody, they too often maintain the system. They often cannot create new paradigms. Usually, they continue to operate in the manner of their predecessors.

If someone comes with a new idea or procedure that has not been in practice, they're going to reject it. Of course, this is not 100 percent true, but it's true for probably at least 9 5 percent of what goes on.

Administrative officials do not want to get crosswise with custody. Custody has a power, through the union, to keep others from getting promotions. It has created an atmosphere where the system is broken.

Inmates and the Chapel

After custody, the second population with significance is the inmate population. Inmates are human beings; I call them "Men in Blue" because they deserve to be recognized. They are 1'Men in Blue" because in the CDCR prison system, inmates wear blue clothing. But they are men first, regardless of the uniform they wear. It is important that all populations in the prison system understand this.

One of the primary changes in prisons is that inmates are divided into ethnic groups,and they are fighting each other. Because they fight each other, they lose their power with the institution. Twenty years ago, inmates banded together and had a common voice and thus had a great deal of influence in the way inmates were treated.

Unfortunately, custody and the system sold them a bill of goods-that each ethnic group was different and that they must fight for their particular racial orientation. It is a tragedy how this orientation has stolen their power.

It is a tragedy how the inmate population has allowed ethnic prejudice to divide and conquer them, and they discovered that they lost what power they once possessed. If they would unite, they would possess power to enrich and enhance their particular living conditions.

The Hispanic population is divided into several groups. Two of the largest and most active are the southern Hispanics and the northern Hispanics. They are all from California but are divided, and they fight each other. Identifying one as Southern or Northern is predicated on where they lived in reference to the city of Fresno. If they lived south of the city of Fresno, they are Southerners. If they lived north of the city of Fresno, they are Northerners. They fight each other at the drop of a hat.

What divided them into these two groups was a pair of shoes.

An inmate leader or "shot caller" in Northern California concluded that an inmate in Southern California had stolen his shoes, and he ordered those inmates north of Fresno, CA to get even. This problem has divided these groups and made them hate and fight each other. There are more riots between these two groups than any other groups in the pnson.

The black inmate community is typically divided between the Crypts and the

Bloods. These groups were formed in the ghettos of Los Angeles. They fought on the streets and continue do so in prison.

In the white community, the Skin Heads or the White Supremacists control much of what goes on in reference to the white race inside the prison.

Their shot callers create significant problems in California prisons. None of the groups have any power except the power that is given them by the ethnic groups that they are supposed to be leading.

Custody is supported by the free staff. They do not have the vested interest and responsibilities that custody officers have, and so they are on the 110Utside." They often provide a positive atmosphere for the inmates, but they have little power to bring about change in the system.

Intimidation of Inmates Attending Chapel

Are there consequences from peers for inmates who come to chapel? Hispanics seem to come to chapel regardless of their gang affiliation on the yard. The same is true for blacks, regardless of whether they are Crypts or Bloods. They can even sit beside each other, since the chapel is a neutral area.

However, among whites, the Skinheads impose their will on everybody. If a relatively young white inmate comes to chapel for two or three weeks, suddenly, he is not there anymore. At least this was true at C and D Chapels.

The reason these inmates stop coming to chapel is that the Skinheads intimidate them. The Skinheads force their will on most of the whites, a:nd those intimidated are afraid to buck them, so they give up coming to church. This indicates the animosity and hatred that exists among the white race when it comes to racial issues and the church.

Lack of Inmate Personal Privacy

At High Desert and administrative segregation at CCC, inmates take a shower in public view. This means that if a female custody officer is on duty, an inmate is exposed to her. This is: demeaning.

I believe an inmate slhould be able to take a shower without females observing him.

The same thing is true when there is a disciplinary problem. When someone gets in a fight, or there is another disciplinary issue, the inmate is taken to the High Desert C Yard's sergeant's office and put in a metal cage without clothing. He would be there for several hours and be exposed to whomever came to the area.

Inmates have rights, even if they are dangerous men. In my opinion, being naked in the front of a female officer is not a requirement for security, and there is no reason for seeing anyone to see inmates that way.

CCC Custody Problems

During my drama club volunteering, the patio custody staff didn't treat me very nicely. They demeaned me because they were angry at the chapel being open.

Often, they wouldn't let the inmates through the Patio Gate. It was my first experience with the degree of animosity that comes from working in the chapel.

The officer who was most offensive had been on the patio for over ten years. He was a royal pain. This experience was a prelude of a continuing custody problem for me as I worked at the California Correction Center.

Plans for Sunday's General Protestant Worship Service

One of my first tasks at the main chapel was to decide how to conduct the Sunday morning general Protestant service. My personal goal in ministry at the prison was to enhance and enable volunteers and inmates to support themselves in their growth (personal and spiritual) and to provide subsistence and inspiration for the inmates.

One of my primary goals was that, as much as possible, the activities of the chapel would be inmate-driven and that they would lead and give direction to all the programs.

Obviously, this was not something they could do by themselves, so it was important to have volunteers to support them. I instructed volunteers concerning this goal. This might have not been a stated goal for them, but at least they understood my desire of the chaplain was that the inmates would have the opportunity to grow. It was a primary goal of the faith based rehabilitation program that was being implemented.

Volunteers were not just to provide the inmates with inspiration and spiritual instruction; they were to enable the inmates to have hands-on learning experiences. It might be unusual to think that inmates could not do the primary teaching and preaching. However, in some cases, because of an inmate's previous expertise and his personal Christian experience, he could be very qualified. I wanted to enhance this possibility.

Unfortunately, most inmates would not accept the word of other inmates. It took me some weeks to learn this. I thought that if their peers spoke to them, it would have more relevance than having some guru or spiritual leader speak to them. It seemed, however, that inmates did not respect each other to the degree that they would accept insight from each other. For this reason, inmates did not do the primary speaking at the worship service, nor did they teach the faith-based materials.

In worship services, I wanted to provide the volunteers an opportunity to share their ideas and inspiration. Since most traveled two or three hours and had significant expenses and time investments, I felt that they had every right to expect to speak on Sunday morning. The question was, how was I going to integrate my responsibility as a chaplain with my desire for them to have the opportunity to minister?

I decided that since we had two hours and twenty minutes of potential worship service that I would take thirty minutes for my part of the program. The rest of the time would be divided between the presentation of visual learning materials and the opportunity for the religious volunteer to give his truth for the day.

It is my opinion that the opportunity to share fifteen to seventeen minutes of inspiration is sufficient for one speaker. I believe the way we structured the program provided optimal opportunities for the religious volunteer and also provided a superb spiritual menu for the inmate.

In the beginning weeks at the chapel, the chapel clerk was responsible for all of the activities that were inmate-driven. It didn't mean he would do it, but he had the opportunity to choose the inmates for the scripture reading, praying, or a personal testimony by one of the inmates.

The service opened with announcements of the activities of the coming week. This was followed by a call to worship, which was usually a portion of a psalm and the invocation. These activities were done by the inmate clerk or by somebody that he had chosen for the task.

After that, I took pulpit for my part of the service. I usually talked for fifteen minutes. I didn't need to do it for my sake, but I felt that I had to do it to provide leadership and credibility for my being the chaplain. Normally, custody and inmates saw me as one of the primary teachers, but I did not see that as my primary role. Rather, my task was to coordinate and enable others to grow lin their ministries. After the talk, I conducted a special prayer time.

Interactive Prayer Time

This prayer procedure evolved over several months. I wanted prayer to be more than a monologue. After I finished the talk, I always offered a prayer regarding whatever participants received from the message. I prayed that what I shared would apply to their lives and help them make a decision to move in the direction of what they learned.

Then we'd sing a meditation prayer. I was introduced to the song at D Yard at High Desert by an inmate clerk. I decided to make it part of our prayer time, because it emphasized the grace of God. The lyrics are as follows:

"Surely the presence of the Lord is in this place. I can feel His mighty power and his grace. I can hear the brush of angels' wings; there is glory in each face. Surely the presence of the Lord is in this place."

After that, I would quote the following verse from Psalms: "Let the words of my mouth and the meditations of my heart be acceptable in thy sight, 0 Lord I my strength and my redeemer." I also shared another Scripture, which is as follows: "Be still and know that I am God." I shared that in the silence that would follow, that we might hear the voice of God or a message that God would speak to our lives. I told them we were going to be silent and listen.

As we listened, we would be conscious of our breath. On the in-breath, we would pray, "The Lord is my shepherd." On the out-breath we would pray, " I shall not want." We did this for a significant period of time. If we were truly focused I was assured that some way or somehow, God would speak a message to us individually. I shared that it was "in the meditations of our hearts" that we find special grace.

What inspired me to include this in our prayer time was the former chaplain at California Correctional Center, Wayne McKibbin. He used meditation as a way to help individuals get free from their addictions. He had developed a program called, "Freedom from Addiction." In that program} they used silent meditation.

So in honor of what he had done over the years in providing a new sense of direction for many inmates, and also because I discovered that breathing this prayer- "I shall not want, the Lord is my shepherd" we used this prayer in worship. I have personally learned to pray in a new way. Through this silent meditation, I find help that enables me to move in a more positive direction with my life.

The silence was usually not more than two minutes. Sometimes it seemed like an eternity, because we are not comfortable in silence. This opportunity for silence was especially important to inmates, because there is very little time when they will be able to enjoy silence. They cannot have it in their housing or on the yard. Even the church does not intentionally provide that option. I am convinced that it is critical that a moment silence be provided for inmates at the Main Chapel. Thus, a moment was available so they could meditate and allow God's Spirit to speak to them in the silence.

I would offer a short, spontaneous prayer to move us to the next stage of our prayer time. Then we prayed the Serenity Prayer, which is the prayer of the twelve-step programs.

They pray only a portion of the Serenity Prayer in secular twelve-step programs. We used the original, as written by Reynolds Niebuhr some decades ago. It goes like this: "God grant me the serenity to accept the things I cannot change, the courage to change the things I can, and the wisdom to know the difference. Living one day at a time, enjoying one moment at a time, accepting hardships as the pathway to peace; taking, as Jesus did, this world as it is, not as I would have it; and trusting that if I surrender to his will, he will make all things right, so that I will be reasonably happy in this life and supremely happy with him in the next."

It's a tragedy that the whole prayer is not used in twelve-step programs, as the complete prayer says things that help us understand how to find the serenity, wisdom, and the courage that we need. The whole prayer helps to design our lives for purpose and freedom.

Another need in prison, as in the outside world, is a need for peace. I needed a moment in church to pray for personal and universal peace. So we prayed St. Francis's Prayer:

"Lord, make me an instrument of your peace. Where there is hatred, let me so love. Where there is injury, peace; where there is doubt, faith; where there is despair, hope; where there is sadness, joy; and where darkness, light. And 0 Divine Master, grant that I might not so much seek to be consoled as to console. To be loved as to love. To be forgiven as to forgive. For it is in giving that we receive. It is in pardoning that we are pardoned, and it is in dying that we are born to eternal light."

We prayed that prayer, and then we prayed the Arsenal Prayer. This prayer was brought to CCC by Mel Novak. He has visited and spoken at prisons and skid-row missions and as a street preacher in the Los Angeles area. He's acted in myriad films as a bit player. He visited CCC and shared the prayer that he had written. It is adapted from apostle Paul's Philippian statement about the armor of God that a Christian is to wear. Following the prayer, we would sing "Sure the Presence of the Lord."

The inmate leader would introduce the next activity. Following the visual presentation, we would sing together. After we sang, the volunteers would share.

Congregational Singing Issues

One of the most critical parts of a worship service is the congregational singing. The issue that we had at our chapel was that the inmates, who played the instruments, were marching to their own drummer. They were not playing for the appropriate reason. They wanted to be rock stars and let others know how good they were, and so it seemed they weren't willing to support a true worship program.

This problem had existed long before I became the chaplain. During the interim chaplain's tenure, he had problems with musicians in the Protestant general worship service. He finally decided they would not use live music; they would sing along with CDs. When I became chaplain, I followed the procedures already in place for Sunday worship.

After a few weeks, I met inmate who purportedly had been a worship leader and played in a worship band on the outside. He seemed to be somebody who could provide responsible worship leadership for the congregation.

He was a white-collar-crime inmate. He seemed bright and articulate, and he played a fair guitar. He considered himself a great singer. My opinion was that he was *not* that good, but we gave him a chance, and it was not long before he started to act out. He wanted to choose which music we sang. He didn't like what was chosen, and he resented having to play it. He even misused the instruments. Finally, I relieved him of his responsibility, and we went back to using CD music.

The Main Chapel Clerk

Several months earlier, when I was volunteering for the drama club with Chaplain McKibbin, I had stopped a couple of times in the patio clerk's office.

The clerk's office is where all the paperwork is processed for the custody officers and the watch commander. It was summertime, and I had been in conversation with the clerks, who were sitting outside the door on the patio, waiting for work to be given to them.

One of the men there was a middle-aged lifer. He and I talked about various things, and I learned that he had been in the army in Vietnam. He had actually come up through the ranks. When he left Vietnam, he was a first lieutenant. I did not know what crime had put him in jail for life.

He already had served more than twenty years.

The reasonI speak about meeting this man is that when I found out that I would be the chaplain, the interim chaplain told me that he had appointed the "lifer" to be the chapel clerk.

I was surprised, but I was grateful, because I did not know anybody, and it would have been very difficult for me to make a rational decision about who should be the clerk for the chapel. I had a staff available to me, and on the other side at Lassen, there was the Lassen clerk who was superb and the custodian guy as well.

Betrayed

Two former custody officers were volunteering at Lassen and Main Chapels. One of them was the interim chaplain. He continued to volunteer for various programs throughout my five years as a chaplain.

The second volunteer was a relative of the only prison chaplain I knew in my early years in the civilian ministry. My friend mentored me prior to my going into the army chaplaincy. This volunteer was a primary support to the previous Protestant chaplain while he was ill. When an interim Chaplain was appointed, the volunteer opted out of volunteering.

When I became chaplain, he volunteered to counsel inmates one afternoon a week. I allowed him to use my office during my days off in order to provide him a reasonable situation for counseling.

He used it for several weeks, and then one day, this volunteer came to me and said he had discovered I had some confidential information about other volunteer, in my file cabinet and on the top of my desk. He said that since I was new in my responsibility, he would not report me, as he should, to a higher authority, if I corrected the problem. I assured him that I would do so.

I checked the folders and discovered that these materials were already in the files prior to my taking responsibility as a chaplain. Since I corrected the situation, I thought no more about it.

About two weeks later, I was called to my supervisor's office. When I got there, he told me that a volunteer purported that I had improper personal information in my office. Since this was inappropriate, he was writing me a disciplinary letter.

He informed me that I would have to take a training course on confidential

109

personal information in prisons. He also told me that I was the only one who could use my office.

I felt betrayed by this volunteer, because he had been so explicit in telling me that he was not going to report me, a statement I had not solicited. Then he turned around and reported me to my supervisor. After giving myself some time to cool off, I decided that I would ignore what he had done and take my medicine. However, I would not trust him anymore.

As a result of his action, counseling had to be done in a corner of the chapel in the future. It was truly unfortunate that volunteers could not use the office.

In the meantime, I found a locked file cabinet in the front of the chapel. It was a two-drawer file cabinet with a locking clasp. I purchased a lock to secure it. I did not want it available when I was not in the office.

Sometimes, custody officers would search my office after hours. When they did a search, they would move things around. Sometimes they even got in my computer.

I believe custody thought I had e-mail and Internet capacity, and they would use it. I was glad that [never had e-mail. I never wanted it, because I didn't want the responsibility that went with it. I couldn't control its use at night or on my day off.

It is my conviction that there were some patio custody officers who would have put pornography on my computer. Then they would have reported to the Computer Office that they believed there was inappropriate information on my computer. I would have had no way to defend myself.

The volunteer, who reported me for having personal information in my possession, continued to volunteer for the rest of my tenure, but he was never very faithful. He would volunteer for a program, get it started, and then he would have an excuse for not completing it. Part of the reason for this was an infirm spouse who often had medical emergencies. He wanted to do many things on Lassen and Main Chapels, but he never followed through. I could never depend on him.

On many occasions,it was reported that he did not like the programming and my leadership. He would act as though everything was hunky-dory, but when the chips were down, he would demean whatever was being done. I discovered he was not able to perform on a consistent basis in any church. He was a church wanderer. It must have been a character flaw.

Conducting Chaplain McKibbin Memorial Service

Chaplain McKibbin passed away shortly after I became chaplain. His wife told me the chaplain had requested that I conduct his memorial service, which was to be at Three Rivers, California, near Visalia.

I contacted the prison administration and asked for permission to conduct the service. They were not excited about my doing it. Reluctantly, I was given permission, if it did not cost them anything. I paid my own way to go, and they gave me one-day leave.

On Monday morning, we had the memorial service, and after the service, I drove back to Susanville, getting in about midnight. Tuesday was my day off, so I was able to recuperate at home.

I scheduled a memorial service at Main and Lassen Chapels. The Main Chapel service was available for inmates, free staff, and custody. There were only four free staff, seven inmates, and no custody other than the chief deputy warden and my supervisor.

Part of the reason for the limited number of inmates was Chaplain McKibbin's long illness- he had been ill for so long that few inmates knew him. Another reason for the paucity of attendance was that many inmates were at work. Some free staff would not attend because inmates were attending.

Food for Inmates

My earliest behavioral brush with custody regarding my behavior took place because I wasn't aware that I could not share any food with inmates. Shortly after becoming chaplain, I started bringing health bars for a snack. I bought them in bulk from Costco and stored them in one of the drawers in a file cabinet

As the faith-based rehabilitation program was initiated in the Main Chapel, I started out-counting inmates for training. At 3:39 p.m., inmates were counted in the houses.

It was policy that I could keep some inmates at the Chapel by following an outlined procedure. A list of inmates was submitted to Central Control, which allowed those inmates to remain in a facility during the count. They would stay at the chapel when everybody else had gone back to the house for a count. I out counted inmates at the weekend noon count and also at the 3:33 p.m. count. All out-counted inmates were confined to the chapel until counts cleared. During out-counts, inmates might be studying or cleaning the chapel.

It was impossible for inmates, other than the chapel clerks, to bring any food through the Patio Gate.. If an inmate came to the chapel at nine o'clock in the morning, and I out-counted him at 11:20 and kept him in the chapel until one o'clock in the afternoon, he would not have had anything to eat since 6:30a.m.

As a courtesy, I would sometimes offer inmates a health bar. I didn't think anything about it, but for some reason, a custody officer discovered what I was doing and reported me to the watch commander.

The watch commander came down one afternoon, when all inmates were gone. He informed me that regulations didn't allow me to give any food to inmates. I thanked him for the information, and he went his way. As I continued to out-count inmates,

I always felt guilty because I couldn't give them anything to eat.

I devised a method to circumvent this regulation. I would take health bars and throw them in the clerk's wastebasket. I would then tell a clerk to empty the basket in the garbage can outside the chapel. I did this for several months.

One evening, I out-counted people from 3:30p.m. through the out-count and the evening class, which was completed at 8:30p.m. There were five inmates, and I gave them some bars. Two of them were sitting out in the chapel, in full view, eating the bars.

An officer, who had a dislike for chapel programming, came in and found the inmates eating. When he saw them, he took a bar wrapper to the watch Commander, who then wrote me up. My supervisor called me in and asked me to explain the incident. I told him that I had thrown all the food away. He did not believe me and thought it was my way of circumventing that regulation. He wrote me up, and a letter went into my permanent file.

I was told if!continued to practice this kind ofbehavior, I was subject not only to a fine but might be fired. The reprimand stayed in my file for one year. After a year, I could request it be removed.

My Greek Fisherman's Cap

When I arrived at California Correction Center, I decided to wear the Greek fisherman's cap that I had worn at High Desert. I wore it at High Desert because the Protestant chaplain requested that I wear something that would identify me as different from inmates. He also wanted it to be different from what free staff might wear. I knew the cap would help me have a special identity.

During my first few months as chaplain, I was told by several of the custody staff that it reminded them of a chauffeur's hat. They wondered if I had once been a chauffeur.

The inmates informed me they saw me as a bike rider and liked that I rode motorcycles.

I had chosen a Greek fisherman's cap because I was a fisherman. I was fishing for men and for their freedom from ever returning to prison. I was working on making them disciples and reducing recidivism.

It is interesting that this cap brought many comments throughout my tenure at the prison. At least once a week, some inmate told me that he liked my cap and wondered that if there was a way that he could have it.

Whenever I was in town and a free staff or custody officer saw me, I was easily recognizable. Since I retired, I have continued to wear the cap in the local community and whenever I go to Reno, Nevada, to shop and see the doctor.

Invariable, someone will speak to me. They recognize me because of the cap I wear.

I'm grateful for the identification and for choosing a cap that speaks to the mission on which I was working while I was active as a prison chaplain.

Need for Repairs at Main Chapel

After the memorial service for Chaplain McKibbin, the chief deputy warden told my supervisor to initiate a work order to replace the altar and aisle carpets. There were frayed and had not been replaced in more than thirty years.

When I left the prison in May 2010,the carpet had not been replaced. I submitted repeated work orders, but nothing ever was done.

The chapel roof leaked badly. It had been leaking for more than five years. Purportedly, it was a priority item in the master plan. When funding was authorized for chapel repair, prison administration redirected the funds to other projects. The roofing was deteriorating, and it was imperative it be repaired. Unless repairs were made, the whole roof would need to be replaced.

Whenever it rained, chapel staff used a laundry cart to catch the water leaks. Even a small rain created flooding. If it snowed, the roof leaked for days. Pails of water were removed several times a week from the laundry cart. This problem existed in the Catholic chapel as well.

Phil S.'s Moving to Susanville

With three evening planned programs at Lassen Chapel, it was going to be very difficult for me to implement much of a program at Main Chapel without additional volunteers. I wasn't sure how it would work out, but I anticipated that local churches would provide the needed help.

A couple months after I became the chaplain, I received a call from a religious volunteer named Phil who had been visiting California Correctional Center from one to three times a year for approximately ten years.

This man was a full-time traveler prison volunteer. He had a circuit of prisons he visited throughout the western states. Two of the prisons he visited were the federal high-security prisons in Colorado and in Illinois.

He usually came to the California Correctional Center for at least three days and would have programs as often as they could be scheduled. He would conduct a seminar for the inmates.

Inmates in informal conversations had told me about him. He had been a full-time volunteer for approximately twenty years. When Phil called} he asked permission to come to CCC for a few days of ministry. We arranged a five-day visit and I submitted a request for approval for the program.

During the five days} he would conduct two days of programs at Lassen Chapel and three days at Main Chapel. After he completed his seminar} he went to San Joaquin Valley prisons.

When he left he said he would call again in a few months. Out of the blue, I received a phone call from Phil, requesting an appointment with me. When he came to my office, he told me that he was going to move to Susanville and would like to volunteer on a continuing basis. He would be available several times a week to help support the programs I was implementing.

It was a godsend to have a man of his stature and experience to help me. After he moved to Susanville, he conducted a Bible study/worship s€rvices. On Tuesday night, he was at Lassen Chapel, and on Wednesday night, he was at Main Chapel.

He volunteered to sponsor the Celebrate Recovery and the Forty Days programs at Lassen Chapel. He also introduced me to the health bars to help sustain my strength during my often thirteen-hour days of programming at the chapel.

I quickly learned thatt Phil was extremely astute regarding security and religious volunteers. He was a strict disciplinarian and held inmates accountable.

It was interesting when I first saw him pray. One of the inmates had already told me that this volunteer always prayed with his eyes open. So, when he first did a public prayer, I saw that this was true.

After the program, he told me that the reason that he prayed with his eyes open was because he was watching the inmates. He didn't want them to act out and do something inappropriate while he had his eyes closed. Since tlhe Scripture said,

"Watch and pray," he felt he was doing exactly what was intended by the Holy Word.

Since he was such an expert at the security issues, I asked him to help me train volunteers regarding their security responsibilities. He conducted three training sessions. With his help, we were able to help several volunteers get the volunteer ID cards.

Volunteers were required to be cleared before they could visit the prison. AID card was valid for a year. In order to renew their cards, they were required to participate in yearly training. With Phil's help, several volunteers were able to continue volunteering.

Phil also had influence with several large churches in the San Joaquin Valley. He helped me get in touch with Capital Cathedral Church in Sacramento. With his help, the church contributed a grant of four hundred dollars, which was applied toward a video projector for the Main Chapel.

Unfortunately, he was very critical of the previous chaplain. He thought the chaplain didn't have a valid Christian faith.

Prior to my coming, the inmate library had been named after the chaplain. When he discovered his name in the library, he told the inmates that if he had his way, the chaplain's name would be pulled off the wall, and it never would be there again.

Since I have great regard for Chaplain McKibbin, I ignored Phil's remarks.

Visit to Substance Abuse Program at Sierra Conservation Center

When we first implemented the Forty Days and Celebrate Recovery programs on Lassen Yard while I was a religious volunteer, the director of the substance abuse program at Sierra Conservation Center visited CCC.

I met him months earlier at the Celebrate Recovery seminar. Sierra Conservation Center is a sister institution to California Correctional Center. (SCC is the southern camp program, and CCC is the northern one.)

He told me that if we wanted him to come to CCC and share their story, he would be happy to do so. He also told me they would welcome a visit to the Substance Abuse Program program by CCC personnel.

A few weeks after I was installed as the chaplain, I asked the warden to approve my visit to Sierra Conservation Center. She authorized a three-day weekend visit and the use of a state car. I drove to Sonora, California, about one hour from Yosemite. I made the trip on Saturday in order to be at chapel programs on Sunday.

I spent Sunday morning at the chapel with the Protestant chaplain. He gave me an extensive tour. He showed me the inmate computers in the clerk's office. The facility was newer than California Correctional Center. The chapel had restrooms and several classrooms. He showed me the Level III chapel and pointed out the substance abuse facilities.

The warden at California Correctional Center had been at Sierra Conservation Center prior to coming to Susanville and was the prime mover in helping the them obtain the first faith-based rehabilitation and faith-based substance abuse program in the California prison system.

Monday morning, at about seven o'clock, I met the director of the substance abuse program (SAP). He was a custody officer and had the equivalent rank of a captain. He was a committed and practicing Christian, and I'd met him for the first time when I went to the Celebrate Recovery summit at Lake Forest, California.

The first thing we did was go to the Celebrate Recovery substance abuse program housing facility, which housed approximately 150 inmates. These inmates were a part of the substance abuse program.

They had been recruited from across Northern California from Level III prisons. To qualify for the program, an inmate had to be eligible for parole in less than three years. I attempted to locate inmates from California Correctional Center, but there were no inmates who met the criteria.

When I got to the housing unit, they had already eaten and were having a joint meeting in the meeting area of the housing facility. There were cells all around the walls. There were rows of chairs.

The opening program began with a short devotional and prayer time. This was followed by a news section, with daily news and funny stories. This was followed by community-building games. The games were all related to interrelational expences.

All of these activities were inmate-led and lasted about forty-five minutes. Each week, a team of inmates planned and conducted these activities.

Following the housing meeting, we went to a modular set of classrooms, reserved for Substance Abuse Program. There were at least five classrooms with a thirty student room seating. There were several free-staff teachers and teaching assistants.

It turned out there was another Substance Abuse Prograam using the facility. All of the classes were inmate driven. A great deal of the teaching was in small groups.

I sat in on two programs led by the inmates. In my judgment, they were effective in opening up communication and helping people to explore their reasons for their substance abuse. I stayed that afternoon and that evening. On Tuesday morning, I returned Susanville, which was a seven-hour trip.

I was grateful for the opportunity to observe the program. It gave me insight on how CCC Main Chapel could be implemented. Although CCC's program was not a twenty-four-hour program, it did provide options for helping inmates to change.

I gave my supervisor an oral report of the trip and wrote a report for the warden. In my reports, I explained options I thought we could implement in the Main Chapel program.

Establishing the Lassen Sierra Prison Ministries Foundation

Thanks to Phil S. and. his foundation, early financial purchases were possible. It was almost immediately that I recognized that some way of purchasing chapel equipment and curriculum materials would require an independent agency as a go-between for the prison and private donations.

Issues concerned with purchasing the chapel chairs indicated I must find a solution to this problem. Providing an income tax deduction to donors was imperative. The solution to the problem would be to establish a 501c3 foundation.

While working at a Missouri state university} I was assigned the responsibility of helping to establish a 501c3 charitable foundation for alumni charitable giving. I worked with the university lawyer to obtain IRS approval and then recruited the possible foundation board meetings.

I talked with some local ministers who had IRS approval for giving} and they recommended that private counsel should coordinate completing the forms. The cost for this support was $11200.

I chose the name Lassen Sierra Prison Ministries, Inc. The mission of the foundation was to support the audio visual, and educational needs of the Protestant chapels at California Correctional Center} High Desert State Prison the Herlong Federal Institution, and the Lassen County Jail.

A designated gift from one of the participating institutions was used to support programs at the chapel.

Undesignated gifts were prorated to all the prisons, based on the percentage of all inmates in Lassen County. This allowed me and others to make gifts to support the faith-based rehabilitation programs at California Correctional

Center.

I completed the IRS forms to the best of my ability. Then I found an expert in the Bay Area to review my material and make corrections in the proposal. Unfortunately, I did not yet possess the money to cover his fee. This meant that as with the chairs, I had to raise the money or give it myself.

Since I was a little boy, I have been going door-to-door to solicit or sell vegetables or ask people to visit my church. So I decided to contact businesses inSusanville and solicit a gift of a hundred dollars to pay for the foundation's IRS approval.

Since the prisons were the primary industry in Lassen County, much of their financial success was directly related to those institutions. I thought anyone might be willing to give to such an ideal way of helping to reduce recidivism.

I went to one of the leading realtors and asked him for a gift of a hundred dollars to support the prison ministry. He swelled up like a toad, and his face got red as he told me to get out of his office; he didn't want anything to do with me. He hated inmates, and he would never do anything to support anything that might help them. He was a man who I had socialized with several times. I really touched a hot button with him, and he sent me packing.

Then I went to one of the leading furniture stores and asked the owner to make a contribution. He got angry with me too and told me to go my way, and he didn't want anything to do with me.

Then I visited the leading motel owner, who owned 90 percent of Susanville motels. I asked for a hundred-dollar gift, and he sandbagged me. He never gave a dime to support the cause.

When you are in the asking business, you must always focus on the next "ask"- that could be a successful one.

I went to the owner of the leading car dealerships, who I knew had a spirit and heart, because I'd talked with him before about prison rehabilitation. He made the first contribution of a hundred dollars to move me toward my goal of $1,200.

I decided to talk with one of the Susanville pastors I knew. I asked him if his church would make a contribution. He told me that their missions funding was committed for the year. So I asked him if he knew of anyone in the community who might open to providing support for my project.

He suggested I see a man who had a medical service. He was generous and was interested in missions.

I told the man my dream and what I needed. He said, "Jack, I'll match anything that you raise from the community} up to $1,200."

This was an answer to a prayer. It was exactly what I needed to solicit additional gifts. When I raised the initial gifts to obtain his match} I could pay for the video projector that I had agreed to purchase from Mr. S.

I contacted religious volunteers who came on Sunday and asked each of them to consider making a hundred dollar contribution so the matching gift could be obtained. I also contacted other friends and challenged them to make a contribution. I was able to raise the $1,200, and the generous matching gift covered these special needs.

My next task was finding people to serve on the board. My supervisor informed me that I was not to be a front man for soliciting gifts from the community. I needed a cadre of local community leaders to help me. Fortunately, I was not aware of this problem when I obtained the funding for the foundation fees and video projector.

It was my aim to recruit leaders from various occupations in the community as directors. I also wanted one director who had had direct custody experience. I went to the former interim chaplain and asked him to consider serving on the board for three years. After several days, he agreed.

I knew a retired judge who I had seen out at the prison doing prerelease presentations, so I made a luncheon appointment with him. I asked him to serve, and he agreed to serve for three years.

Someone suggested I contact the retired Lassen County sheriff, who had an awesome reputation in the community. He did not want to be a director, but he said he would make a charitable gift each year to the foundation.

Then I went to the auto dealer who had been so generous in making the first gift for the match. I asked him to serve. After considering it for several days, he told me it was not something he wanted to do.

I decided to contact a lay pastor, who had recently been appointed assistant superintendent of Lassen County of the Board of Education. I asked him to serve on the board and he agreed.

I called a meeting of the group, and each of them assumed a leadership role. This information was required on the IRS application.

The proposal was sent to the Bay Area expert for his review. After three weeks, he sent it back exactly as I had first written it. He did not revise it all and said the IRS would approve it. I had board members sign it and submitted it to the IRS. Within six weeks, the IRS sent an approved form.

Obtaining a DVD Projector for Main Chapel

I was struggling on how to purchase a DVD projector for the Main Chapel so we could conduct Forty Days and Celebrate programs for a chapel full of inmates. Mr. S. told me he had a projector that I could use temporarily until I was able to find the funding for one.

I graciously accepted. his offer. When he brought the projector/ he also had a movable screen and two speakers for sound projection. We used them for several weeks when he told me he would be willing to sell it to me for $1,500.

Although it was a used one, it was a better deal than anything else I could get. I knew it would serve us until we could purchase a new projector that could be mounted in the ceiling. I bought it.

One of the reasons it was a temporary fix was we needed a more powerful project to take care of the more than two hundred inmates who sometimes might view a program. I received authorization for a more powerful projector that was mounted in the ceiling. I purchased a large motorized ten-foot-by-twelve-foot project that was mounted in the front of the chapel. When these items were installed, it served the program effectively and is still operational.

Visiting Great Susanville

Shortly after my appointment as chaplain, the interim chaplain told me there was a local minister's group that met once a week for fellowship and prayer. He told me I should consider joining.

I thought, 'Well, yeah, it's something that I would consider, but I want to be sure that I am welcome." I wasn't sure after my experience with Susanville businessmen.

I knew there was strong animosity against the prison in some local churches. The Susanville 110ld guard" disliked the prison because it had changed their community from a timber town to a prison town. With the demise of the timber industry Susanville would have been a ghost town without the prisons.

I decided to contact one of the local pastors and he invited me to their meeting} which took place in one of the oldest restaurants in Susanville. There was a large room in the back of the restaurant which had served as a community meeting room in the 1900s. The owner had a small auxiliary floor heater} because he couldn1t afford to heat the room for a small group.

A maximum of ten ministers attended the meeting.

One of the pastors at the meeting was JJ, who was on the foundation board. He was a pastor of an independent community church. He founded the church when he graduated from the university and began to teach school in Susanville. He started it as a house church and his inspiration for founding it came from a book called Body *Life*. This book described a church from the California Bay Area. The church met in his home for several years.

When it outgrew his home, they purchased a California fire facility. They remodeled it as a church facility. There was no paid staff.

One of the other senior pastors had been in Susanville for more than fifteen years. He had a significant number of custody officers in his church.

I often ask him to volunteer at the chapel, but I could not enlist him. He told me that earlier on in his Susanville ministry, he had decided to never work with inmates in the prison. My judgment is that he recognized such a ministry was controversial with custody, and he decided he would not endanger someone attending his church.

Two of the ministers from the Evangelical Free church were also members of the group. Their church was located downtown, but they had outgrown it for Sunday worship, and they met in the local high school. During the week they used the church. They had building plans for a new church.

One other pastor from an independent Bible church in Janesville completed the core of the active participants in the group. He rode a motorcycle as his primary transportation.

Several pastors from other churches were attendees but were not present each week. I was a member of the group during my tenure at the chapel. I had been looking for fellowship, because I know no one can be a lone ranger when it comes to Christian ministry.

The meetings were on my day off, but they were so important to me that I made it in spite of the inconvenience. I recognized that I needed fellowship, so every week I came to this program. It was a high priority for me.

About seven months before I retired, I enlisted four pastors from the group to volunteer at the prison. They also referred members of their churches to me for consideration as religious volunteers.

I told Phil S. about the group, and one Wednesday, he came. I learned much about Phil by observing his behavior with these pastors.

After several months of participating in the group, I asked each of them to give me five minutes on Sunday to share with their congregation my dream for a faith-based rehabilitation program at CCC.

Books, Bibles, and
Literature for Inmates

As we prepared to start Celebrate Recovery at the Main Chapel, it was discovered that Celebrate Recovery handbooks now cost $2.17 a copy. Unfortunately, five books were required for the program, which would be a cost of ten dollars an inmate. Sixty inmates would cost six hundred dollars. If we repeated or enlarged the program, the cost would be prohibitive Since the Main Chapel participants were transient because of obtaining a camp assignment, it would require at least $2,000 a year for the program. Now I knew I had a major problem.

The CCC chapels had a shortage of Bibles. The only Bibles available were recycled Gideon hard-back Bibles. They were formerly in motels and were being replaced so the Gideon's donated them to pnsons.

Unfortunately, inmates cannot have hard-back books in their houses. In order to use them, inmate volunteers carefully removed the hard-back covers. These Bibles were recycled on Saturday and Sunday mornings. There was minimal success, but these were the only Bibles available.

New Bibles from the American Bible Society cost 20 percent of the market value of the Bible, which paid the postage. I order fifteen different samples of Bibles. Some of the translations were the New King James, the New English Version, the American Standard translation, and two different Spanish translations.

I was double and trijple tithing from my chapel income to provide resources needed in the program I had committed to. I purchased $1,500 worth of Bibles from the American Bible Society, and we distributed them over the next two years at Lassen and Main.

Fortunately, an organization called Living Waters, out of Oregon, decided to provide us with the New King James Version of the *Nelson Study Bible*. It was a resource for inmates who wanted to be students of the Bible.

In order to be accountable to Living Waters, a form was developed, which the inmate would sign, indicating that he got the Bible. On the form, the inmate would give a history of his past, his church relationship, and his relationship to God.

Periodically, the forms were sent to Living Waters to let them know that we were accountable. Living Waters would send us about fifty Bibles a month. We would distribute them throughout the pnson.

At least twice a year, a case of these Bibles was sent to each of the eighteen camps that were a part of the CCC fire camp program. The Bibles were an incredible resource to religious studies at CCC.

A similar form was developed for the American Bible Society. Twice a year, the forms were submitted to the American Bible Society so they would know we were making the distribution and that their contribution was valuable.

One of the contemporary translations, which is very helpful with inmates, is *The Message*. It's a contemporary translation of the Scripture in English. Many traditional Christians do not like it, because it is in contemporary English in the form of a story.

It's a story. It's a story of how God wanted a relationship with another creature. That creature he called man and woman. The first human family failed, and the relationship he anticipated was thwarted. So the story of the Bible is how God went about reconciling and brought us all back into this relationship he had dreamed that we would have. That's why it is a story. We need to understand it that way and recognize it that way.

I made a purchase of about five hundred of these Scriptures. They cost six dollars a copy. We used them as special awards throughout the years that I served as the chaplain.

Two sources gave us books during my tenure. One was Dr. James Gills, who is a medical doctor in the Deep South. He has written a series of books regarding the Christian faith that are very readable and are popular among inmates. Once a year, he would send us several boxes of these books. We used them extensively, especially in administrative segregation, because they were paperback and easy to read.

A prison library organization from Georgia sent Christian periodicals, books, and videos to the chapel. The first shipment was a monstrous mailing seven or eight hundred books. Included in that delivery were copies of the New Translation of the Scripture with a leather cover. It was a soft cover, and it became the primary gift that I would give to individuals who served the chapel well. I would give it to them in a box.

In some cases} I suspect} they sent it home as a representative of what they had accomplished. The distribution from this special library program was made both to Lassen and Main Chapels. It was wonderful.

Guidepost magazines were sent bimonthly. It was information that most inmates would read. It was also an item used for visiting in the infirmary and for administrative segregation.

Buck Steele and the Bill Loucks Volunteers

The first Sunday that Buck Steele came to conduct the worship service, he brought Bill and Lisa Loucks. Lisa Loucks had a great voice and sang a solo to a CD accompaniment. It was a very meaningful time and the inmates, as well as me, appreciated her contribution to the worship service.

They continued to come each month when Buck Steele was there. Bill Loucks was a principal of a small school near Weaverville, California, and Lisa had a pet grooming business. They had terrific spirits, and they were significant to me because they were the first new volunteers during my tenure as chaplain.

Changing Chairs for Pews
in Main Chapel

In the middle of our second Main Chapel 40 Days program, I realized we had to make a change in the seating arrangements in the chapel. It was required if we were going to implement the program that I told the warden to expect, and I anticipated it would work.

That change was to find individual chairs to replace the pews. This was a major project, and I needed to get a cost estimate for the project. I estimated we would need two hundred chairs for the chapel.

My sources told me it would cost fifty dollars a chair. That meant it would cost ten thousand dollars to refurnish the chapel.

I knew that the prison would not do anything about it. If I would submit a proposal, I would have to guarantee funding for the purchase of the chairs. The funding would have to be contributions from individuals or institutions outside the walls.

As I prayed about what I should do, I quickly recognized that if I was going to make this suggestion, it was very unlikely that I would get a contribution pledge ahead of time. This contribution would have to be a faith act. I would have to trust that the idea, which I had, was a God-given idea and that somehow the way to do it would become apparent.

I finally recognized that if the chips came down, there was one way that it could be done. I would have to be willing to step up to the plate and personally guarantee the money myself. Ultimately, the whole program depended on my willingness to make any necessary sacrifices to make it happen.

It took me a few days to digest this idea, and I came to the conclusion that if I was to remain in this position, I must decide. I decided that regardless of whether there was any money receiv,ed from any outside source, I would guarantee that the ten thousand dollars wolilld be provided to buy the chairs.

I wrote the proposal and submitted it to the warden and gave a copy to my supervisor. I didn't know if there was going to be any response.

A few days later, I was called to the warden's office for a meeting. I met with my supervisor, the warden and the chief deputy warden.

We talked about moving the pews. I informed them that I had already spoken to the vocational cabinetry program, and they would accept the pews and dismantle them. The wood would be used for projects within the prison. They would be willing to use some of the wood to provide cabinetry and storage in the chapel, which was so desperately needed.

I informed them that we could have the two hundred chairs for ten thousand dollars. I said that I would continue to look for other options. I shared that someone said Sam's Club had a chair that would work and was less costly.

I went to the Reno, Nevada, Sam's Club and discovered a plastic/aluminum stacking chair, which was called a Lifetime Chair. It was very comfortable. Seven chairs could be stacked together, and each chair was only twenty-five dollars.

I purchased one chair and took it back to the prison. I made contact with my supervisor and requested that someone check this chair to see if it would meet the requirements of security.

The second-watch commander approved the chair and said that it would pass the security test. She requested that two screws be secured before we installed the chairs. I researched the issue and found that the local hardware store had a screw that would secure the screws.

The price of the chairs was only half of what I had anticipated. With ten thousand dollars, chairs could also be purchased for the Catholic chapel.

I went to the Catholic chaplain and asked him if he wanted any chairs.

He agreed he would like to have the change, because it would allow him to do programming that he couldn't do with fixed seating. I made an arrangement that we would buy five hundred chairs. The Catholic chapel would have 250 chairs, and the Protestant chapel 250 chairs.

Unfortunately, we still didn't have any funding. I called a couple of leaders in the Redding Prison Fellowship program and shared what the warden had approved -I could get five hundred chairs for ten thousand dollars. I asked them to pray for the project.

A few days went by, and I got a call from the Ralston's, Volunteers from Redding, CA. They told me that they had just talked to their senior pastor, and he had agreed to give forty-five hundred dollars to purchase the chairs.

I heard from another source that the large church in Redding, which had never made a contribution to the chapel, had decided that they would give forty-five hundred dollars. That was nine thousand dollars.

In the meantime, I had written a letter to five hundred churches in Lassen and the surrounding counties, requesting that they make contributions. I also sent letters to friends and inmate parents for contributions. From all these sources, we collected fifteen hundred dollars.

Phil S's Foundation agreed to accept the gifts and purchase the chairs.

I contacted purchasing at Sam's Club in Reno to order the chairs. They informed me they would make the order when they were paid. It took two weeks to make the payment.

After another two weeks, Sam's Club called to let us know the chairs were at the store. It took four days to make the arrangements for a CCC truck to pick up the chairs. They put them in storage.

The next problem was getting the pews removed. The vocational cabinetry shop agreed to dismantle the pews when I got permission for some inmates from the shop to come to the chapel. I obtained permission, and they sent over a crew of six men to dismantle the pews. It took two days to finish the dismantling.

It took another day to get a truck to take the materials to the vocational shops at Main and Lassen. On Friday, the chairs were brought to the chapel.

The Catholic chaplain had some resistance from Catholic custody, who didn't think it was a good idea. He backed away, and I ended up with five hundred chairs. The chairs were stored along the chapel walls.

After three months, seating at Lassen Chapel also became a problem. The inmates were dismantling the wood chairs and stealing the wood and some of the bolts to make weapons. Custody wanted to replace the chairs. We took ninety chairs from the Main Chapel to Lassen Chapel. The chairs at Lassen were also used in the Lassen visiting room when Celebrate Recovery was conducted there.

As you can imagine, the chairs changed the whole atmosphere for small group activities. It allowed us to be flexible in our seating.

If we were going to have a small group, we could arrange chairs so that people would be sitting close to each other. Inmates preferred to sit alone, rather than close to another inmate. It was a matter of trust. Being able to limit how many chairs we had on the floor, we were able to limit how the seating was arranged. It made for more effective communication.

It's hard to believe that the decision I made to put up the ten thousand dollars, if needed, never occurred. It is a picture that the resource that is available on the outside is more than adequate for meeting the need. It taught me a great lesson about the possibility of getting help when help is needed.

Finding Outside Funding

During my time as a volunteer at Lassen Chapel, I learned that if any faith-based rehabilitation programming was to occur, it was up to me to find the funding. If funding was to be, it was my responsibility to figure out how to do it.

I made a decision to use some of my tithe money, which I normally use for charity and my church, for the programming I had instigated for Lassen Chapel. During my volunteer days at Lassen Chapel, anything that was done there was a result of the funding that I was able to find out of my own resources.

I spent more than five thousand dollars as a Lassen Chapel volunteer to fund programming. I decided to do this voluntarily, because I was committed to seeing the 40 Days of Purpose and Celebrate Recovery programming succeed.

Long ago, I learned that if anybody was going to realize something, it was going to cost-in time and often in monetary resources. I expected that it would cost me money, which these programs did.

During my five years as Protestant chaplain, there was a never a budget. I would ask about it and would be told there was no money or budget. There were two occasions when funding was provided for the Protestant chapel.

The first time it was an inner-faith rehabilitation program. I presented it to the warden, and she promised to pay for the curriculum materials for the first portion of the program. The teaching materials could be used again. The package cost a thousand dollars.

She agreed to fund it in two installments since it was an inner-faith program. An invoice of six hundred dollars was paid. When I submitted an invoice for the remaining five hundred dollars, she informed me the budget would not allow the purchases because of budget revisions. It was my responsibility to find funding if the program was to continue.

The second funding was for purchase of a piano, which would allow the presentation of classical concerts to Main Chapel inmates. The chapel piano was tinny and could not be tuned.

My supervisor also served as chairman of the Lassen County Arts Council. He had asked me if classical concerts would fit my faith-based rehabilitation program. Of course they would, I told him.

He was able to find budget funding to purchase an electronic organ-piano. Itcost $1,500, and it provided many musical options not normally available in a chapel. The instrument was used in normal chapel programming, as well as serving as a concert instrument. The piano was the only equipment purchased by the prison during my five years as the Protestant chaplain.

Main Chapel's First 40 Days Program

In scheduling the first Forty Days program at the Main Chapel, the chapel clerk served as the inmate leader. He introduced the DVD program on a fifty-inch television.

Because of the small image, it was not possible to have a full chapel. The class was limited to fifty inmates, in small groups of six. Eight groups were the maximum we could have in the available space-the chapel seating was pews, so there was little flexibility. Two additional groups could be seated on the chapel stage.

The text for the course was Rick Warren's *Forty Days of a Purpose-Driven Life*.As we prepared to order the books, Saddleback Church initiated a policy that each prison had to pay a portion of the cost of the book. Each book cost $1.25.

In future planning of the program, it would be necessary to have a minimum of five hundred dollars to cover book costs for one year of programming. The only way to increase these numbers would be to change the chapel seating.

Out-of-Town Volunteers' Sacrifices

After I became chaplain, I discovered the extreme generosity of the volunteers who came to the chapels on weekends. They came from miles away and had to find housing for themselves and pay travel and food expenses.

I felt they should receive a small token of appreciation for their sacrifice but there was no resource at the prison. I decided that I should provide some script for a noon meal at the snack bar each day when volunteers traveled farther than fifty miles from Susanville.

Since most of them also supported the faith-based programming} I believed the small token of appreciation would help them know that the prison appreciated their work. It cost approximately $220 a month to cover the cost of the volunteers who traveled more than fifty miles to the chapel.

I purchased script, which is the prison money, at the cashier's office. When an eligible volunteer worked in the chapel, I would give him or he.r five dollars, which would purchase a snack bar meal. I continued this program for the next th.ree years.

We would not have been able to accomplish most of the programs at the chapel if it had not been for these volunteers. I felt that my financial contribution to them was worth every dime. Even more than that, it was critical to the ongoing success of the program. I was grateful that I could do it.

In addition to supporting volunteers, there were the expenses for buying office supplies, which were not available through prison supply.

Prison Fellowship Seminar

Following our first Forty Days program} the Redding Prison Fellowship group presented a seminar in the Main Chapel. It had been more than five years since they had been to the prison. The leaders of the seminary were Roger and Joan Ralston. They brought ten othe.r volunteers from their Prison Fellowship program.

The seminar was a small group program. Each of the volunteers led one of the groups. Approximately one hundred inmates came to the seminar.

The only way to accommodate the small groups was to have the pews set back-to hack; the inmates sat in the pews with a space between them and the next pew.

The volunteer leaders sat at the end of the pews, with approximately ten inmates in their groups. We survived the program, but it was not easy.

During the program, I talked with two of the volunteers who were lay leaders in two of the largest churches in Redding. I told them I was considering presenting a proposal to the warden to replace the pews with chairs. My big problem was how to finance it. After a short discussion we went on to another subject.

Climate in Susanville Church Community

In my early months as a chaplain, I visited about twenty different churches, attempting to encourage the pastors to become involved in prison ministry. I didn't do very well. I did discover that some of them were isolationists when it came to prison.

Three churches had great animosity toward the 40 Days Program and any other Rick Warren material. They thought it was heresy.

Speaking in a Local Church

One of my first programs was at the Christian Fellowship Church in Janesville. The Pastor didn't just give me five minutes; he also asked me to speak for the worship service. Two custodial officers were there with their families. One was from High Desert and the other was a CCC lieutenant and member of the church board. He worked a different shift, so I had never met him. He was extremely gracious.

Visiting a Large Church

One of the largest churches in Susanville asked me to share about the CCC chapel program. I shared the dream and some of the excitement that was taking place in the chapel.

After the service, no one spoke to me. The pastor left immediately after the benediction for another meeting.

Several weeks later, the pastor told me that during the previous two Sundays, two families had come to him to say, "We're back, Pastor."

He hadn't known they were gone, but he wanted to know why they had not been attending services. He discovered that the reason they had left was because they were angry over my presentation and so they had decided to leave the church. After they calmed down, they came back.

He told me that there were five families that left the church because I'd been there. That's quite a cost to have somebody speak. It made me evaluate my sharing with local churches if I created that kind of animosity.

Engaging a Custody Officer
at Church

I also spoke at one a church whose pastor was a leading clergyman in Susanville. I wasn't the primary presenter, but I had opportunity to speak for about ten minutes at both the early service and the later service.

At the early service, one of the CCC custodial staff was there. He had confronted me and demeaned me in public on the CCC patio. He was angry and had continued to create problems on the patio.

I usually am able to engage people when I talk, and I worked very hard and moved all over the front of the church, trying to get his eye. During the whole time I was there, he would not honor me by looking at me.

After the service was over, he was standing in the back of the church, and I went back and greeted him. I wanted to be sure that he recognized that I would reach out to someone, regardless of how he felt about me.

Meeting with the EV Free Congregation

I had an opportunity to speak at the EV Free Church, which met in the high school recreational center. The pastor was gone that Sunday, so I was the primary speaker. After the services, young people crowded around and wanted to talk to me.

The older people of the church tended to shun me-even though I was standing with the lay leader, they did not speak with me. I believe it was because churches in prison communities do not often have a prison ministry.

A Susanville Fellowship Group

The final church I'll mention was one of the fellowship churches in Susanville. They were very gracious and the pastor extremely so.

The next week, he called me to say the church had agreed to take care of the cost of the books for one year for Celebrate Recovery, and the 40 Day Program. I was able to purchase approximately a thousand dollars worth of books because this church made this contribution.

It was a great boon to us, and I appreciated it more than you could ever believe. I couldn't believe that he was so generous. The other churches didn't make any contribution to the prison ministry, although the one church, where there were five families who were disenchanted, did make a contribution later to support the ministry.

About six months prior to my retirement, I was able to enlist three of these ministers to get gate clearances, which meant that they could come to the chapel if they came with a beige volunteer card.

Traveling Vietnam Wall
Susanville Visit

On July 4, 2007, the Susanville Minister's Association, along with civic organizations, sponsored the Vietnam Wall visit. The keynote speaker was Bob Wayland. He wrote a book titled *Walking across America.*

During the Vietnam War, he lost both of his legs. He made a decision to walk across America, using his arms as legs, and as he moved across the continent, he kept a diary about his experiences and then wrote a book.

I worked with the project coordinator, and Mr. Wayland agreed to speak at the Main Chapel on a Saturday afternoon. When he got to the chapel, he came in a wheelchair, because his walk across America caused him to have severe bursitis and arthritis.

During his presentation, he got out of the wheelchair and onto the floor and used his arms. I'm sure it was very painful, but by doing it, he illustrated his message of hope and reconciliation. He talked about how it was possible to turn your life around, and lack of recidivism was not a dream. He inspired the inmates who were there.

As a result of the wall visit, I was able to recruit several local ministers to serve as keynote speakers for the Purpose Driven Life graduations. At the program, we had a baptismal service. Six different local ministers came to the prison and baptized new believers. Normally, there were at least forty inmate participants at each baptism. This experience gave them an opportunity to experience the validity of prison ministry.

Forty-Day Book Outline

The inmate assignment lieutenant was part of a worship team in a local congregation. After he read the The Purpose Driven Life book, he outlined it, pointing out the major message in each day of the forty days of lessons.

The interim chaplain told me about it, and we were able to get a copy of it from the lieutenant. He gave us permission to reproduce it. It became one of the instruments we gave to the inmates who became a part of the 40 Days program.

It was extremely helpful. It took all of the ideas that were in each chapter of the book and broke them down to the very minimum. Thus, the lessons could be understood and maintained in the inmates' memories for a longer time.

The Louckses' Volunteer Commitment

In June 2005, Bill and Lisa Loucks, who came to the chapel with Buck Steele on the third Sunday of the month, called me to say they were moving to Susanville. They were moving because they wanted to support the programs that I was designing for faith-based rehabilitation. What a godsend- we needed volunteers at the Lassen Chapel.

They had purchased a rundown old house in Susanville that had once been a classic home. They had received a grant to partially restore it.

Bill Loucks was a teacher and had been working in a small school district just outside of Weaverville. They were coming to Susanville to work and volunteer, although they had no prospects for a job. This was a major faith step for those folks. It turned out that their walk with the church had not been very long, but they were awesomely committed.

Before they got here, Bill started to look for a position. He went to the county school superintendent's office. It turned out that there was a position open to work with students who had learning disabilities, and that was one of Bill's specialties. He got a job working with troubled seventh and eighth grade students who were failing in school.

He did this for four years and was extremely successful. The county superintendent told me that he felt fortunate to have found Bill to do the program. Lisa, after coming to Susanville, took her GED and then went to Lassen Community College and obtained her AA degree as a licensed practical nurse. They were God's answer to a great need.

Gate Pass and Beige Card Approvals

One of the most continuing problems for volunteers was getting a gate pass. The vital information required was their names on their driver's licenses, their birth dates, and their social security numbers.

These items are used to search the records to find if they have any misdemeanors or other issues that could prevent them from being a volunteer. This information must be submitted by the Community Partnership Manager's Office.

As chaplain, I couldn't gather this information. The clerk submitted the information to the gatehouse for their action. Often, there was a time lapse in the process that delayed the issuing of the gate pass. Sometimes the personnel lost the material, and it had to be resubmitted. This problem existed throughout my tenure as chaplain.

The second issue was getting prison ID cards or beige cards for volunteers so they could function without the chaplain's presence. Religious volunteers were considered unpaid state employees by the administration. Many of the custody officers saw them as interlopers and not qualified to supervise inmates.

These passes had to be renewed annually, and it was difficult to track them. Many times, after volunteers had traveled more than one hundred miles, the beige cards did not clear.

Much of the problem was with the Personnel Office, which issued the cards. The lack of timely approval was a continuing problem during my tenure as chaplain. A written procedure for this program was n,ever addressed by Personnel.

Annual Training for Volunteers

Volunteers had an annual training requirement. The specific courses or programs were never stipulated. It ended up being at the whim of the training lieutenant as to what was required.

When I first went to work at the prison, the training lieutenant had been there for many years and was nearing retirement. He required volunteers to attend the appropriate classes in the free-staff training program. It was offered once a month and could be completed in one day.

The new lieutenant, however, did not want volunteers in a class with the free staff; he wanted a special class for the volunteers. The training was completed in one afternoon and consisted of four classes.

Each time a new officer took control, the way volunteers were trained was changed. At the end of my tenure, the procedure was to offer volunteer training four times a year.

Volunteer Supervision of Inmates

The major issue I faced during my five years as chaplain was how many inmates a religious volunteer could supervise. When I came to the chapel, the rule was twenty five inmates per volunteer.

And there were only two exceptions to that rule: the two retired custody officers. They were eligible to have full chapel; otherwise, a volunteer, no matter how long he had been a volunteer, was limited to twenty-five inmates.

This created major problems on weekends. Weekend attendance at worship and Bible studies was much higher than twenty-five. Thus, a program required the chaplain be present so that all inmates coming to the meeting could be approved.

Volunteers for self-help groups were authorized for fifty inmates. The argument was that free staff was better trained to supervise. Free staff received a stipend for supervising, but religious volunteers did not cost the prison anything.

Volunteers were doing it as a mission, as a project, as something to which they personally were committed, yet they were limited in how many people they could supervise.

It seemed to me that was an inequity, especially when a volunteer may have been coming to the chapel for as many as five to twenty years and still could not supervise more than twenty-five inmates. My arguments were never accepted. There were no exceptions to the rule.

I conducted a survey of all thirty-four state prisons regarding the number of inmates a religious volunteer could supervise. Most of them had a rule that a volunteer could supervise the number of inmates that were authorized for a given room. In two cases, prisons limited new volunteers to fifty inmates. The only prison with a limit for supervision was Old Folsom.

From my first day at High Desert, I was able to supervise as many inmates as a facility would hold. There was no requirement that I have training. It is a Level IV facility, whicih gave volunteers more trust and responsibility than CCC, a Level I or II prison.

I submitted a proposal to the warden for a relaxation of the 2 5J 1 rule. Chaplains met twice a year with the warden to discuss chapel programming. I brought up my proposal request at the meeting. The warden turned to my supervisor and asked him if he had read the report; he hadn't. The warden did not say a word and went on to the next agenda item.

After three years as a chaplain, I submitted a new request for four volunteers to be given full chapel clearance. To my great surprise, it was approved. This allowed flexibility in planning for weekend programming.

Frank K. and Bill L. were also authorized to visit the administrative/segregation unit. For the remainder of my time as chaplain, I was able to get more and more volunteers authorized to supervise more than twenty-five inmates.

Inmate Clerk Frank W.

Frank was the Main Chapel clerk for the first thirteen months of my tenure at the prison. He was scheduled to be paroled in July 2006 after serving a sentence of more than twenty years. He had started out at Pelican Bay and spent some months in what's called "the Shoe," the most segregated and regulated program in all the prisons.

He finally adjusted to prison and decided to rehabilitate. During his last years at Pelican Bay, he worked with the chaplain very closely. He obtained a licensed minister credential as a result of the training he took with the chaplain.

In 1996, he was transferred to CCC and eventually ended up on the Level II yard. Prior to becoming the chapel clerk, he was lead clerk on the patio. While housed at Cascade Yard in the main division of the prison, he had gone to work in the patio as the clerk for the custody officers. The interim chaplain knew him there, and he ended up hiring him as the chaplain's clerk about three weeks before I took my position.

It was a very positive move for him, because I would not have had the experience to have made a very good decision about it. Frank was smart, streetwise, and prison-wise, and he knew how to work the system.

Recently, I met an inmate who was housed with him during the time he was the chapel clerk. In his house and on the yard, he was with the old guys, "the old fish." He worked with them, used their language, lived their kind of existence, and followed their rules. When he came to chapel, however, he put on another face. He acted like he was holy, and he conducted the services for me because that's what I wanted. He did it effectively.

About six months before he was ready to parole, he talked to me about what he planned to do when he got out of prison. He had decided to go back to Southern California, near where his parents lived, and establish a program to help inmates who were getting out of prison. He hoped to provide them with clothing and an employment service. I was excited about his dream and suggested he share it with other volunteers.

Mr. Herring, a religious volunteer, was retired from the men's clothing business. He had contacts that could help Frank with his dream. It appeared Frank had discovered a purpose.

Patio Problems with Custody and Whistle-Blowing

From the inception of my service as chaplain, I had continuing problems with three or four custody officers. They were intent on limiting and controlling what went on at the chapel.

Two of them were elected officers for the local chapter of the labor union. They continually discredited me and talked ugly to the inmates as they cleared them through the gate.

I talked to my supervisor about this issue on many occasions and was extremely frustrated by it. One day he said to me, "Jack, your predecessor was over here to see me at least three times a week on the same problem. And he did that for three years, and we didn't get anything done. So what I want to tell you is, put up or shut up. That's all I want to tell you."

After mulling it over for several days, I decided, "If it is to be, it's up to me." I decided to file a discrimination suit and became a whistle-blower.

I talked about it and ruminated on it and finally decided, "Well, what's the worst case for me? If I do this, what's the worst that could happen to me? The worst thing that could happen to me is that I get fired.

There's nothing that's going to cost me. If I get fired, I go back into retirement, and my lady would be pleased."

Before I filed, I talkecll to the prison Equal Opportunity Employment officer. He told me to submit my complaint, and a few days later, an instructor from the Education Office interviewed me on the legitimacy of my claim.

After the interview, he told me I didn't have a case and should drop my complaint. I interviewed with the associate warden, who was also the chief Equal Employment Opportunity officer, and he said I should file the claim.

Based on his recommendation, I filed with the state for discrimination by the president and vice president of the local union.

I knew that within a few days, the two officers would receive the word that somebody had filed against them. After a month, I received a letter from the state Office of Equal Opportunity that they had rejected my claim of discrimination and that the problem I had was a workplace problem. I needed to solve it through the local workplace.

When word got out, all hell broke loose. I was mistreated by those two officers as well as by their fellow officers. Everybody was after my hide. I was shell-shocked by what was going on.

If I took papers down to the Watch Office with the name of inmates for a program, they would lose them. They would not go to the gate at the time when inmates were supposed to come through, and they refused to let them through because they claimed they didn't have a list. I would take a second list down, and they would wait an hour before they would let the inmates in.

It often took an hour before inmates would get to a program. This went on for months.

For the whole of my tenure as chaplain they created problems daily for the chapel program. They never forgot. They fought me. They did whatever they could to demean me.

I tried to have the administration schedule a meeting between the three of us. They refused to meet. In any other work situation, when staff had problems, they met and worked it out, but not at CCC.

One of the officers told me he did not ever want to speak to me. Even so, I would always say hello to them, because that seemed to me to be the professional thing to do. But they would. never acknowledge my greeting or presence.

One winter morning I was at the back of my car, picking up my lunch and carrying case. I was putting my belt on when I heard someone walk by. I said,

182

"Hello. Hope you're having a good morning."

I looked up to see who it was that I'd greeted and discovered it was the vice-president of the union. I got my stuff together and started into the prison.

I was at the sliding doors when I heard somebody holler, "Hey, Carmichael." I turned around, and there was this officer who had been giving me trouble for months. He came up to me and said, "You need to quit harassing me. You are giving me a bad time, and I'm sick of it. I don't want you to do it anymore. I'll do whatever is necessary so you don't continue it."

"I didn't do anything," I said. "I haven't harassed you. I was doing what was professional."

He swelled up like a toad and said he was a professional. I didn't respond. I wrote a report to my supervisor but nothing happened,

Eventually, those two guys were voted out of their positions. When they left the patio, things improved.

Incident with Prison Fellowship Seminar

A few weeks after I received my rejection letter, we were having a Prison Fellowship seminar. At 1:00 p.m. on Saturday, there were more than fifty inmates standing at the gate.

There were twenty-one volunteers who had come from Redding, California, to participate in the weekend, and they were present at the chapel. We were waiting for the unlock at 1:00, which was the appropriate time to unlock, but it never came.

I was watching with a couple of other volunteers as the custody officers, which included one of these men I have talked about, were going out to the gate to let people in. They did not have any list in their hands. They turned on their heels, went back to their office, and didn't unlock.

They did not come back, because during the next hour, there was a watch change, and they went home. At 2:15, the new shift allowed them to come in.

Think how this demeaned the twenty one volunteers. I wrote this up and submitted it but received no response from the authorities regarding this kind of behavior.

The next day we were having a Sunday unlock, and the officers claimed they didn't have a list. I went out to the gate with a list for the officer to use. The officer looked at it, and he rejected it, saying, "I don't want it." I said, "Well, here it is. You better take it. If you don't, I'm going to the watch commander."

The officer made a crude remark to me, but he did take the list and let people in. I went down to talk to the watch commander about what I felt was insubordination.

I realized that for the rest of my tenure at the orison, I would be demeaned by many officers.

Handling the Mail and Tobacco

When I went to the chapel on my first day, there were two large mail baskets full of mail. Much of it was sixty days old. Most of it was advertisements and Christian literature that could be distributed to inmates.

I also picked up the mail from the mailroom. The Catholic chaplain was not at Main Chapel during the day, so I also picked up his mail. Shortly after I started picking up the mail, the mailroom consolidated the chapel mail to one drawer. When I brought the mail to the chapel, I would have the lead clerk help me open it.

Over time, Frank, my clerk, opened more and more of the general mail and literature packages. I later regretted the trust I had given to Frank.

It was less than two months before Frank was to be released on parole, after having served more than twenty years in prison.

I was in the office, and Frank was in his area.I had given him the mail to open.I was sitting at my computer, when all of a sudden, all hell broke loose.

There were all kinds of custody officers coming into the chapel. It turned out that it was the investigative branch of the prison. They came in, looked at what I had, and then they went into the other office and found Frank.

Frank had opened some mail, and in it was tobacco that had been dyed. He had dye all over his hands from having opened it.

Tobacco was not acceptable in the prison. He had gotten some from an outside source. They took him to administrative segregation.

After two or three days, I went over to see him. He never apologized; he just owned that it had happened. He was going to take the tobacco to his yard and sell it.

It was beyond my wildest imagination that with so short a time to go before he was to be released that he would do something like this. It could extend his time significantly. He was calm about it.

After a few days, he was released from administrative segregation and assigned to Sierra Yard. He was released from prison within a few days of his original release date. He came to church after several weeks. I did not give him any opportunity to speak or to do anything.

All the volunteers who had promised to support him on the outside with his ministry also felt betrayed. After he was paroled, I called him one time, and he told me that he had a job.

I tried another time to call him, but his number had changed. I haven't been able to reach him since. He was a very gifted man, but for whatever reason, he made some really bad choices.

Recently, I talked with someone who was in his house. He believed that Frank's colleagues had the tobacco sent to him, and they were forcing him to bring it to them. If he hadn't done it, they would have abused and misused him.

It's hard to believe that after all he had been through that they could intimidate him. I guess that those who want will get it, no matter what they have to do to get it. I guess that's the way it is on the outside as well.

Loss of Replacement Clerk When Frank Went Down

I also lost my unpaid clerk when Frank went down. I needed clerical assistance, so I went to the Inmate Assignment Office to get a clerk. They told me to see the correctional captain.

He told me I couldn't choose a clerk. He said he would choose two inmates clerks for me. He took the clerks' eligibility list and checked two names. He said, 11These are the guys who are going to be your clerks." He didn't know who they were; he just chose them arbitrarily.

I took the two names down to the Inmate Assignment Office, and they made out ducats for them to come to the chapel the next day.

The first man came, and we talked. He had actual orders for him to go to the Arnold Unit for training for fire camp. That made him ineligible for my program, and so he went his way.

The next man was a young Hispanic in his early twenties. He and his brother had been adopted by a minister in one of the leading churches in a residential community in Greater Los Angeles. Both he and his brother had gotten involved in gang activities and both went to prison. He was at California Correctional Center, and his brother was at another prison.

We talked about the clerk's job and some of the requirements. He told me that he didn't think that he would like to work in this position but that he certainly had the skills. He was very good on the computer and had the clerical skills that were required, but he didn't have the interest in the religious programming.

I told him, "Maybe this is an opportunity to learn some of the lessons that your adopted father wanted to teach you." He held his adopted father in very high regard. He thought he had not treated his dad very fairly. He had no excuses for the way he behaved.

His stepmother had passed away, which may have been part of what traumatized the two boys, because she was very close to them.

I continued to talk to him about taking this opportunity to change and said he could look at this as a chance to explore areas that he hadn't before. "I would like to have you consider doing this," I said. "You can do it for as many weeks as you feel you want to, and if I reach a point where I don't think you are supportive of what I want to do, I will let you know. If you reach the point where you feel it's no longer something you want to do, you can excuse yourself."

He agreed that he would take the position as long as he wouldn't be the lead clerk. He would do what he could to support the program and give him an opportunity to see if this was a chance for him to change direction. He went back to his housing, and he indicated he would return the next day to the chapel to work.

I took the information I had gleaned from both of these applicants over to the Inmate Assignment Office, and the inmate assignment lieutenant told me that I should see what I could do to find another inmate for the position. He indicated he had been in contact with the custody patio clerk, who was a very experienced clerk, and he had great clerical skills. The inmate had an interest in the position and said that I might want to interview him.

I went down to the custody clerk's office and asked Mike S. to come to the chapel at his convenience. When Mike came to the office, I liked him, although he was certainly crusty. He had been in prison at least four different times. He was back in prison for a three-year stint for a drug charge, while he was on parole. He said he was married and had a fourteen-year-old stepdaughter, and he was truly devoted to his family.

He said that as a youngster, he had had a very deep, personal religious experience. This experience had s,et the tone for his whole attitude about God and about the church and Jesus Christ.

He indicated that although he didn't necessarily always talk like he ought to, he certainly had a deep conviction about his spiritual nature and that there was a reality bigger than himself that he needed to identify with. We talked for quite a while about his experience, and then we talked about his clerical skills.

He informed me that he had three different businesses on the outside and had developed significant computer skills. He would be able to do whatever I needed in the way of computer skills-if I was fortunate enough to get an inmate computer. He indicated he would like to go to work for me.

I told him about the required lists and some of my expectations. I indicated that he would not be expected to give program leadership but would take care of the clerical needs of the chapel and develop the computer programming we would need when we obtained an inmate computer. I did not contact the Watch Office about the switch, as an inmate can make a job change if he decides he wants to.

Mike was able to work with the young clerk, primarily because Mike had a reputation on the same yard.

Finding a Copy Machine

One of the major concerns for the chapel was the ability to make multiple copies of lists and curriculum materials. We needed a minimum of six hundred copies per week. I was told, in no uncertain terms by the Watch Office, that this was not possible.

I had a great problem with this, because the copy machine in the Instructional Office was only available during working hours, from 7:00a.m. until3:00 in the afternoon. On weekends, when I had a big need for it, I could not use it.

In that case, I would have to find another place to do it. One of the places I could have done it was on the patio. Custody had a copy machine, but I was told that I couldn't use it.

Patio custody resented any time I tried to use the copy machine. I had a key that would open the copy room when the administrative officer, the watch officer, and the sergeant would allow me to use it. The key that opened the chapel was a key that would open this particular copy machine.

The few months I used it, there was always a sense that custody felt I was misusing it. And eventually, they were able to have it put in their office, where they spent the bulk of their free time.

Much of the copying that I was to be able to do was when they were doing unlocks. After failing to find a solution, I used my personal printer to print the lists and curriculum materials we needed. This was how I solved the problem for the rest of my tenure.

Obtaining an Inmate Computer

In order to perform the mission mandated for me, I need a computer for inmate clerks. I initially contacted Automated Services to authorize it.

The supervisor told me in no certain terms that it would never be possible for the chapel to have an inmate computer. After she transferred to another institution, the new supervisor was someone who had worked in the same office for more than a decade, and I feared she had the same prejudices.

Before I approached her, I decided I would check with other state prisons to see if inmates had computers there. I contacted Pelican Bay, which is a Level IV prison, and was informed that there were several computers used by inmates in the chaplain's facility.

They had been donated by private sources. The chaplain had been able to get private individuals to donate a new computer, and it was accepted as a gift and became a part of the chapel property.

I also contacted our sister institution, where the fire camp training is done in Southern California. They also had computers used by inmates in religious or substance abuse programming.

I presented this information when I contacted Automated Services. When I suggested a private gift of a computer, I was informed that this was not possible.

They told me that this was not their way of doing things and no computer would ever come to the chapel as a private gift. I attempted to get a computer out of the inventory, which the computer supervisor controlled, and she refused to do it. She said that she wouldn't do that under any circumstances.

She did authorize special programming for my computer, which Automated Services installed after it was purchased by private donations.

During my semiannual meeting with the warden, I made my pitch for an inmate computer. She didn't say that I could get it, but she listened. And my supervisor was open to our having a computer for that purpose.

Eventually, we did get a computer when they got a significant number of new computers and used them to replace most of the antiquated computers in the lieutenant's and the sergeant's office.

The inmate computer was antiquated. It was initially housed in my office, since Automated Services did not trust the inmates to have it in their office. Nothing could be printed directly from the inmate computer. It had to be transferred to my computer for printing. We did it by floppy disc and jump-drives. I was required to check all materials before they were printed. This meant that all printing was done while I was in the office.

Automated Services gave us minimal upkeep support. When maintenance was needed, it was like pulling teeth to get any help. They refused to set a maintenance schedule for any of the chapel computers. They had maintenance schedules for all the other offices, but refused to do it for the chaplain's office.

On several occasions, the Automate Services staff descended on us and requested to review the contents on the inmate computer. They always felt that there might be something there that was inappropriate.

I believe custody either used my computer or tried to get e-mail through it. I always was fearful that some of the custody officers would put pornographic material on my computer and then report it. Administration would inspect and find it. I would be in deep "doo-doo."

The typewriters that had some capacity for word processing apparently failed. One of the clerks looked at these two word processors and said the motherboard had failed. I went to the Internet and found some antiquated motherboards. This agency also restored them, and I was able to purchase two boards.

A donation request was made to the warden, and they were purchased. The motherboards were put in place in less than five minutes, and they gave us an alternative way to produce the attendance lists.

The only two programs that could be used on the inmate computer were Word and Excel programs. Inmates could not use PowerPoint and Access.

Custody believed that the PowerPoint might be used to generate tattoo patterns or some pornographic material and so that program was off limits. And Access was off limits because inmates could maneuver and work with material in a more sophisticated way which they felt inmates should not ever be able to do.

Excel and Word ended up being sufficient for chapel needs because we had some very innovative clerks with computer experience on the outside and they were able to implement what they knew for our programming.

Mike designed an Excel program that allowed us to gather or put in place the appropriate identification material for each of the inmates who were participants in the chapel programming. He also developed a way of keeping a record of the attendance for each of the programs we had.

Ultimately, we had twenty-six different options available at various times for inmates in the rehabilitation program. Mike told me when he interviewed for the position that he would be able to do this, and over a several-week period, he was able to get it done.

After Mike paroled, another clerk improved on it. Without Mike's contribution, the faith-based rehabilitation program would not have been as successful as it was. I am grateful for his gifts and his willingness to use them in the chapel program.

Celebrate Recovery Leadership at Main Chapel

In the summer 2006, the Celebrate Recovery introduction seminar would sponsor prison chaplains and volunteers with free tuition. At that session, I found literature and videos that supported inmate leadership. Two keynote speakers, Henry Cloud and Rick Townsend, had several video programs that could be used in faith-based rehabilitation.

Although Inmate Ack was no longer a chapel clerk, he was eligible to come to chapel. He assumed responsibility for coordinating the Celebrate Recovery program. He was an excellent planner, and he assigned different inmates to teach the lessons.

The soundboard continued to be a problem, since the operator had to be sophisticated about audio sound. The board provided twenty-six options for sound.Since many inmates had sticky fingers, support batteries were often taken.

An inmate, who had been attending the chapel for several years and had participated in the previous chaplain's band, was knowledgeable about sound boards.Jon had been adive in chapel for several years and volunteered to man the soundboard.

Jon was a keyboard player. He was becoming more proficient, because he practiced when possible and always volunteered to play in the band. For months he had volunteered to maintain the soundboard when he wasn't playing in the band. He was knowledgeable and proficient in supporting the audio needs of the chapel.

Cory, the First Fruit of the Program

After about three months, one of the inmates became eligible to transfer to a fire camp. Since he was deeply involved in the leadership group, we decided to have a sending service, where we would challenge him and bless him in his camp ministry. He was instructed to carry out the principles, and he was advised to use what he learned at the fire camp.

We formed a prayer circle, had him sit on a chair in the middle of the circle, and various inmates touched and prayed on behalf of their dream for him. Every member of the group prayed for him, and he left the chapel.

I didn't hear from him for well over a year. When I got a letter from him, I learned he had paroled to Yuba City, California. He said he went to a Yuba City church and talked to the pastor about the 40 Days and Celebrate programs.

His pastor had authorized him to initiate both these programs in this church. He had purchased the curriculum out of his earnings. He informed me how he had purchased the equipment for the curriculum to do this out of the earnings as well. Making the curriculum purchase was a sacrificial gift on his part, since he had a marginal job as a day laborer on a ranch.

Cory was the first fruit of the mission to reduce prison recidivism.

The leadership group continued until winter came. It was severely cold at that time, and custody were forced to stand at the gate for a minimum of thirty minutes and sometimes an hour. Often, custody would not come to the Patio Gate until 8:00a.m. Even when inmates came to the 9:00 worship service, they often stood in the cold for an hour or hour and twenty minutes. Thus, it was not reasonable for the leadership program to continue.

Developing Inmate Leadership

A major miscalculation at the inception of the faith-based programming was when I allowed inmate-clerk Frank to conduct the entire program. He was expected to train assistants for the programming.

Unfortunately, Frank did not enlist other inmates, other than a couple of his friends. So when he was no longer the clerk, there was a leadership vacuum.

One of the problems we had was checking out library books. Since Frank was leading worship, another volunteer was needed in the library. Some inmates were not checking books out according to procedure.

An inmate started coming to the chapel who had checked out books. He volunteered to serve as library clerk. He was a university graduate and knew what it meant to be responsible.

After he had served for a few weeks, he told me a book from the library had helped to restore his faith. After graduating from Boston College, he'd moved to Tahoe. He got into a car accident and was sentenced to five years of imprisonment. He was bitter, because he felt he had been treated unfairly by the court.. He spent several months out on the yard, nursing his resentment and anger.

One day, he came to the chapel and checked out a book. It was about the disciples of Jesus and the people around the cross. In it was a story about the man observing the Crucifixion, and when Jesus couldn't carry his cross anymore, a Roman centurion enlisted the man to carry the cross. It is probable the man was of a different race and that was what caught the soldier's attention. What happened to the man as a result of this encounter touched Matt and became the catalyst for him to begin his faith walk again. Over time, he began to do more and more volunteering.

Gene and Redd, Religious Volunteers

E. Herring said he could cover some services, and Len and Jerry, retired custody officers, also agreed to help. Unfortunately E. Herring could only supervise twenty five inmates, even though he had been a prison volunteer for thirty years. I kept praying that God would provide some volunteer alternatives, since we had such a loss in Mr S leaving us.

One Friday afternoon, I was in the office when Redd, one of the motorcycle volunteers at High Desert from Redding, called. He said he and his partner, Gene, would like to come and talk with me. I made arrangements to meet in the snack bar, where we could have a cup of coffee and talk.

When they arrived, they told me they were staying in Susanville on the weekends. They volunteered to come on Friday nights at Main Chapel. On Saturday, they would continue to volunteer during the day at High Desert and then help at Main on Saturday evening. After chapel at Main, they would go back to Redding.

They wondered if there was something they might be able to do at the chapel. What a boom that was. I had a volunteer to cover 40 Days and Celebrate Recovery on some weekends.

Gene Beer came three weekends a month. He and Richard were willing to continue to support weekend programming if I could get beige cards for them. A beige card is individualized to a prison and may or not be recognized as valid at a prison, unless it is issued by that prison. CCC does not recognize other prison's beige cards.

CCC beige cards were stored at the lobby desk. Each time a volunteer came to the chapel, he would pick up his beige card and surrender his driver's license. At High Desert, volunteers kept their beige cards with them.

As Gene and Richard continued volunteering, I began to bond with them. Gene Beer was an awesome man. He had spent a lifetime as a truck driver. One of his legs was shorter than the other, and he wore a shoe that extended his leg. It was amazing, the work and time he volunteered at High Desert. Although he had heart issues, it did not detour him; he had a deep passion for helping inmates.

It was late in life when he made a decision to become a Christian. Since he had lived a rough and tough life, he understood an inmate's issues. He was not able to read very well. He claimed he couldn't read at all before he became a Christian and wanted to read the Bible.

He'd obviously had a learning disability since childhood. At that time, they didn't help people with that problem; they dropped out of school.

Gene and Richard had good favor with custody because they were tough-minded and they were tough on inmates. When the inmates were wrong, I learned early I didn't have to worry about their ability to maintain security. If someone got out of line, they could easily confront them and dispatch the issue quickly.

When the weather was good, Gene would stay over on Saturday night and cover Celebrate Recovery. If the weather was not good, he would go home in the afternoon after he completed his work at High Desert.

At High Desert, he visited inmates in their cells on Friday and distributed literature on Saturday, and he conducted eight services in the reception center. It was a strenuous day for him, and I was amazed that he could volunteer at Main Chapel on Saturday night.

He had a small camp trailer and rented a space adjacent to the prison. It was only a half mile from the prison. He had no discretionary income, since he lived on his and his wife's social security.

In time, Gene Beer was issued a full chapel clearance. This allowed him to cover all full chapel programming. He also was authorized to visit the administrative segregation unit. It was difficult for him to do it, since his day activities were at High Desert. Sometimes he would visit in the evening and on Sunday, if he stayed over.

As much as possible, he went home on Sunday to go to his home church. He was deeply involved with his church and their ministry to the parolees who attended that church. His church welcomed parolees. I think that's part of the reason for his prison-inmate passion. He caught a passion for prison ministry, because his pastor had a passion for inmates.

Gene was loyal to me and the faith-based program. Over time, he was as passionate about faith-based rehabilitation as I was. I am amazed that we came from such different backgrounds, but a common passion for reducing prison recidivism bonded us. Richard did not come as often and finally dropped out.

Gene will always be honored because of his passion for the Master and His kingdom's work. Because of the Louckses and Gene, it was possible to develop additional midweek programming.

Phil S.'s Departure

Phil S. played a strategic role in the success of the early months of the faith based program. He provided resource, expertise, and invaluable volunteer service. Because of his help, I decided that the fifth Sunday of the month, which had no volunteer assignment, would be offered to Mr. S. It was the chapel's general Protestant service, and he had preached three times.

One of Mr. S.'s special ministries was his prayer ministry following the worship service. His prayer time was radically different from a typical Protestant service.

I had no quarrel with this ministry during a denominational service. In those services, the worship leader had the privilege of using the techniques that he felt the Lord had given him.

However, at the Sunday general Protestant worship service, the order should be in keeping with general Protestant worship practices. This service should meet all worshipers' needs, not fulfill the interest of the worship leader. I expected that service to follow the worship pattern that was generally accepted on Sunday morning in most of the churches in the United States. Mr. S.'s prayer service didn't meet these criteria.

Since I was responsible for the total chapel program, it was imperative I discuss this issue with Mr. S. I talked with him about my criteria for worship and informed him that having his prayer time on Sunday morning as part of the general worship was not acceptable.

I requested that the prayer service be conducted at the end of worship in another area. Individuals who wanted prayer would go there, and he could conduct the service in his usual way. The rest of the worshipers would sing songs and be excused to their housing.

He didn't ask to discuss it,but his nonverbals expressed clearly that he was not happy. I assumed that he had accepted the decision.

Several weeks later, I was at the door of the Lassen control room, where the keys were to Lassen Chapel were issued. As I was waiting for the door to open,Mr. S. came through the door. As I greeted him, he said, "I want to tell you, Carmichael, I'm out of here. I'm gone, and I won't be back as long as you're chaplain."

I was nonplused, but I didn't try to defend myself. I didn't try to talk him out of it, because I long ago learned that a person filled with anger needed time to cool off. I anticipated I would have another discussion with him. He went his way.

That night, he was scheduled for a denominational service at the Main Chapel. Fifty inmates waited at the gate for more than an hour, but he did not come. I never saw him again. He moved to the Sacramento area.

I was chagrined at the loss of his help. He was a great asset to the program. I have learned not to hold grudges because you are hurt, not the one you hold a grudge against.

About three weeks before I retired, I got a phone call one Saturday morning from Mr. S. He said he thought he owed me an apology. I thanked him and told him I didn't have illfeelings toward him. I said, "I can't afford them, I have to go on with my life. I continue to pray for you, as I have for months." I then suggested he apply for the chaplain's job, since he was an effective leader. I sensed that one of the reasons he came to the prison was because he recognized that my tenure there would not be very long. Itturned out to be a couple years longer than I ever would have anticipated.

Rogers Family Volunteers

The Rogers family, who lived in Chester in the summer and Southern California in the winter, wanted to conduct a midweek Bible study. They did not want to support the faith programming.

I explained to them that it was my policy that there were no free lunches to religious volunteers. Everyone who volunteered was expected to support the faith-based programming. If they were authorized a Bible study, they were expected to volunteer to support a faith-based program.

I explained to them that the purpose driven church had a program called "Four Bases." I suggested that Mr. Rogers support a program called < second Base," which helped inmates to share their faith effectively. Reluctantly, Mr. Rogers agreed to do it during the summer.

I asked Charles T. to be the inmate coordinator of the program. The Rogers Family provided the volunteer support. Charles gave the Rogers a section of each evening's programs.

They usually had fifty inmates at the Wednesday night program. The Rogerses became enthusiastic supporters of the program and supported it until they went to Southern California for the winter.

Studying Purpose-Driven Life
Church Book

At the next meeting of the leadership group, I brought a copy of *The Purpose Driven* Church book and shared the table of the contents of the book. The group decided to study the book. I wrote a proposal to the warden, requesting that I would be able to purchase these books and loan them to the individuals who were participating in this program.

The primary proble m with the proposal was that these books were hard cover. There was a stipulation that hard cover books could not go through the Patio Gate. Inmates could check out hard-cover books in the yard library, but no one was allowed to take a hard-cover book through the Patio Gate.

Patio custody officers enforced this rule without exception. The proposal was approved. Inmates could take the book between the chapel and their housing. All agreed that we could have these books, that we could loan them to the people, and that they could take them back and forth through the gates.

The first two times inmates took the books to the Patio Gate, the custody officers refused to allow them to take the books to their housing. To help off-set this issue, a copy of the approved memo was attached to each book. After administration intervention, this issue was solved.

An inmate, who had been a part of Cascade Yard for several years, was a Bible student. I enlisted him as coordinator or study leader of the group to lead the discussion of the book.

In spite of continual counsel about following the book, he would develop a lecture that had little to do with the chapter. Most of the time, he was pushing a doctrinal interpretation that was not relevant to the book.

I counseled him for several weeks and finally had to relieve him of his responsibility. I assumed the leadership. After a couple of weeks of my leadership, I was able to enlist the former clerk at the chapel, who had been disqualified to work as a chapel clerk, to lead the program.

At the Celebrate Recovery leadership seminar, I purchased several DVD series by Townsend and Cloud. One of them was on *Twelve Concepts of Leadership*. Bill Hybels donated several years of DVD programming from his national leadership seminar. Leaders from all over the United States presented their ideas about leadership.

John Maxwell, author of *Twenty- One Laws of Leadership*, had a series of leadership DVDs. John had been a pastor of a mega-church in San Diego. For several decades, he developed leadership principles and shared them with national and international church leaders. He decided to leave the ministry and build a leadership program for the church and corporate leaders. I purchased his video programmmg.

For the next few months, the group studied these leadership materials. It was a very rich leadership training opportunity, and the inmates continued to come every Saturday morning to study. A great deal of personal sacrifice was required by them to make the early morning meeting.

The Leadership Group

Since Celebrate Recovery and 40 Days were the flagship programs, and I wanted additional inmates trained to support these programs, I called a meeting of inmate leaders for the 40 Days and Celebrate Recovery programs.

We sat down together to brainstorm a leadership program that would meet at 7:00 on Saturday morning. I had already submitted a request for the administration to approve the meeting.

Twenty inmates who were already involved in 40 Days and Celebrate Recovery were eligible to become members of the leadership program. In order to participate in this program, however, an inmate might need to miss breakfast.

At the first meeting, we sat in a circle and introduced ourselves and told the nickname we had on the yard. It was expected that each would explain what the nickname meant and the characteristics that earned the moniker.

After that, we discussed the mission of the program. It was decided that the mission was "*Make disciples; reduce recidivism.*" Then we brainstormed about what kind of program could make disciples and reduce recidivism.

Over the next few meetings, we talked about our individual goals and why we were willing to make 1 the sacrifice to make this early morning meeting. One of the major goals for members was leadership training. A second goal was to understand the meaning of a purpose-driven church.

An Experiment with a Chapel Pass

Over time, Main Chapel had twenty eight different weekly program options for inmates each week. This became a clerical nightmare when it came to making the attendance lists.

Inmate Clerk Mike S. hadna suggestion to cut down the number of lists required. His suggestion was that we developed a chapel pass, and this pass would have the various options that an inmate was eligible to attend each week. The next month, we would issue a new pass with all updated options on it.

Not only would it serve as a chapel identification card, but it also would keep the inmate informed about this chapel schedules. Housing custody could use it to release inmates to the chapel, and patio staff could use it as an approval for access through the gate to the chapel.

I had the clerk design a model of what this would look like. I took it to the yards and talked with custody, sergeants, liuetanants, and yard captains on the two watches affected by the changes to get their reactions. They generally thought it might work, and a pilot project of two months was suggested.

After I had yard consensus, I took the proposal to the two watch commanders for their reactions. The second watch commander was open to it but said the problem for third watch was there was no one lieutenant assigned to the position. Several different lieutenants were assigned to work each week. I contacted them for their reaction. They were open to idea.

I did not contact patio custody, because they resisted all change. Finally, I took it to the correctional captain for his review. He was willing to implement it if I could get the warden's approval. I submitted the proposal through channels to the warden. After review, it was approved for a two month trial.

It was working extremely well for two weeks, and then suddenly, the warden reversed her decision. It turned out the president and vice president of the Custody Union had rejected it. They had other custody officers, especially those on the patio, oppose it. This indicated the lengths the Custody Union would go to have their way.

This incident illustrates the vindictive spirit of many custody officers. When I came to work, I didn't realize that the new programming under my watch was bringing change to the prison.

Custody is opposed to any change. They like the things the way they are. If the change helps inmates, this truly raises their hackles. If things are the same, there is no judgment or exceptions required. Every new program or change I suggested was not what they wanted.

Unfortunately, I recognized that patio policy change was imperative to the faith based programming.

When I filed a grievence against the union leaders, they were committed to paying me back in spades. If I sound like I'm paranoid ove.r this, it's probably true that I am. I recognize that I have a jaundiced view of what had been going on the patio for years. I could never bring myself to live with it. I continued to confront it until I retired.

One of the ways the custody officers continued to hassle the chapel was to refuse to open the chapel for the clerks. Patio custody, after accessing inmate through the Patio Gate would go back to their office and leave the chapel clerks outside the chapel.

Their work order required them to open the chapel for the clerks1but they ignored it. They would leave the clerks sitting in front of the chapel on occasion} for several hours. The union leaders intimidated the other custody to follow their lead.

It was a continuing problem} and my requests for solutions were largely ignored by patio administration. When the two men who I filed the grievance against} worked on weekends it was especially harrowing. The watch officer was almost always a different person, who often was not aware of procedures, so he followed the lead of custody.

Almost every weekend, I would call the Watch Office before a program was scheduled and report on custody. In some cases, the lieutenant would not answer my phone call, so I would go to his office to get the issue settled. Some weeks, I did not have any backup volunteer supervision to allow me to leave the chapel, so programs were delayed.

One of the third-watch custody officers was persistent in creating issues for me. One time I had fifteen inmates in a program and was walking by the chapel. I went out to challenge him, and he proceeded to read me the riot act. He said he was writing me up for leaving inmates unattended. I wasn't out of the chapel for more than a minute and decided to write a memo on him.

As a result of this encounter, my supervisor designed a report on which I was to report each incident that occurred. I was to submit it to him, and he would work it through channels. I ended up writing eight or nine a week for several months. In spite of these reports, there was no change in patio policy.

Christmas Support for Inmates

Two programs supported inmatesand their families during the Christmas holidays. These programs were the way that inmates and their families dealt with the isolation that incarceration creates.

The first program was the Prison Fellowship's Angel Tree program. This program provided Christmas gifts for the children of inmates. Inmates completed questionnaires in late summer, listing the names and addresses of their children. A catalog of possible gifts was used for the inmates to choose an age-appropriate gift.

The chaplain collected the applications and forwarded them to Angel Tree Prison Fellowship. These applications were distributed to participating churches that made the Christmas gifts available to the children. Each year, CCC submitted a minimum of three thousand forms.

One year, Prison Fellowship called me, concerned about the number of children that some CCC inmates claimed as their children. There was no way I could check this, but we did ask inmates when they returned their forms to talk about their children. Multiple applications were necessary, because there were inmates who had nine and ten children.

The other program was a Christmas card program, which a nonprofit organization from Missouri provided. Christmas card companies donated the cards to the agency, and they distributed them to prisons. A prison was required to pay the freight on shipping the cards to the prison.

I chose to give two cards to each inmate, beginning with the first Christmas I was at the prison. We distributed eleven thousand cards each Christmas, enough for every inmate assigned at CCC and the eighteen fire camps. The cost of the program was more than five hundred dollars, which Lassen Sierra Prison Ministries funded.

Disciplinary and Laudatory Certification

Custody and free staff write a "128 statement" when an inmate deserves special recognition. A 128 can also be disciplinary in nature.

One evening1two inmates came to the chapel. After a few minutes, they requested to go back to the Patio Gate. I told them if they went back to the gate, they would be eligible for a disciplinary 128. I asked them to stay at the chapel, since they had volunteered to participate in that evening's program. They got angry and called me names. So I wrote a disciplinary 128 and put it into their personnel file.

A 128 remains in a personnel file until the person who wrote it requests it be removed. One of the inmate clerks at Lassen Yard, who was a lifer, received a disciplinary 128 during his second year in prison. It was the only disciplinary write up he received during his prison term.

Fifteen years later, when he was eligible for parole consideration, that 128 came up to bite him.

So I only issued two disciplinary 128s during my career, and six months after I wrote them, I requested they be removed from the inmates' personnel files.

I placed uatta-boy 128s" in hundreds of inmates' files. When students graduated from the 40 Days program, a 128 was placed in their files to honor this milestone in their recovery. Other than for 40 Days, I did not issue many 128s, because I felt too many might be a detriment in some disciplinary hearings, because those inmates might be held to a higher standard of behavior. If an inmate was a leader in several programs at the chapel, I did authorize that recognition by a 128.

Another way inmate achievements were recognized was by issuing a certificate of completion. The certificates were given to the recipient for his personal record or to send home to his family. Sometimes inmates participated in a program in order to receive a certificate that they could send home to their families.

I reconciled this issue by deciding that something positive would result from completing a program, even if the reasons participating in the program were less than I would have liked. I recognized that inmates needed positives to help their families accept their incarceration. We continued to use certificates of completion while I was at the chapel.

When Phil S. was at the chapel, he gave certificates to participants in his programs. They were expensive and impressive.

To give a high-grade certificate at an affordable price, I bought reams of high-grade paper, and we printed our own certificates. One was given to each baptismal candidate for his permanent record, or he might send it home.

Fallout from Warden's Meeting

A few weeks after a warden's meeting, a memo was sent to me, prohibiting chaplains from issuing inmate ducats to the chapels. For at least ten years, chaplains had issued ducats to authorize individual inmates to come to the chapel.

The Catholic chaplain used this method for small group counseling. Now, we had to get prior approval from the inmate assignment officer or arrange with the yard sergeant to issue a ducat. Obviously, I issued more ducats than had been issued in previous years because of the extra activities.

This new policy prevented volunteers from doing any counseling when the chaplain was not in the chapel. One of the times that ducats were invaluable was when an inmate was having trouble in his house or with a gang.

I would have a chapel clerk take a ducat to the inmate, and no one knew he was coming to the chapel. For the same reason, I often used it was when I found out that somebody was having difficulty on the yard.

This facilitated the program without letting other inmates iknow that the person was coming to the chapel. Often, coming to the chapel was seen as a sign of weakness, and many inmates would not come to the chapel for that reason.

With the new system, there was no privacy. A ducat list had to be in the Inmate Assignment Office at least twenty four hours prior to the event. Initially, unit officers were reluctant to issue ducats, but by the end of my tenure, there was no hesitation in filling my request

Early in my career, the Inmate Assignment Office mistakenly issued priority ducats for an evening program. At that time, I was told that when an inmate got a priority ducat, he had to honor it, or he was eligible for a disciplinary 115.

Based on the climate among custody regarding the chapel, I feared they would charge the inmates, so I wrote a note to all inmates on the priority ducat list, informing them of this possibility. I was attempting to protect them.

When inmates were being cleared at the Patio Gate, a couple of inmates complained because they were required to attend chapel to avoid a 115.

One of the patio custody officers got upset about it. Shortly after the program began, he came into the chapel lobby and announced that he wanted all those who were in chapel because of their fear of a 115 to be released to the patio immediately. He said, "No one on my watch will ever have to go to chapel out of fear of discipline."

He started into the chapel, but I stopped him. I told him it was my chapel, and I would make the announcement. I stopped the program, went to the front of the chapel, and said, "Anybody who doesn't want to be here is free to go back to his house." Only one man walked out.

This was one of the most intense encounters I had with custody during my tenure.

As I came out of the chapel, the watch commander came in and asked the officer and me to go into the inner office. We discussed the issue, but there was no way of resolving it. I wrote a report of the incident. In the report, I expressed my opinion that the officer was out of line and had showed an intense animosity to the chapel and the chaplain.

Getting Equipment to the Chapels

Whenever equipment arrived at the warehouse, it was checked for contraband. Normally, the warehouse delivered the items to the chapel every month. Occasionally, I would check out a vehicle from Transportation and personally bring the materials to the chapel. I would bring it to the Sierra Sally Port Gate, where it was checked again by a security officer. It was then cleared to drive the vehicle to the Patio Gate.

Often, I had to wait at a gate for up to forty-five minutes, because activities on the patios had to be completed before anyone was allowed through the gate. When I cleared the Patio Gate, I would proceed to the chapel. The inmate clerks would unload the material into my office where I reviewed it before placing it in the chapel.

If I had equipment for Lassen Chapell I would have to follow the above procedure by personally taking the materials to the chapel. This project would take a minimum of four hours.

When I first went to the chapel I was able to bring Christian. literature through the Main Lobby Sally Port Gate. After I got crosswise with certain custody officers} they made an issue of my bringing materials through the lobby. I had to check out a vehicle and bring the materials through the Sierra Sally Port.

Meeting with Administration on Chapel Access

One Monday morning after a very blatant disregard by patio custody of the chapel program, I went to talk with the correctional captain. He proceeded to tell me he wasn't going to do anything and was disgusted that I continued to make issues for the custody staff.

I reported this to my supervisor, and my supervisor said he was going to the warden. He went to see the warden and shortly thereafter, I got a telephone call, requesting that I come to the warden's office in ten minutes for a special meeting.

When I arrived at the warden's office, all associate wardens were present, along with the correctional captain and investigations lieutenant. There was frost in the air.

The warden asked me to discuss my issues, and a free-for-all ensued. The main associate warden and other patio administrators wanted to restrict the number of inmates who could come to Main Chapel. Fire regulations limited the capacity to five hundred. There was a procedure in place to limit the number to three hundred, which limited each yard to 150 inmates.

The officers took exception to the present policy. They recommended that only one hundred inmates could be in the chapel. I suggested that we limit the attendance to 130 inmates from each yard. That was half of what the fire regulation limits were for the chapel. The warden agreed with my suggestion, and that became the rule. The correctional captain wanted to disallow my ability to out-count inmates during count. I sometimes out-counted as many as seventeen inmates. Normally, this out-count was at Saturday or Sunday noon counts, after the worship services.

This had never been an issue before this meeting. If they could not disallow

229

my having out-counts, they wanted to restrict them to seven inmates. I had four clerks, so it meant I could only have three other inmates.

I explained that I conducted a small group activity that I called "The Chaplain's Hour," and I needed at least twelve out counts to take care of the chapel clerks and the small group.

After a long discussion, the warden said I could out-count ten inmates. I asked her to authorize twelve1because Jesus had twelve disciple, and she said "Yes and there are Ten Commandments.And that stopped the discussion.

The ten-inmate limit created problems but we learned to live with it. It meant that two of my clerks had to go to their housing.

The fallout from this meeting was judgment and hostility from several ofthe administrative o:fficers for the rest of my tenure as chaplain. The correctional captain was especially resentful and often would not speak to me.

Upgrading Chapel Audiovisual Capability

Inmate Jon, the audio-video and soundboard technician, turned out to be a gem. He was bright and had a thorough understanding of the faith-based rehabilitation program for the chapel.

I spent a great deal of time with him, talking about my dream for the total program. I explained that I wanted an upgraded sound system, which included additional options for simultaneous programming in different parts of the chapel. I hoped we would have four or five different programs in various areas of the chapel at one time.

I asked him to design the ideal audiovisual system to provide for these options. I obtained catalogs from audiovisual equipment companies for him. He spent several weeks choosing the equipment and writing a proposal that justified his choices.

After he completed his proposal, I had three different prison free staff review it before I submitted it to the warden. Each of them had audiovisual expertise. After they shared their opinions with me, I asked them to write an endorsement of the proposal.

Some of the equipment we requested was state-of-the-art and costly. The equipment we needed!. was applicable for singing groups and classical concerts. It took a few weeks to gather the letters. They were attached to the proposal, which I submitted through administrative channels to the warden for approval.

The cost of the equipment was $5400.It was a steep price to pay, but I wanted it to be a quality sound system. I used my tithe to fund it.

After obtaining approval, I had to follow purchasing requirements for buying it. A list of equipment was sent to two vendors for the best price. Lassen

Sierra Prison paid for it through my contribution.

Partners in Faith - Based Programs

I decided when I came to the chapel that I would attempt to provide the Catholic chapel with similar equipment to what was provided to the Protestant chapel. I believe that a rising tide raises all ships, and the best way to ensure the improvement of the Protestant chapel was to help other programs as well.

So a video projector, sound speakers, and the mobile screen that Mr. S. sold me were donated to the Catholic chapel. Religious groups must support each other due to secular forces that would prefer to reduce religious activities. It was also important to have the Catholic chaplain as an ally in the fight for the faith-based rehabilitation mission.

Legal Library Clerks and Administrative Segregation

The inmate clerks-in the main legal library got in trouble. An inmate volunteer in the library, who had been relieved by the free-staff coordinator, attempted to destroy the staff and workers.

He claimed that the clerks had misused the prison telephone by making personal calls. These inmates were authorized to call some legal numbers for information that would help them assist inmates with the legal cases. The frustrated inmate claimed the clerks were using the phone for personal calls to their families.

Ultimately, all of the inmates were sent to administrative segregation and the free staff coordinator was pressured to resign. After several weeks, he found another job with the federal government and resigned. It was a significant loss to the law library, since he was diligent and caring about his mission to serve inmates.

One of the clerks, a seventy-year-old inmate, had helped with Christmas programs. He had been charged with a white-collar crime, which was on appeal. His resume was impressive, as he had worked in international circles.

He had pictures of himself with the President Mikhail Gorbachev of the Soviet Union. He had also worked at the United Nations. He was very caring but also a very straightforward man. He had helped scores of inmates draft their appeals.

In administrative segregation, he was placed in one of the end cells, which was farthest from any heat source. He told me, in my visits to him, how cold he was and that he had requested an extra blanket but it was always refused. When I went to see him, I always took him out of his cell there was no privacy in the cells; whatever was said in the cell could be heard in several cells-and he was placed in a cage, where we could talk privately.

Initially, when I asked to talk with him in a cage, custody resented it and would put him in the cage next to the sergeant's office.

I always moved to the backside of the cage so that I could talk to him with some privacy.

He was deeply concerned about his wife, because he had never been incarcerated before, and she was retirement age. His concern had deepened, because he had not talked to her for several weeks.

They kept him in administrative segregation for over seventy-five days without charging him. In a sense, they had put him out to pasture. About three weeks before he was to be paroled, they returned him to his housing unit on Cascade Yard. They never did charge him, which was improper.

Whenever I visited him, I felt judged by custody, because I was attempting to help him. They did mistreat him during his time in administrative segregation, but I never appealed it, although I did talk to the main associate warden about him.

After getting out of prison, he continued to work internationally. He told me federal authorities had the person for whom he had served his time in prison, and he was being returned to the United States for trial. Then he would be exonerated. In a recent telephone call, he told me he'd had surgery for the injuries he received while he was in administrative segregation.

The New Muslim Chaplain

I resumed my alternative-faith coverage for several months.

One day, my supervisor told me he had found a half-time Muslim chaplain. Josef Mohammad, a native of Ghana, had been in the United States for more than twenty years and was a lifetime Muslim. He turned out to be a prince of a man. He was a Sunni and knew his faith intimately. His strength was working individually with an inmate. He held inmates accountable and was great working with them on an individual basis to help men grow in their faith.

Purchasing an RV for Volunteer Housing

One of my acquaintances from Redding, California, called me to say that a Redding nonprofit had a first-class RV for sale.

He told me an elderly lady had lived in it until two month ago. He claimed it was in first-class shape and would be a good investment. The price was five thousand dollars, and he had ensured that everything was working in it. If there were any problems, the charity would correct them.

My reason for considering it was to provide housing for the religious volunteers who came on the weekends to support the program.

I also knew that Dr. Harold a retired prison chaplain, might come, and he would need housing. Since he had marginal income and would only have a half-time salary, I decided to purchase the RV and fix it up for him. I stored it for three months in a trailer park about five miles from the prison. Itwas a park where I thought Harold might prefer to live.

A trailer park adjacent to the prison had five trailer spaces. I had approached them several months earlier, but they had no openings. Then the owner called me and told me he had an empty space.

I had the trailer moved to that space. It would be convenient for volunteers' housing if Harold didn't want it. I used my AAA card to have the trailer moved to the new location. I assumed what I had been told by the charity about the trailer being ready to use.

The day Dr. Harold arrived was the worst snowstorm during my tenure at the prison. The trailer furnace would not work. I called a local RV service to check it. They discovered it was filled with wasp nests because it hadn't been used in years.

The charity had sold me a bill of goods. I called them, and they said they hadn't tested the furnace, and it was my problem.

Additionally, the roof leaked. It was supposedly repaired by the charity1 but they only did a cosmetic fix, and roof had to be replaced. The leak caused electrical failure that had to be repaired.

So what the man who sold me the RV had told me was not true. He hadn't tested any of it. I had to have the roof fixed and a new furnace, as well as repair the refrigerator.

I had bought a pig in the poke and was stuck with it. The charity wouldn't talk with me, and my friend would not own up to anything either.

It cost another seven thousand dollars to get it all fixed up. During the time the RV was unusable, I put Dr. Harold in a local motel and paid the bill. Actually, before he could move in, I had to pay for another week at the motel. He finally moved into the RV and settled down for a week.

One morning, I went in a local motel, where the chaplain had been for a week while the furnace was being repaired. It turned out that he came back to the trailer and the furnace still wasn't working correctly. So he went back to the motel for another week, and I had to cover that.

As he settled in to the regimen, he had significant success. Not only was he helping with the alternative faith, but he was also helping with faith-based programmmg.

The prison administration approved his covering faith-based rehabilitation programming, if it didn't interfere with the alternative-faith programming. We also decided to share our time, so we could have a four-day workweek. The proposal was submitted to the warden for her approval.

On a Saturday morning, Chaplain Harold was scheduled to share a short homily, but he didn't come to the chapel.

During the noon hour, I went to the RV. No one was there. I got the key from under the rug and opened the RV. Nothing from Dr. Harold was in the RV.

Chaplain Harold didn't show up at the chapel for two programs, so I went by the house where he was supposed to be. There was a sign on the door that said he had gone back to Florida.

On Monday, I went to my supervisor, and he told me Dr. Harold had a medical condition with his legs, and he had returned to the Veteran's Hospital in Florida for treatment. What a bummer.

Working with the Main Chapel Muslim Community

Muslim inmates were irresponsible in their demands from the inmate clerks. I had to talk often with the Muslim inmate leader about this issue. The inmate leader was chosen by the group. Since there were divisions among the inmates, sometimes some didn't want to abide by the group decision.

I gave a copy of the Islamic DVD to the inmates to help them understand the historical basis for the Muslim faith. Most of them became Muslims while in prison. In many cases, it was not as much a faith issue as a cultural prejudice against how they had been treated 110Utside the walls" and prison culture. They felt discriminated against, and becoming a Muslim was a way to react against this discrimination.

Of course, this is a judgment on my part, but I think it's a fair one. Since they didn't have a background in their faith,

I suggested they study these DVDs in the weekly Monday study.

I also got a DVD about the first mosque established in the United States. It was in Grand Rapids, Michigan. The Muslim who founded it worked in an automobile assembly plant. His story is of a mainstream Muslim mosque established in the historic tradition.

I continued to monitor this program. My supervisor told me that there was a possibility that they could have a half-time alternative-faith chaplain. Even though he was not a Muslim, he could administer all the alternative-faith programs.

I thought of my friend, Dr. Harold, who had retired as High Desert Protestant chaplain three years before. He needed supplemental income.

So I went to my supervisor and told him about Harold. He knew Harold while he was at High Desert. He had high regard for him. He talked to the warden, and they called him with a job offer. He agreed to come if Sacramento approved his hiring. This took several months.

Toastmasters Club

I researched the possibility of having a Toastmasters Club as an inmate self-help program. Toastmasters International sent information for establishing a club that would not require the normal costs connected with a Toastmasters Club. There was a minimal annual fee and the expenses for the curriculum materials required.

My supervisor asked me to draft a proposal for a self-help group. Unfortunately, another office assumed responsibility for the chapel, and my supervisor never processed the proposal for approval.

If I had realized the roadblocks to a self help group, I would have developed it as a chapel program. I had written the proposal for the class to be conducted in the chapel} since there was audio equipment available as a resource.

Communication skills are imperative to success for staff members and the inmate clerks.

Federal and State Legislation Affecting Chapel Programs

There were four bills passed by the California legislature and federal government that impacted chapel programmmg.

The first was the federal law that authorized that every inmate had the right to have a worship experience once a week. This allowed an individual with his own private faith to have a time each week to practice his faith. A person could develop his own particular religion and could have a time to experience or share it.

The second law was a California law that allowed volunteers and chaplains to contact inmates after they were paroled.

Prior to this law, it was not appropriate for either chaplains or volunteers to make contact with any parolee they had known mpnson.

The law recognized that contact with a parolee was as important as contact and counseling were with inmates when they were on the 11inside." This law allowed former inmates to receive help from individuals they had learned to trust on the inside.

These contacts increased a parolee's opportunity to stay out of prison. It was a very important move to help a parolee's rehabilitation.

The third and fourth. laws were laws regarding the physical and mental health of inmates.

Two case laws in federal court indicated that California prisons did not serve the mental health and physical health of inmates. In fact, the federal government ultimately took responsibility for California Health Services. It was done because in twenty years, they had not solved their medical and mental health services to inmates.

This law impacted the chapel programs, because it increased the workload of patio custody. The increase in workload also required the hiring of additional patio custody.

Of course, having to work harder did not set well with custody. They resented it. Ultimately, they had two cadres of officers - one that served medical and the other that served the rest of the patio services. With two unlocks, one of medical and one for the rest of the patio, there were issues as to when an unlock could be scheduled. This created an issue for the chapel, because the regular custody officers would not do their unlocks in a timely manner, as often the only inmates at the gate were chapel participants. It was a continuing problem during the remainder of my tenure as chaplain.

About two years into my tour, the California Department of Corrections changed its name to California Department of Corrections and Rehabilitation (CDCR). The change of name turned out to be a political move and was a face dressing.

It did not change policy, at least at CCC. It did not impact programming at all, from my perspective. It may have made a difference in some prisons, but it certainly didn't make any difference at CCC.

The chapel faith-based rehabilitation programming served the warden well when she went to CDCR meetings with other wardens. She could share about programs at CCC that were significantly greater than other state prisons. No accolades were awarded the chapel, but it did serve a larger cause.

Carmichael at Work

One day I came to the chapel, and when I opened the door to my office, I saw an 8x11 envelope on the floor. In it was a picture of a grizzly bear, standing on its hind legs, roaring as though he was going to devour something.At the bottom of the picture, one of my inmate clerks had written, 11Carmichael at work."

It was a caricature of me, and I really got a kick out of it, so I posted it on the outer door of my office. The caricature stayed there until I retired.

I always felt like, in some ways, I was a bear, especially when people were out of line. On the other hand, I could be a pussycat. I would like to think that I was a balance of both.

Whatever I needed to be, I believed I did it. Others will judge whether that was the case.

Alternative to Violence Workshops

A friend's organization from the Bay Area sponsored a program called "Alternative to Violence." It was a weeklong workshop during daytime working hours.

This program was the highest priority at the prison in the daytime. The leaders had talked with the warden about this program.

Although it was faith-based in origin, they didn't want anything to do with the chapel. It was conducted in the visiting room.

Since they had priority ducats, their program took place regardless of other activities. Even when there was a lockdown, they would meet. The volunteers came from the Bay Area, and they stayed at the warden's home. They gave her insight into how custody operated on the patio.

Several of the chapel inmate clerks were leaders in the program. The Spanish speaking clerk was the facilitator for the Spanish segment of the program. He often was on loan for a week at a time. I was honored to have the clerks involved in the leadership of the program.

The California Rehabilitation Opportunity Program (CROP)

The California Rehabilitation Opportunity Program's leader was Frank Genetti. The program was not a sponsored activity of the chapel.

CROP was a special project of the warden. Mr. Genetti had contacted the warden's office with a proposal to provide a faith based program for the Main Division.

They sponsored a course on family relationships and anger management. Classes were conducted in the gym classrooms. The gym was accessible to both yards. An organization called Friends on the Outside had conducted these programs but had lost their funding so CROP agreed to pick up the slack.

CROP's primary mission was to have several self-contained farms throughout California for inmates. Their mission was to provide an educational and housing environment to reduce recidivism.

It would be a place where inmates could live for up to three years while they were developing a vocation. It was this larger vision that interested the warden. The classes at CCC were to be a bridge for CCC inmates to be assigned to a farm when they were operational.

My introduction to CROP was when the associate warden for Main told me that CROP had given ten thousand dollars' worth of musical instruments to the chapels. After several weeks with no further word about the donation, I made inquiry concerning the donation. I was told it would be given to the fine-arts program rather than the chapel.

One day, I met the warden and was invited to a meeting of his administrative staff and CROP. All the top administrators were present at the meeting.

Mr. Genetti made a presentation on CROP. He shared his dream about the farms and the teaching program at the gym. It was an excellent presentation.

The warden asked if anybody had any questions. Everyone sat on their hands. It was something beyond me. I knew some of the officers, and their behavior did not fit what I knew about them.

Finally, one of the captains, who believed in programming for inmates, asked a question. That was the only question asked.

After it was over, I spoke to several of administrators individually and asked them why they weren't more involved. They said that programs like this were old hat to them. They had seen stuff like this come down the pike several times during their tenure at the prison. They didn't buy it. It was the warden's project. They were going to wait and see.

About two months later, Mr. Genetti got permission from the warden to come to the 40 Days Purpose-Driven program. He came with his wife.

I found out later that the reason his wife came with him was that his son was an inmate at Lassen Yard. His son had been at High Desert State Prison and was now in a Level III facility. I didn't know anything about this until months later.

Charles Turner was responsible for the program. He impressed Genetti with his gifts. Weeks later, he approached Charlie about working with him when Charlie got out of prison.

Three or four weeks later, the warden had another meeting with Genetti. At that meeting, Genetti brought a former inmate named Monty and his friend, who was the director of a halfway house in Florida. Monty's friend related well with inmates as he shared about his farm in Florida.

The warden authorized a chapel meeting where Monty could share his story. At the Friday meeting, Mr. Genetti shared his dream of rehabilitation with the inmates. Another meeting was scheduled for Friday morning with a prerelease class, where Monty shared the CROP story.

In his talk, he shared about possible educational programs that might be presented at CCC and how computers could be used to teach English as a second language and help inmates obtain aGED. Monty was just sharing his dream.

Under the circumstances, it was probably premature to share the dream, because one of the inmates in the class started to complain that they couldn't do anything for him, since he was getting out of prison in two weeks. He said he didn't have any place to go when he got out. He didn't think it was fair, and he began to get angry. Monty talked with him and worked with him and got him calmed down.

A teacher in the back of the classroom got excited, because she perceived this would possibly cause her to lose her teaching position. She talked to the principal and other teachers, and they went berserk.

It was rumored that education positions could be cut, and they felt this might mean they would lose their jobs. None of this came up; they just assumed that this would take their jobs. They really got angry.

That same day, the warden called a meeting of custody administrators. He also invited two teachers. They were angry about Genetti's program.

It was a tragedy that this happened. It would have been far better if Monty had never shared. It created a great deal of animosity. The principal of the education program was really resistant to any kind of idea like this. I don't know how it all worked out, but it was a very difficult time.

Each time Genetti would visit his son, he would normally come to the 40 Days program. While he was there, he would meet new inmates who had recently become active in chapel.

One of the new inmates was Shane. Shane was a very gifted young man. He got the attention of Mr. Genetti.

Shane had been at CCC for several years. Recently, he had gotten involved with a faith-based program sponsored by the Friends Church. It was a pet project of the warden. She had the instructors stay at her house when they were in Susanville.

The program was titled "Alternatives to Violence." The classes were conducted in the visiting room, and special ducats were issued to all participants. Come hell or high water, the program went on, regardless of what was taking place at the prison.

Shane volunteered for the program and ultimately became their lead inmate instructor.

Before he got involved with this program, he was a wiccan. His mother was a wiccan, and that was one of the reasons he identified with them. He was antagonistic toward the church and toward anyone who was part of the church. As he got involved with the Alternative to Violence program, his heart began to soften, and he developed a new worldview.

It turned out that Todd, the lead chapel clerk, was on the same yard, and they became good friends. The clerk invited Shane to the chapel.

Shane didn't want to go to any of the services but the clerk had Shane watch DVDs. One of the programs that touched him was the program called NOOMA, a series of videos by Rob Bell, which we used at the Sunday morning worship.

Rob Bell also had a lecture titled "Everything Is Spiritual." It was a part of a Midwestern tour.

In his presentation, he used a twenty five-foot white board. As he lectured, he filled the white board with notes. The presentation grabbed Shane's heart and intellect.

His second presentation was titled "The Gods Aren't Angry." The inmate clerk showed Shane other DVDs that piqued his interest.

As a result of these materials, Shane came to chapel. When he showed an interest in the chapel, Charlie Turner and Todd, who were in the same house as

Shane, enrolled him in the 40 Days program.

At the end of the 49 Days program, Shane made a commitment to Christ and was baptized. His actions caused a stir in Cascade Yard, as he was an inmate with influence among all inmates. Shane watched all of the DVDs that presented the Christian faith as a rational faith, not pie in the sky.

Sometimes, he didn't want to attend a worship service, so Todd would set up a DVD for him to review. Shane became a symbol of faith as few inmates had been during my tenure as chaplain.

When Mr. Genetti, the CROP founder, met Shane, he was entranced by him. He made arrangement to keep in contact with Shane when he was paroled to the Greater Los Angeles area. He told me he planned to give Shane a job in his CROP program.

Frank Genetti made arrangements with the warden to bring some parolees to Main Chapel to share the CROP dream. CROP had been working with the women's prison in Chowchilla.

He made arrangements with the warden to have an afternoon s,ession at the chapel. Prior to that program, he had a meeting in the gym with the CROP classes.

There were several administrators present at both sessions. They used the used the gym for this meeting. Following their meeting, they participated in a graduation for people in the anger management program, and there and then, he brought them over to the chapel. We had quite a number of administrative officers there.

Shane shared his story after having been out of prison for only ten weeks. A parolee from the women's prison also shared. They both were impressive with their stories.

Charles was the third inmate presenter, and he talked about his children and their relationship with him while he was in pnson.

After he finished, Todd B., the lead clerk, shared a video clip and talked about inmate responsibilities. This program was presented while I was on sick leave.

I came back for the presentation because it was part of the futur•e of faith-based rehabilitation programming at CCC.

When the meeting was over, I still didn't understand its purpose. No one in administration of the CROP program ever discussed it with me. It wasn't really any of my business, since it was a CROP program conducted in the Main Chapel.

Tobacco-Smoking Inmate

After Robert came to the chapel, he was regularly treated by a physical therapist.

It was rumored that the therapist brought him tobacco.

The therapist was fired, but the clerk was not disciplined. Later, I discovered he was smoking in the Catholic chaplain's washroom.

When I discovered it, I relieved him of his duties and sent him back to his housing. After my report, I expected him to be disciplined. Nothing happened; he continued to live on the yard.

He continued to have physical therapy and would drop by the chapel, unauthorized, to talk to the clerks. He propositioned the lead clerk to notify him when tobacco came through the chapel mail for him.

The clerk said no and came to me privately and said that tobacco would be coming to the chapel through the mailroom. I immediately told my supervisor about the request.

About a week later, I got a phone call in late afternoon from the mailroom that there was a lot of mail in the chapel box. I looked for a clerk to go with me to get the mail, but none was available, so I proceeded to the mailroom.

When I opened the mail drawer, there were only two pieces of mail in it. I couldn't understand why I'd been called, but I didn't say anything to the mail clerks, because they were all busy. One of the mail pieces was an eight-by-ten-inch envelope.

I stopped in the chapel lobby to open the mail on the counter. I tore the envelope open, and there was a plastic package inside. Inside the plastic were three two by-four-inch packages.

I realized they were packages of tobacco. As soon as I recognized the contents, I knew I had been set up.

I grabbed the packages and headed for the mailroom. The mail sergeant was there, so I took the package of tobacco over to him and threw it at him, and he caught it.

I didn't realize it had been salted with dye. I had dye all over my hand, and I had wiped it on my forehead and face.

In my anger, I left the mailroom and headed for the investigations lieutenant's office. I wanted to tell him what I thought of his attempt to involve me in another tobacco issue.

As I was walking by the Sally Port of Sierra Yard, I spotted the warden watching the proceedings. When I saw him, I told him what I thought of the procedure in no certain terms. Then I headed for Investigations.

The warden followed me, and when the lieutenant came out, the warden asked him to come to the chapel to talk to the chaplain. I was still unaware that I had dye on my hands and face.

After another ten minutes of emoting, the warden and lieutenant talked to me and calmed me down. The warden told me to go to the restroom and take some of the dye off. It didn't all come off until after I had a long shower.

Thank goodness the sergeant also got some dye on him. Much of my anger stemmed from the fact that I was the one who had warned them about the tobacco, and they still used me. I believe they didn't trust me.

Within a few days, the inmate who caused the incident was back on the yard, with no disciplinary action. I found out later that tobacco is not an illegal substance in California, so inmates caught with it usually receive little or no disciplinary action. However, the chapel's reputation suffered.

Chief Clerk Todd

When Rick, my chapel clerk for several monsths, left the chapel, we were in need of somebody who had special computer skills. I had no one in the chapel who was qualified.

Todd was the chief Cascade Yard clerk, and I approached him about considering a position in the chapel. The clerk's reputation was impeccable.

He'd had more than one hundred employees in his business in Sacramento, but a marital dispute had put him in prison. It was the first time in his life he had ever been at odds: with the law.

While on Cascade Yard, he had gained the respect of inmates, custody officers, and administration.

He had not been to chapel, but as CT broached the subject, he came to a general Protestant service. He continued to come. I invited him to come for an interview.

After our visit, he told me he would take the position if I got him cleared of his position as Cascade clerk. What a boon it was for the chapel. He had integrity, skill, and a personal presence that touched everyone he met. He was an accomplished public speaker and obviously led and supervised faith-based programming. He was also a Cascade Yard representative at the monthly meeting with the warden.

I worked well with him, and he took a major responsibility in keeping the faith based program operating. He coordinated the Financial Peace University program, which taught inmates how to handle money.

After I left the prison, I received a letter from him, telling me that I had helped him discover that Jesus of Nazareth was the Master of the universe. I was honored by the opportunity to help him discover a renewed faith in God and his world.

The Financial Peace University Program

During most of my tenure as chaplain, I looked for a program that would teach inmates financial responsibility. For a time, we used a program titled "God's Way of Handling Money." Inmate Clerk A. taught it, but it did not attract many inmates.

One of the Susanville ministers introduced me to the Financial Peace University program. It was expensive, but I worked out a deal with the publisher so we could use it at the chapel.

After it was approved by the administration, we offered it on Monday and Thursday afternoons. TB taught it, and he attracted a new clientele to the chapel. It was a continuing program when I retired from the chapel.

DVD Video Library for Camps

In early 2010, an inmate returned to the Main Division Cascade Yard because he had to have a medical checkup. While he was in the yard, he came back to chapel. He had been coming to chapel prior to his going to the camp, but he was never too active. He seemed to be playing games.

I had a couple of conversations with him in my office. He didn't appear to be sincere. I was surprised to see him when he came back for his medical. He was really energized about being involved in the church.

He said that while he was at camp, he gained a new understanding of how important it was to begin to change if he was going to be able to stay on the outside when he was released. He felt that the church could do much to help him in that way.

He had talked to his camp lieutenant about the chapel's developing a DVD lending library for camps. The DVDs would be faith-based programs that would be loaned to a camp for a few days and returned in order to obtain another DVD. I told him I thought it was a great idea, and I would work on finding a source to fund it.

We would need an inventory of as many as one hundred different DVDs to provide for the eighteen fire camps on a regular basis. One of the chapel clerks and I went through video catalogs to find what might be available. I determined that a grant of three thousand dollars would be sufficient to begin the program.

I contacted the CROP Foundation, and they agreed they would fund it. They also agreed to provide three hundred dollars to purchase Spanish videos for Main Chapel. My next task was to write a proposal for CCC administration to authorize the project. I went to the Associate Warden for Camps and

265

proposed the idea. He thought it was a good idea but asked that I survey the eighteen camps' administration as to their willingness to support the idea. He wanted me to include their ideas in the proposal.

I was able to touch base with seventeen of the eighteen lieutenants. They agreed it was a viable program, and their camps could benefit from it.

I was working on the final draft of the proposal when I injured my back.

As a result of the injury, I was only able to work half a day at the chapel. I was required to have a volunteer with me at all times. I finally submitted the proposal to my supervisor a few days before I retired. Since my retirement, no action has been taken on my proposal.

Inmate Program Coordination for Celebrate Recovery

One of the first coordinators was a clerk at the Sierra captain's office and had been a high school teacher. While drinking, he had an injury. He was sentenced to five years in prison. His educational background allowed him to enhance the Celebrate Recovery curriculum for small groups. During the remainder of my tenure, we practiced the program he suggested.

Another of the leaders was Michael. Michael was the yard representative for the Crypts. At the time} I was not aware of this. He used his own experiences out on the street, which were pretty vivid, to describe what addiction does.

His favorite illustration was a dog he found on the street. He put him in his backyard and treated him kindly for several months. His dog finally trusted him, and he became a prize for him with his buddies on the street.

Lonnie was a crack addict. He had been in prison on eleven different occasions. He didn't have any teeth as a result of the crack addiction.

As a leader, he was extremely motivated and articulate. His energy and emotion was evident in his talks. Unfortunately, he would not share his leadership. After several months as a Celebrate Recovery leader, he had to face another charge. He was gone for six months, and when he came back, he expected to take over again as coordinator.

I didn't allow him to do it. He became very emotional and got in my face about it. It showed that he was not about being a servant but being somebody in front of an audience.

Inmate Clerk Jon became the leader after Lonnie left. He reorganized the PowerPoint programming and made it possible to use them with a USB drive. As a result, the material could be presented on the screen without needing any wireless assistance.

It was an effective teaching tool, but when custody learned about this, we were not allowed to use the technique, because a flash drive could not be available to inmates.

Michael H. had been a successful businessman on the outside. His home was in Arizona. One weekend, he came to California and ended up in a bar fight and had a five-year sentence.

He was the lead clerk in the Sierra captain's office. Because of his crime, he was not eligible for the camp program. Because of the respect he gained with the captain and yard custody, they waived the camp restriction, and he went to fire camp. He has paroled and is in Southern California. He was restricted from going back to Arizona until he is off parole.

He has a business in Long Beach with several employees. He .said he has two patents in reference to waste management that he expects to contract with a community in the Los Angeles area. If what he tells me works, he will be a rich man.

Others who led the program were Dr. Bob, Don R., and Barry M. When Barry was reassigned, Todd B. became the lead clerk and very soon assumed leadership in Celebrate Recovery.

He had the respect of the inmates, custody staff, and administration. He represented his yard in the monthly meeting with the warden. He worked as lead clerk until I retired.

The Faith-Based Rehabilitation Programs

As previously stated, I had agreed with the warden to install a faith-based rehabilitation program, led by inmates, supported by volunteers, which would help reduce prison recidivism. From the outset of my mission, the 40 Days of Purpose and Celebrate Recovery programs were the flagship programs.

It was hoped that thls pilot program could be a model for faith-based rehabilitation programming in other California state prisons.

40 Days and Celebrate
Programs

The 40 Days of Purpose program was a seven-week program, and the Celebrate Recovery program was a twelve-step program that could be a part of an inmate's life during his time in prison and also on the outside.

Celebrate Recovery was applicable to all addictions, not just substance addiction. All human beings are addicted to something, and the Celebrate Recovery program is aimed at helping a person deal with his particular issue.

At CCC, the 40 Days of Purpose program was the introductory program for the chapel's faith-based programming. The 40 Days of Purpose program introduced the small group to inmates.

The first program was in the Main Chapel in October 2005. During the first six months of my tenure, I continued these programs at Lassen Chapel, where they began while I was a volunteer. I did not have any volunteers who would support the program during my first few months as chaplain.

The first two 40 Days programs at Main Chapel were led by Inmate Clerk Welty. After he left the chapel, I enlisted several other inmates to be inmate leaders. One of the first was Inmate Clerk Ackerman. He not only led the program, but he also organized the book distribution and curriculum materials.

Approximately twenty-five 40 Days of Purpose classes were conducted during my five-year tenure at the prison. The average number of participants in each of the offerings was sixty. At least twenty-four hundred inmates took the program during the five years.

Each inmate had a book plus office supplies and video equipment. All these costs were covered by Lassen Sierra Prison Ministries.

During the five years of the program, a number of different inmates were the coordinators for the program. They made the public presentations and coordinated the small group leaders. A DVD presentation by Rick Warren was the primary focus of the teaching. After it was presented, small groups consumed the remainder of a session.

Groups were limited to no more than seven inmates and were ethnically balanced. It was difficult to obtain ethnic balance, since many inmates were resistant to the idea. It was imperative to have the balance to counteract the prejudicial practice in housing and on the yard.

To qualify as a program coordinator, an inmate was required to have completed this program and serve as a small-group leader at least two times. These experiences gave him an appreciation for the program and how the program was conducted.

During most of the years of the program, the overall coordination from the chapel was the responsibility of Charles. He made recommendation of possible coordinators and small-group leaders.

We gave certificates of completion to all of the inmates who completed the program. I also wrote a 128 < atta-boy" statement, which was placed in their permanent file. Atta-boys were not a normal result of having completed a program.

The 40 Days program was life-changing, since it helped inmates to set goals and find a new direction for their lives. Thus, it was noted in their permanent files.

The other flagship program was the Celebrate Recovery program. It had twenty-seven different weekly presentations. John Baker, the creator of the program, had PowerPoint presentations for each session. The coordinator presented the session or chose another inmate to do it.

Inmate Clerk W. led the program for approximately nine months while he was the clerk at the chapel. When he paroled, Inmate Ack assumed the responsibility.

Boundaries

At the Celebrate Recovery annual seminar, I discovered a program on DVD by Cloud and Townsend called "Boundaries." Cloud and Townsend are two Christian clinical psychologists from Orange County.

The focus of the program is helping individuals set boundaries for their lives and their behavior. There are eight lessons, and we used a small-group format. A workbook was given to each inmate.

One of the problems that inmates have is that they don't have boundaries almost anything goes. And the only way one is successful is when he is able to have boundaries to help govern his life. This program does that.

It was one of the more popular programs in the faith-based arsenal. Ken K. was one of the first to coordinate it. Charlie T. served as coordinator when Ken left.

Angry Heart

Another program that we started very early in my tenure was called *"Angry Heart."* Lisa Revere taught Angry Heart, which dealt with the issues of how we handle our anger, especially when it comes to our family.

Don Bemus and his wife introduced it to the chapel; they showed the DVD of the program on Saturday morning. After seeing it, I was as able to get the videos, and we implemented it to chapel. We used it more than any other videos, other than 40 Days and Celebrate Recovery.

Anger issues are endemic to the human nature. But they're even more so when it comes to inmates and individuals with drug issues, because the drugs let down the bars, and whatever anger you have is much more able to be displayed.

One of the reasons violence is present in inmates is because it has been bottled up and needs to be released. The Angry Heart program provided a formula for doing that.

"Undercover"-Living under Authority

John Revere has a program called *"Undercover."*

Volunteer Jerry P. introduced the program to the chapel and taught the first class. He contacted the Revere Organization and they sent videos of several of his seminars. We had enough that we sent them to the fire camps. Undercover was a program to help individuals learn to live under authority. The first story of the Bible was about two humans whose problem was that they were not willing to live under the authority of their Creator. As a result they made some horrendous errors.

This has been a problem for all humans since that time. We've been irresponsible, because we like to fight authority.

Jerry P. got permission to reproduce copies of the workbook, which were used extensively throughout my term at the pnson.

We always gave certificates for this program. The title of the certificates was "Undercover." Some inmates took the certificates back to the yard, and some of the crazies there said that these chapel guys were undercover agents for the custody security, and they were going to nail chapel inmates.

There was a big crisis on Cascade Yard, and the lieutenant on the yard asked me to write a memo explaining the program.

So I wrote explaining that Undercover didn't have anything to do with being a secret police; it had to do with living under authority. It was major flack for about thirty-six hours, until we finally got the crazies to settle down and recognize that this was a title of a program that had nothing to do with being a sneak.

One of the things I often did was to take the story or the title of whatever program we had and give it a new title that was more secular in nature, especially if we were using it as a means of telling the world that we were doing something that could affect the behavior of people on the outside. We were not just selling a theory of some "pie in the sky" idea about where somebody might go after he died.

Second Base

Rick Warren's Saddleback Church had a new membership orientation program called Four Bases. The first program encouraged new members regarding their decision to follow Jesus and steps to begin the process. The second was about sharing with others what we have discovered so far on the journey of faith. Third base was helping new members to discover their gifts and how to use them to serve others. Fourth base was finding ways we can serve our community of faith.

We chose to do the Second Base program on Wednesday night, with the Rogers family as the volunteer sponsors. The Rogerses were already sponsoring a Bible study at Lassen Chapel. Mr. Rogers agreed to sponsor the program for three months as his token of support to the faith-based programmmg.

Since the program was in the middle of the week, it was very popular. Inmate Clerk Charlie T. designed the program, so Mr. Rogers had an opportunity at each session to teach. The program used the small group format.

Mr. Rogers initially didn't approve of small groups, but as he experienced Second Base, he had a change of heart. He admitted it was an effective program for inmates.

Saturday Early Morning Leadership Program

We conducted the leadership program at 7:00a.m. for approximately nine months. The curriculum consisted of leadership materials from Cloud and Townsend as well as John Maxwell's leadership materials.

Willow Creeks Church had contributed several years of the National Leadership Seminar to the chapel. Twenty inmates attended the program. The program was led by Matt H. and Ken A. They were both university graduates and did a great job of leading the program.

Throughout the entire program, custody resisted giving inmates access to the chapel in a timely manner. In the winter inmates waited more than an hour to gain entry to the chapel. The excessive mistreatment of the inmates finally made me cancel the program.

Seven Steps to a Turnaround

T. D. Jakes developed a motivational series using biblical principles, titled "Seven Steps to a Turnaround." Jakes purported there were seven steps to a successful life. Each presentation was approximately fifty minutes, which was followed by thirty minutes of small groujps.

Inmate Clerk BobS. was the inmate director of the program during his tenure at the chapel. Bob had a graduate degree in psychology, which enabled him to lead the program most effectively. His leadership enabled the participants to discover ways to change.

In the first session, Jakes introduced the idea that one of the first things needed is an exposure to as many aspects of life as possible. In order to have a plan for success, one needed to understand the myriad options available to all humans. Limited experiences and knowledge of these options is one of the first issues that a person developing a success orientation must experience.

It is my sense that inmates too often have limited exposure to life. Many inmates come from the inner city and have spent their whole lives within ten to fifteen blocks of their birthplace. They have never had an opportunity to discover the fantastic world we live in and the options they have to experience it. Unfortunately, opportunities are too often not available. It is no wonder that too many of them made poor choices.

Unsafe People

Townsend and McCloud had a program called "Difficult People." It submits that some people are toxic by nature. If you are around them, you pick up their toxicity, and it gets you in trouble.

Humans tend to choose certain types of people to be around. If a significant other is toxic, we may well repeat the choice in a new relationship.

This is also true when it comes to our neighborhood. We must figure out a way to get free from whatever sources and people lead us to the destructive behavior.

It was difficult to recruit participants in the program.

Twelve Steps to Freedom

Twelve Steps to Freedom was presented by Dr. Ed Young, pastor of the Second Baptist Church in Houston, Texas. It's one of the largest Southern Baptist churches in America, with seven campuses. *Twelve Steps* to Freedom is an eight-week program.

We used the supplement materials for our Celebrate Recovery program. Inmate leaders could choose segments of the program to support the particular twelve steps under consideration. Since Dr. Young was a powerful and articulate speaker, his material was often significant to the Celebrate Recovery participants.

The F-Word Program

The F-Word program dealt with the issue of forgiveness. Most of us have another word in mind when someone says the "F word."

Forgiveness is a signiificant problem for most of us, and we need to figure out a way to do this significant act. One of the quotes I remember goes like this: "I can learn to love myself and others by forgiving rather than judging." The forgiving we do is not for the other person's benefit. Any time we forgive, it is primarily because it releases and frees us.

Most inmates, as well as the rest of the world, have issues with forgiveness. There are people they resent. There are people who they have not been able to get out of their minds. These people still control them. They need to be free.

This five-lesson series was truly helpful to many inmates.

Saturday/Sunday Afternoon Faith Based Programs

Saturday and Sunday afternoons were dedicated to providing multiple faith based offerings in the chapel. We offered up to four options at a time.

Some of programs we used were Angry Heart, Under Cover, and Boundaries, as well as a program on personal finances.

Ken Ackerman taught the personal finance program. It was interesting that there were few takers for this program. Typically, five or six inmates would come to the program. Actually, this program could have benefited all participants in the faith-based programming.

Financial Peace University Program

A few months before it was time for me to retire, I came across a program called *"Financial Peace University,"* a financial planning program. It was a fifteen-videos program that was taught by Inmate Clerk Todd. It was offered on Monday and Thursday afternoon. Normally, there would be up to fifteen inmates from the two yards.

It was interesting that the inmates attracted to this program were not involved in any of the other chapel programs. I don't know exactly the reason for it, but Inmate Clerk Todd was very articulate and was respected by all inmates in his housing unit. His personal reputation helped to recruit participants.

Spanish Programs

A major problem we had throughout my tenure was providing resources for the Spanish-speaking people.

I went on the Internet, looking for instruction materials, but was not able to find them. It might have been because I couldn't recognize them, because I'm not a Spanish speaker.

One of the things we did, however, was have a program for Spanish speakers on Saturday mornings. Typically, we would have two volunteers who were Spanish speakers, and they would conduct a program, sometimes on a Saturday night, but when we got Celebrate Recovery moving, it wasn't feasible for that to happen.

So we decided to use the Catholic chapel in coordination with the Protestant chapel on Saturdays. We didn't have them go over there on Sunday, because Sunday was a general service, and we were able to facilitate Spanish speakers with the use of the multiple hearing aids.

On Saturday, we ran the program, and one of the Spanish-speaking inmates led what was called "En Familia." It provided teaching on how the family works. It was a powerful program. Normally, the class had more than thirty participants.

It was the best attendance we ever had for a Spanish-speaking program.

Life Connections

One day my supervisor came back from a state meeting and told me that he had been introduced to an interfaith-program.

He asked me if I would look into it. I had been looking for an interfaith program, and his program seemed to fit. I wanted something that could be used with different faith groups, such as Muslims, Buddhists, Odinists, and Jehovah's Witnesses, as well as Christian groups.

The program was developed for use in the federal prison system and had thirteen different modules. A presentation was made, and the group was divided into triads to discuss the material. As our program developed, we didn't use triads exclusively.

I asked BobS., one of the chapel clerks, to teach the program. We chose five modules for our program. Our reason for choosing five modules was because the class only met twice a week, and a module usually took a minimum of a week to complete.

In the beginning, we had a class in the morning for Cascade Yard and one in the afternoon for Sierra Yard. It was hoped that bringing one yard at a time would facilitate access to the program.

After we determined our schedule, I called the company that sold it concerning the cost. I was informed it would cost a minimum of $1,100. We could not copy any of the materials, so we would have to use a lesson several times to be cost effective.

We developed a folder for each student in which he kept the materials.

It was anticipated that the prison would pay for it, since it was an interfaith program. All other faith-based curriculum used at the chapel was paid for by the Lassen Sierra Prison Ministry Foundation.

Before the warden would approve the expenditure, I met with her and explained the project. She agreed to fund it. She requested that I only order half of the materials in this fiscal year, and the second half would be ordered next year. It cost almost six hundred dollars.

After about six weeks, I requested the second half of the program, and the warden informed me that there wasn't any money in the budget for the program. She told me I would have to find another source of funding for the additional materials. I asked Lassen Sierra Prison Ministries, Inc., to step up to the plate and fund it. They did.

BobS. designed the program and taught for almost two years. When he paroled, I ask Charles T. to take his place. He was working in the chapel as a unpaid clerk.

He used many other programs in the chapel library to supplement what BobS. had developed.

After Charles T. became the instructor, we decided to have only one session for both yards on Monday and Thursday afternoons. The last year I was chaplain, that was the way the program was conducted, and so I asked him if he would come to work at the chapel in an unpaid clerk's position. He agreed to it, and he took responsibility for that program for the next two and a half years.

We redesigned it very differently. He was able to bring materials from many other sources. We used much of the DVD material that we had acquired for our library. He was extremely creative, and he did a really good job.

Ultimately, after he took responsibility for the program, we had a difficult time keeping the numbers up for two groups. We finally decided that we would have just one group, on Monday and Thursday afternoons. And that worked out for the last year of the program. We had Muslim participants and some Skinheads in the program.

I was very pleased that we were able to offer so many options for inmates to learn skills that could help them be successful on the outside. Some of these programs can be used by groups on the outside who are working to help individuals in recovery. Often, church programs use the lecture method of presentation, when small group programs, like the programs addressed above, might serve them more effectively.

Alternative Faith Based Programs and Supervision

When I came to CCC, the Muslim chaplain was a half-time position. He also covered High Desert State Prison. His family lived in the San Joaquin Valley, and it was a real hardship for him to work in Susanville. Finally, he found a position as chaplain in a prison near Sacramento. It was a half-time position, so the CCC religious supervisor gave a half position at CCC so he could transfer.

Sacramento administration recently had authorized a full-time Muslim chaplain for all California state prisons. Thus, High

Desert had a full-time Muslim chaplain position, but CCC only had a half-time position, because of the transfer decision. With only a half-time position, it was difficult for CCC to recruit a Muslim chaplain.

As a result of this problem, the Catholic chaplain was given responsibility for supervising alternative-faith programs.

Muslim inmates were allowed to meet under custody supervision. Their meetings were conducted in the back of the Catholic chapel A temporary barrier separated the Muslim area from the Catholic chapel. Thus, Muslim worshippers couldn't see the Catholic images in the front of the chapel. It wasn't a perfect solution, but it worked.

DVDs-Faith-Based Rehabilitation Programs

Invaluable resources for faith-based rehabilitation programs are the DVDs and movies that speak to everyone, regardless of the chapel affiliation. The DVDs from national leaders in many fields are available for purchase and serve the chapel programs well.

T. D. Jakes's Videos

One of Bishop Jakes's most powerful presentations was a DVD titled *He-Motions*. I was introduced to the program by lifers who attended Lassen Chapel. He-Motions was a key national program that he shared with groups throughout the United States.

He postulated that men had different emotional makeup than women. He talked about fathers and sons and how they behave. Initially, he was going to share it only with men. Then he decided to share it with women as welL He discovered that women gained as much from it as men did. It was one of the most powerful talks that I have heard in my lifetime.

After being introduced to the program at Lassen Chapel, I purchased a copy of it for Main Chapel. When we first showed it, I was overwhelmed.

It was even more interesting to watch the inmates view the video. Among the participants were several white lifers. They were centered on the materials in a way I had never seen before. Of course, the blacks endorsed it, as Jakes was one of their favorite preachers.

There was one video clip I will always remember. A mother was coming down the church aisle while Jakes was giving an invitation to come for prayer. She had a young boy by the hand and was dragging him to the front. When she got to the front, Jakes asked. "What do you want me to pray about?" She said. "I want you to pray the devil out of my son."

As he looked at the boy, Jakes could see that the boy was deeply embarrassed. So he asked the mother where the boy's father was. She proceeded to rant and rave about what an ugly person his father was and that her son was just like his father.

Of course, the boy was shrinking, and Mr. Jakes wanted to respond in kind to her accusation, but because he instead, he said a simple prayer. The mother left with the boy, and she didn't understand that her little boy had changed..

He said that about nine or ten years of age, boys, who until that time thought their mothers and fathers were infallible, become aware of their peers and their opinions. And like all males, that boy wanted to relate to male figures.

About this time, we discover the power of playing the game. We are built for competition and want to be winners. This boy had discovered the game and that his mother's rules didn't help him play the game. His allegiance changed. He was listening to other voices.

Jakes then illustrated the different ways men play the game and what motivates them. His illustrations were provocative. This DVD was shown at least three times a year in prime time to chapel participants.

Another DVD program of Jakes's was called *Seven Steps to a Turnaround*, a program on goal setting. Although some of the illustrations were biblical, it was as great a motivational program as I have ever encountered.

Rob Bell Programs

Rob Bell has two programs that are masterpieces.

The first presentation is *Everything Is Spiritual* and the second is *The Gods Aren't Angry.*

They will grip you intellectually and emotionally. In *Everything Is Spiritual,* he described how everything in our universe has a relationship to the spiritual. It is not a pantheistic argument but a Christian one in every part of his presentation. The Christian faith is not pie in the sky; it explains the reality of our universe.

The *Gods Aren't Angry* speaks to guilt that humans have and how we act with the possibility that God is angry with us. Bell's visuals enhance his ideas, and his arguments are invaluable for helping searchers understand the Christian faith.

The second program is a series often minute programs called NOOMA. He has produced twenty-five different programs. These programs were a part the Main Chapel Sunday morning worship services for three years of my tenure.

Tony Campolo Sermons

Tony Campolo was a popular presenter in the 1980s. Tony was a professor at Eastern University, St. Davids, Pennsylvania. Tony grew up in a black Baptist church and spoke with their power of persuasion. Two of his seven DVDs that are at Main Chapel should be viewed by aU inmates.

The first one was titled *If I had to Live It Over Again.*It's a survey of ninety elderly seniors. It describes what they would practice if they could live life over again. This speech not only speaks to those who have already lived their lives, but it also is invaluable for those just beginning the life's journey.

The second DVD is titled *The Kingdom of God Is a Party.* Dr. Campolo talks about various aspects of what the kingdom is. The kingdom is *shalom*, which is defined as a wholeness that makes up life. It's also jubilee, which allows life to start over again. He ends the sermon with an exquisite story when he talks about when "the kingdom of God is a party."

He tells a story about when he was in Hawaii, conducting a seminar. He couldn't sleep one night, so he got up about three o'clock in the morning. He went out looking for a place to eat. He found a diner, went in and sat down at the counter.

The cook served him eggs toast and coffee. While he was eating/ a whole raft of prostitutes came in.Before it was over there were about thirty of them.

The diner was where the prostitutes gathered after completing their night's work. They ate and talked together.

In the course of the conversation, one of the prostitutes told her friend that tomorrow was her birthday. The friend said in a caustic way, "What do you want us to do? Do you want us to give you a party?" She said, "No, I don't want a party. I've never had a birthday party in my life, and I'm over forty years old. I don't need a party."

After they all left, Campolo said to the owner, 11What about us throwing a birthday party tomorrow for the lady who has never had one? When they come in tomorrow night, we'll have a birthday party. I'll get all of the decorations, and I'll buy a cake."

The cook said, "No, no, I'll make the cake." Tony looked at the cook's hands and the way he was rubbing them on the dirty apron. Tony thought that after seeing the man's hands, he didn't want to eat what he had already ordered.

They agreed they would have a party the next night for this lady. The next night, just before three o'clock, Tony arrived with all the decorations, and they decorated the diner. The cook had made the cake.

All the ladies waited until the birthday lady came in. When she came in, they sang "Happy Birthday" to her. She was overwhelmed. The cook brought out the birthday cake, and she fell apart.She asked if she could take the cake to show her mother, who lived three houses from the diner. She took the cake, showed it to mother, and brought it back. Then they finished the celebration.

After the women had departed, Tony and the cook continued their conversation. The cook asked Tony what he did, and Tony said that he was a preacher. The guy said, "No, you're not a preacher." Tony said, "Yes, I am a preacher."

The owner asked Tony what kind of church he had. Tony said, ui have a church that throws birthday parties for whores at three o'clock in the morning." The owner said, "If there was a church like that, I would join it."

Tony said that the kingdom of God is a party for people who are lost. People who are down and out are the mission of the church. There is no better message for inmates than the understanding that God throws parties for inmates just as well as he might for ladies of the night.

The Film Fireproof

A recent film that impacted inmates was *Fireproof.* It speaks to what one needs to do to restore one's marriage. It was in secular theaters at the time it was shown at the chapel.

After the film was shown, a lively discussion concerning its content was conducted in the chapel. It was also shown on Saturday morning, as well as Celebrate Recovery.

Promise Keepers Seminar DVDs

We obtained a significant number of Promise Keepers Yearly Conference DVDs.

One speaker who spoke clearly to inmates was Joe White.

He presented dramatic programs where he carried a cross into the auditorium and played the part of a cross maker. It spoke vividly to every inmate.

In another session, he told about a martyred pastor in Uganda. The terrorists came and took him from his church and killed him.

Before they came, the pastor posted his manifesto of faith on his home door with a knife. It mirrored what Luther did. The piece is called 11I Am Part of the Fellowship of the Unashamed." Using his knife he stuck manifesto on the outside door of his home. The following was staked on his door because he was willing to die for his faith: *"The die has been cast. I have stepped over the line. The decision has been made.I am a disciple of jesus Christ."*

It is a very powerful piece, which Joe White uses to explain the need for all of us to make a commitment that allows all of us to stand against evil in whatever form it appears. If anyone needs to do this, it is men in prison, because in my estimation, that is one of the most difficult places to follow Jesus, the Master and Savior.

Bill Hybels National Leadership Conference DVDs

There are several pieces in Bill Hybels's national leadership training program for ministers that were valuable to the Main Chapel programming.

Bill Hybel's church in Illinois contributed six years of DVDs to the chapel. It is the only nonprofit organization that contributed their materials with no cost to the chapel. These materials were used in a myriad of chapel programming.

One DVD talked about success not being a one-person project. We all depend on others for our success. There are no self-made men. This program speaks to inmates about their addictions.

We have to recognize that in order to get out of our addictions and our failures, we need to be willing to give ourselves to a power bigger than ourselves.

Dave Roever DVDs

Dave Roever is a Vietnam veteran. While he was in Vietnam, a bomb exploded at his stomach. He lost one of his eyes and an ear, as well part of his face. He is tragically scarred that way. He also lost several fingers.

The video tells his story of rehabilitation and recovery. His humor makes him a telling communicator. Every one of his humorous stories has a punch line, and it strikes to your soul. Tlhe original DVD is in black and white and vividly describes the power of the Christian faith.

Life without Limits Videos

Nick Vujicic was born without limbs. He has small fins as arms and legs. He lives alone and is self-sufficient. Nick is an Australian man whose parents gave him no slack because of his handicaps. He swims like a fish and does his own household duties.

He is also a superb communicator and has a strong Christian faith. When he is in front of a church he is helped to get on the top of a table. He is able sit upright on his own. His voice is strong his articulation is terrific and his message has touched inmates, lives.

All who see this film cannot leave without being thankful for what God has done for them. Obviously inmates need to find a way to be thankful for their circumstances. This video helps them to do that.

We used Nick's video often as a way of stimulating inmates to see life in a different way.

The Pay It Forward Film

An older film called *Pay It Forward* had a message that it was more important to "pay it forward" when someone does you a good deed. If someone does you a good deed, you pay them back by doing someone else a good deed.

This is a great concept for inmates, because they need to figure out a way to quit looking at the past and how they can make restitution. The best restitution they could ever make is to live life fully, give life to somebody in the future, and not worry about their past.

Land of the Giants Film

There is a Christian movie titled *Land of the Giants*, which is a football story about a public school team that had believers playing on it. The coach is also a Christian. The film shows how they are able to deal with unbelievable adversity and come out the winner. It speaks to team spirit and the commitment it takes to make a team work. The inmates liked it.

Special Programs

The following speakers and groups had a significant impact of the CCC inmates:

Follow-Up Ministry of Concord, California

The Concord Study Group conducted a weekend seminar, four weekends a year, at Main Chapel.

Tim W., their leader, was bilingual and a powerful communicator. His primary assistant was a retired high school principal.

They had been at the chapel at least fifteen times, but once when they arrived at the chapel for a seminar, the retired principal was not cleared for the weekend. His pass had expired.

I still have difficulty understanding how this happened, as my policy was to check with the Visiting Office prior to an event to assure that everyone scheduled for the program was cleared.

He had in his possession three beige cards from other state prisons, but these cards were not recognized at CCC. He came into the chapel on Friday night, and I anticipated talking to the administrative officer on Saturday morning to attempt to get a temporary clearance for the volunteer.

On one other weekend, I had a problem with a volunteer's clearance, and it was handled by the Administrator of the Day for the weekend.

The Administrator of the Day came to the watch commander's office, and I went down to visit him. He was adamant in his refusal to allow an exception. He basically told me to take my kite and fly it. So the volunteer spent the weekend at the motel.

Victory Outreach of San]ose

Victory Outreach is a church that focuses on helping people in recovery. Their members are from all walks of life and have learned about how God can enable people to recover from their addictions.

When their possible volunteer applications were sent to the Visiting Office for clearance, several of them were not eligible because of brushes with the law.

The volunteers who were cleared had a powerful message to share. Their leader was Fernando Rios, a powerful speaker. He had had a problem with drugs but had overcome them.

All of the volunteers spoke with passion, and their experiences resonated with the inmates. They were one of the most effective groups that came to the chapel.

Bit-Part Movie Actor Mel Novak

Mel Novak is a household name among people who are involved in skid-row missions and the Los Angeles County Jail. He is a bit-part movie actor, and he told me he had been killed eleven times in films.

An inmate at Main Chapel told me about Mel and how powerful he was. I contacted him by mail and asked him to visit CCC.

When he came to the chapel, scores of inmates recognized him.

One of his strengths was his ability to memorize Scripture. He knew more Scripture than any man I had met in a long time.

Since his mission was independent, and he was a faith-based person, I knew he was using his own money to come to prisons.

Since I believe that the servant is worthy of his hire, I told him that I would cover the cost of his airfare from Los Angeles to Reno. I would also pay for a car rental and his housing costs while he was in Susanville.

Following his first visit, he told me that during his entire prison ministry, no institution had ever given him anything to help him with his expenses.

He introduced the inmates to his "Arsenal Prayer." This prayer became a part of my Sunday morning worship time. It is a prayer that many inmates could use every morning as they started their day.

He visited the chapel on four different occasions and blessed many inmates with his sharing and testimony.

University Cathedral of Los Angeles

In 2009, the University Cathedral Church of Los Angeles contacted CCC and requested a seminar at Main Chapel. They had been going to Soledad State Prison and two other state prisons in San Joaquin Valley.

Pastor Melissa Scott had a vacation home at Lake Almanor, about fifty miles from Susanville. She would!. be at the chapel on Friday evening and Saturday morning and afternoon.She would fly back to LA for the Sunday service.

She knew seventeen languages and was a biblical scholar. She was fluent in classical languages connected with the Old and New Testaments.

She brought a five-piece band with her. They sang older gospel hymns. The music was refreshing to me, since it was the kind of music that was a part of my ministry.

As they were preparing to leave, they asked me if there was anything they could do for the chapel. Did we need Bibles?

I said we needed Spanish Bibles. They said that they would send a hundred Bibles. The Bibles were leather-bound and beautiful.

They were given as an award for an inmate's faithfulness to the Spanish program. If the inmate leader recommended someone, a Bible was awarded. If a Bible was awarded, a letter of thanks, written by the inmate, was sent to the church. The second time they came, they brought English Bibles. As they were leaving, they again asked if we needed anything. I mentioned that the Fourth

Annual Celebrate Recovery Celebration was scheduled for the next month.

As a part of that program I wanted to provide pizza for the inmates} which would cost approximately five hundred dollars. I didn1t expect any response;

I was just telling them a story. The pastor's assistant told me they wanted to do something special and that it was probable that they would sponsor the pizza party. About two weeks later} a check arrived for five hundred dollars.

The third time they came Pastor Scott presented a program titled "How the Bible Came to Be." She gave each participant a textbook on how the English Bible came to be. Unfortunately, the material was not received very well be the inmates. It was probably because it was very academic.

Dr. Sam Huddleston, Master Preacher and Former Inmate

One of the inmates on Lassen Yard told me about Sam Huddleston, who had been an inmate at Sierra Conservation Center, a sister institution to California Correctional Center, as one of twoCalifornisa fire training center. He had been released from prison eighteen years ago and had gone to college, seminary, and graduate school.

After serving at an Assemblies of God church in the Bay Area, he had been elected as an associate superintendent of the Northern California Nevada District of the Assemblies of God. In visiting with him, I learned that he was one of two African Americans serving as administrators in the United States Assemblies of God.

He agreed to visit CCC on a Friday night and Saturday morning and afternoon.

It was almost impossible to get him clearance to visit the chapel. CCC has a long-standing policy of not allowing former inmates to volunteer at the chapel. Even though he had been out of prison for twenty years and was a leader of one of the largest Christian groups in Northern California, he was not welcome.

Anybody who was a former felon was a real anathema to the prison staff. For me, it seemed that former felons, if they had gotten straight, would be some of the best people to speak in the prison. Dr. Sam was only the second former felon I was able to get cleared to speak at the chapel. Finally, the warden agreed he could come to the chapel, but I was to be his escort during the time he was at CCC. I had to be with him at all times.

He was one of the most terrific volunteers we ever had at the prison. He was a master storyteller. He had a feeling for where the inmates were, because he had been like them.

Actually, when he came to prison, he had a life sentence, which was commuted by the governor. He had a state document that said he was no longer considered a felon, but CCC would not honor it.

One of the things that he shared was that he saw himself as a representative of all Men in Blue-of all inmates-both incarcerated and on the outside. He stated he could never fail to live appropriately, because he was a symbol of all of them, and he realized this and had decided to carry the responsibility. Wherever he went, he was their representative to the world on the outside. It was a great lesson.

He also wrote a book about his experiences and gave fifteen copies to be loaned to inmates. His autobiography is a story about reconciliation, recidivism, and all the things that were a part of my dream for inmates who came to California Correctional Center.

I was never able to have him back again. I told the new chaplain about him, but I don't know if he will invite him back. Every prison ought to listen to this man!

Oroville Bible Church

The coordinator of the University Cathedral's program lived in Oroville, California. He commuted back and forth to Los Angeles.

After he had been here a couple of times, he called me and asked permission to bring a Native American group with drums to the chapel. I was not present for that weekend, because I was injured and was at home on sick leave. But I understood it was a great program and that these people spoke with real authority.

The coordinator of the University Cathedral program wasn't always required to be in Los Angeles for their programs.

He was a CPA and the financial officer of the church.Much ofhls work was done in his office in Oroville, where the University Cathedral Church was born more than fifty years ago.

The financial officer's church in Oroville had an outreach group that visited jails and prisons. The pastor and a men's quartet visited CCC on Friday night and Saturday morning and afternoon. Because of my illness, I was not at the concert but was informed it was a huge success.

The Covenant Players

During my third year at the chapel the Covenant Players contacted me. The Covenant Players was founded fifty years ago. Youth were recruited for a two-year volunteer service. When I was in Paradise the Covenant Players made a presentation.

I received a phone call from the Northern California group} requesting the privilege of coming to the chapel. In the conversation} I toldl them about the audience at the chapel. They indicated they would come at no expense to the prison. I obtained a clearance for them to visit the Main Chapel.

The first team consisted of two women and one man. They shared their dramas with minimal costuming. They provided a list of all items for their programs, which was finally cleared by the administration. The inmates were enthusiastic about their programmmg.

The drama team enjoyed their experience at the prison. I made a contribution to cover part of their expenses at the prison. My gift was stimulated by a request from the team leader for funds to pay for their expenses at the prison.

About six months later, I received a call from the new team.] was explicit with them that we didn't have any money for sponsoring and that if they wanted to come, they would have to find their own sponsor for the program. They agreed to come. They performed at Lassen Chapel on Friday night and tthe Main Chapel on Saturday morning and afternoon.

Lassen Chapel seats a maximum of ninety inmates. Fifty inmates came to the program.

Because of the proximity to inmates, which to the performers was a problem, the team stayed in the storeroom and came to the front for their presentations. At the end of their presentation, I was planning to invite the team to mingle with the inmates, but the leader of the team told me they were not comfortable talking to the inmates. They felt intimidated. At the Main Chapel, they also didn't want to meet with Main Chapel inmates.

Early in 2010, I received another call from the Covenant Players. Since I was retiring, I asked the Catholic chaplain to sponsor the program. He told me he would sponsor them, and I got the paperwork approved for them. Whether they came or not is not a part of my knowledge.

Jim P., a Volunteer Who Helped

In early 2010, I got a phone call from a prospective volunteer by the name of Jim P. Jim was a retired forensic clinical psychologist. He was also a student of the classic biblical languages of Hebrew and Greek. During my final weeks at the chapel, he served as my volunteer helper. Even with all his qualifications and experience in the prison system, I was unable to get him cleared for beige ID card.

After I got injured, I conducted my part of the Sunday general Protestant worship service from a wheelchair. Unfortunately, I was somewhat handicapped by my injury, and I could not move around the platform as I was prone to do.

My Last Sermon at CCC

The last two Sundays at the chapel were special to me. I would like to share both of those times with you.

On the next-to-last Sunday, I shared the story of Mark 2, regarding the paralyzed man whose friends let him down through the roof into Jesus's presence. The crowds prevented them from getting him to Jesus in a more traditional way.

What happened when they let him down through the roof is not clear, whether the roof was an emergency opening to the residence or they tore a hole in the roof to let their friend into Jesus's presence.

When they let the man down into the house, Jesus stopped his teaching and talked to the man, touched him, and healed him. This created uproar among all present.

My question to the inmates was, which of the many groups present at the meeting could they see as their group?

I introduced this question with the following story: During and following World War II, a German pastor and theologian named Theilicke was a factor in opposing Hitler and helping in the rehabilitation of Germany. One of the books he wrote was *The Waiting Father.*

In the introduction of the book, he tells a story about when his son was a baby. He would place his son on a table in front of a mirror and watch his son to see what might be going on in that young mind. He watched him week after week.

One day, as his son was looking in the mirror, it seemed that a light burst

341

on that little face. Theilicke said it was as though his son recognized the image in the mirror as an image of himself. It was a moment of inspiration and excitement for the little boy.

Theilicke said, "When we read the Scripture, we should attempt to discover if any of the characters in the story resonate with us."

Gospel stories are the easiest to identify in this way. He said we should continue to read the story until one of the characters leaps out at us. We should use our imagination to help us learn some important lessons about ourselves.

His formula for learning in this way from the Scripture is as follows: First, we must immerse ourselves in the passage or story. Second, we should identify with a character in the story. Third, we should look for the good news in the story, for that character and for us.

There is good news in every story in the Bible, and we should search to discover it, because it will give us a new sense of our worth and value. I suggested that we use this formula in our study for the day.

In this story, there are many people we could consider. We might be the invalid man. We might be paralyzed in our condition, and we need somebody to touch us in our pain. We could be the friends of the invalid man. We may desire to bring somebody into the presence of the Master, so that he can have healing.

We could be the disinterested crowd who were busy trying to find out what was happening. We could be a religious leader, who was there to judge Jesus. We might identify with the owner, who is worried about the value of his property. We might even identify with Jesus. Maybe we have a gift for someone in a paralyzed condition. Maybe we could set that person free.

We could be one of the people or groups or maybe we can see ourselves in several of the characters in the story.

It is important that we know where we are hurting and need help as well as understanding the gifts we may have to give help. It is important to know our strengths as well as our weaknesses. We can be enablers for those around US1 if we know our strengths and our hurts.

I suggested that we pray for wisdom to be the men God wants us to be.

When we prayed I was truly energized, because I had a vision of inmates being set free to be all God intended them to be. I was also inspired that some of them might use the formula I had used to explain the Scripture as a tool in their personal study of the Scripture. I felt truly inspired by this my last talk to inmates before retiring.

An Experiment in Leading
Small Groups

For my last service, I decided to try the Chaplain's Hour in a large group setting. I asked participants to build a personal coat of arms, with specific events described in the drawings and symbols.

I had participated in this sharing with hundreds of inmates on the Saturday and Sunday Chaplain's Hour. For many months, I had wanted to see how it would work with many small groups sharing at the same time.

There were approximately 120 inmates at the service. I broke the inmates into triads, with inmates who they were sitting next to. The groups spilled over into the aisles. It took several minutes to form the triads.

After the groups were formed, I talked to them about the kingdom of God being a kingdom of relationships.

God has four relationships that he wants every human to have. These are 1) a relationship to God, 2) a relationship to ourselves (we know who we are), 3) a relationship to the significant others in our lives (our families and intimates), and 4) a relationship with the world at large (people outside our in-group).

I said this exercise would help them in all four of our relationships. It was my conviction that only in a sharing, small group relationship could some of these learnings take place.

The inmate clerks distributed paper and pencils to each inmate, so he could begin to build his coat of arms. I explained that there needed to be boundaries for the picture and that symbols were both words and pictures. So the coat of arms could be pictures or words or a combination of the two.

They were to create four major pictures, representing four different experiences in their lives.

The first picture or symbol was to represent a *happy experience* they remembered between the ages of eight and twelve. I suggested that some of them might not be able to remember any happy experiences during those years.

It could be an experience with parents, a holiday, or something good that happened at school. If they couldn't remember any happy experience, one likely would come to them during the meeting. I gave them a few minutes to work on that in silence.

The second picture was to be a tough, difficult, or excruciatingly hard experience they had between the ages of twelve and seventeen, what many call our adolescent years-a difficult time for most teenagers. The difficult time could be a family breakup, a death in the family or among friends, or a difficult or bad experience in school. All of us have had a bad time we remember from those years.

After a few minutes, I explained the third experience to them. They were to draw a symbol to represent the most significant thing that had happened to them in the last three years. It could be bad, or it could be good. It could be coming to prison, the loss of a family member, or something good that had happened to them.

After they had spent some time thinking about this issue, I brought up the last picture.

The last picture was to be a symbol to answer the following question: what would you do if you discovered you had only three years to live and there was nothing that could stop you from doing it - no money problems, no prison problems or other problems that could prohibit you from doing what you wanted to do. What would it be?

I explained that every coat of arms had a motto- a special saying or thought. Then

I said, 11The last thing that you do with a coat-of-arms is develop a motto. So for our motto today, I would like you to write five positive characteristics about yourself five things about you that are positive.

346

"For example, you could say, 1I'm honest.' That doesn't mean that you are honest 100 percent of the time but that in reality, you see yourself as an honest person. You don't go around lying all the time. You may slip on occasion, but in reality, you see yourself as an honest person. Write five positive characteristics about yourself on your page."

I then told the group that we would share our stories. To begin, I would share a couple of my own experiences to serve as a model. Then I asked them to go around their triads and share their stories.

The happiest experience we had between the ages of seven and twelve was our first story.

I shared about my childhood family. My mother was what we might call a practicing Christian. In my growing- up years, we often identified practicing Christians by their behaviors. They didn't smoke, they didn't drink, and they didn't associate with people who did. They didn't play around, and they didn't associate with people who did. My mother was that kind of Christian.

My father wasn't a practicing Christian. I don't mean that he wasn't a Christian, but he didn't abide by the behaviors my mother thought were Christian. He didn't show up at church every time the church doors opened. He didn't necessarily read his Bible every day. He might, on occasion, use pithy words that the church people wouldn't approve of. He smoked, and smoking, for a lot of churches, was forbidden.

Smoking wasn't forbidden in many Southern churches, but it was for my mother. My father was addicted to smoking. He didn't quit until he had emphysema and his lungs were so collapsed that he couldn't breathe. Finally, at the very end of his life, he quit smoking.

So, I talked about my family and how my mother judged my dad. She also judged a lot of other people.

A lot of Christians are good at that. We want to be judges.

I appreciate one of the principles of the attitudinal-healing program, which says, "I can learn to love myself and others by forgiving rather than judging." I think that that is a principle that applies to everybody. We could be a lot better off if we forgave rather than judged.

I told them that in the fifth grade, the teacher announced to the class that the class was going to have an ice skating party at the gravel pit outside of town. It was the only body of water that was big enough to ice skate on. She said we would be meeting on a certain Friday afternoon, and there would be hot dogs and side dishes offered to us. She hoped we would be able to come.

I didn't think that my parents would let me-first, because my mother had restrictions on the kind of activities she felt were appropriate for her boys; and second, because my dad didn't like public gatherings.

I went home and asked them, and after a couple of days, they agreed that I could go. About three days before I was ready to go, my dad came home with a pair of ice skates. I don't know where he got them.

I don't know how he could have afforded them. But he got the ice skates, and although I had very small feet, they fit me. Arrangements were made for someone to take me to the gravel pit, and my dad was going to pick me up.

I knew that when my dad came to pick me up, I would have to go home immediately, because he wouldn't stick around. When he came after me, he expected me to leave immediately.

The skating party had hardly gotten started when I looked up and saw my dad's Dodge panel truck coming over the edge of the horizon, down to the gravel pit.

I was distraught, because I knew I was going to have to go home. I hurried to the other side of the gravel pit, as far away as I could get from him, so it would take him a while to find me.

I watched him as he stopped the truck and got out. He went to the back of the truck and fumbled around for a little while and then closed the panel truck door. He came down toward the gravel pit, I saw that he had a pair of ice skates- the kind that clip onto your shoes.

He went over and sat down on one of the stumps and proceeded to put on his ice skates. When he got up and started to skate, I saw that he could skate better than anybody else on that pond.

It was awesome. It was the first time I ever felt like my father was number one. Even when I tell it again today, I feel so emotional about the wonderful experience of being able to think about my father as being number one.

I told the men, "Your stories might not be as dramatic as mine, but I'll bet you all have a story about a happy experience.

It might have been with your father. It might have been with a grandfather or a grandmother. It could have been with a mother or one of your siblings. So please, share your story with your colleagues."

They started sharing, and the hum of their conversations resonated through the chapel. There were more than forty different groups, all talking at the same time. Since the triads were close together, there was no problem being heard. They talked and they talked, and when the talk began to subside, I suggested we move on to the second symbol.

The second item was to describe an experience that was frustrating, difficult, or hard for them, when they were between the ages twelve and seventeen.

I told them that I had been very good in math. In the seventh grade, there were seven seventh-grade math classes. When the teacher gave an achievement test, she listed the top four scores on the test from all the classes. I invariably would get my name up there. I was one of the better math students. I had the sense of being a good math man.

"When I took algebra in Nebraska," I said, "I was top man in the class. In the middle of the year, my dad decided to move the family to San Jose, California. It took us a couple of weeks to get to San Jose. When I went into my new algebra class, it was as if I was in Greek class. They had completed factoring and several other critical ideas in algebra, and I didn't have a clue about what was taking place in the class.

"I failed in an area where I thought I was the best. It did not matter that I maxed the class the next year with very little effort. By knowing the steps, I understood the program and excelled. Unfortunately, that was a failure that still smarts."

I asked them to share their stories. As they shared, the noise level rose again, and when it started to subside, I asked them to go to their third story.

I did not share my third story; I asked them to start the process themselves. They talked about the most significant thing that had happened to them in the last three years. When the conversations subsided, we addressed the last story. Then we went to the fourth experience. We imagined a genie would appear out of bottle on the platform. The genie said, "What would you do if you could do anything? If nothing could stop you, what would you do? No money problems. No parole problems. Share the story that represents that dream." As with the other stories, the sharing was awesome, judging by the noise level.

I talked about the human tendency to think negative things about oneself. I said, "It takes about one-fourth the time to write down five negative things about ourselves as five positive characteristics." This is especially true of inmates, because the prison culture is a negative culture.

"Everybody is negative, for the most part, in a prison culture. But that isn't what God sees. God sees us as positive, so let's share the positive things." They did that.

About ten or fifteen minutes was left at this time. So at that point, all the clerks came to the platform to give me a send-off and a blessing from the chapel inmates. Each of the four clerks shared something of what had happened to them while they were working at the chapel.

Todd shared some things that he had learned from me. Then Joel gave me a card that had been signed by his Hispanic brothers. Then T. talked about what we had done with our faith-based programs. Charles T. was last, and he gave me a notebook that he had developed during my five years at the prison. It had stories and "atta-boy" letters from inmates to me.

Then the clerks gathered around me and prayed a sending prayer for me. It was a rousing and wonderful experience for me.

It was a highlight of the many good-byes I'd said over the years.

My Last Day at the Prison,
May 10, 2010

The last Sunday service was May 9. 2010. I retired on Monday, May 10. On Monday, all I did was come to the office and say good-bye to the inmate clerks and check out with personnel.

In Conclusion

As you followed me on my journey of a thousand barrels through the prison recidivism desert, I trust you learned something about your journey through your own personal desert. We all have one.

I hope you will discover, as I have, the inmate poet's truth: "We are all brothers."

APPENDIX I

MUSINGS AS A HIGH

DESERT VOLUNTEER

My First Meeting with High Desert Prison Protestant Chaplain

I made a phone call to the chaplain's office and talked to him. He suggested that we get together for an interview. The easiest way to do that would be for us to meet in the snack bar in the Administration Building at the prison. We set a time and date for a lunch meeting.

I arrived at the snack bar a little early and waited to see who might be the Protestant chaplain. I wondered what he might look like and if I would recognize him.

A few minutes went by, and a man came in with a great big hat- bigger than a cowboy hat. He was gray-bearded. I looked at him and thought, *Maybe that's the chaplain.* He came over and asked me who I was. I gave him my name, and he introduced himself. He was Chaplain Green.

Chaplain Green had opened High Desert as the Protestant chaplain. He was the first one of the chaplains to be hired.

He had been in prison ministry for many years. He worked in several states, throughout the West.

He was a Southern Baptist minister. He was very articulate and erudite-it was obvious in the way he carried himself and how he spoke. I could see that from the moment he arrived.

He introduced himself as Dr. Harold Green-that's always a mark of somebody who thinks or feels like he has something to share.

I think titles are actually detrimental to communication. They build walls, not bridges. I have the privilege of feeling that way, since I have a degree that would allow me to be called by a title.

I don't want to be called by my title. "My name is Jack," I tell people. And I told him that. "My name is "Jack." I didn't share anything about my education or my history.

He sat down, and we talked together for quite some time. He told me some stories about his life experience. He talked to me about High Desert Prison. He told me that it was a prison that was primarily a Level IV prison.

In the California prison system, there are four levels of prisons. Level I doesn't require two fences around the facility. Level II has two fences, and security is more stringent. Level III is more secure, because the individuals assigned there have committed more severe crimes.

The inmates are housed in cells. In Level I and Level II they are often housed in dormitories, where people live within bunk beds. Level IV are lifers and others who are more dangerous.

High Desert has mostly Level IV inmates. He said it was the equivalent to Pelican Bay and Corcoran Prison when it came to the kind of prisoners they housed.

He told me High Desert had a Level III yard and that's where his office was located. B Yard C Yard and D Yards were all Level IV yards.

He explained to me that the Catholic chaplain was located in B Chapel and the Muslim chaplain was located in C Yard Chapel. The D Yard Chapel office was covered by a Catholic volunteer who served along with the Catholic chaplain.

He told me that he would like to have me go around with him, and he would introduce me to the way he wanted things to be done.

He informed me that he wanted all his volunteer chaplains to wear clergy shirts and collars. I had never done that before, but in order to serve as effectively as possible, I agreed I'd do that.

He said the reason for the collar was that it enabled people to know who I was. Thus, I would be more able to share what

I needed to share. I was not sure that I agreed with him, but that was his position, and I agreed to do it.

At High Desert, each yard was separated by walls. From one end of the prison to the other was approximately one half mile.

To get to the chaplain's office, I went through the gate that moved me inside the fences and then to the gate where keys were issued. There were two of these gates, one for the A Yard and the B Yard and the same for C and D Yards. Mter I got through the gate, I would go either left or right, depending on whether I was going to A orB Yard. I turned to the left and went toward A Yard.

A Yard was separated by a fence from the access area. There was a guard in a tower. When appropriate, he opened a gate to let me go in. The chaplain's office was the second door on the right side.

Access to the chaplain's office was available to the inmates without going through a gate. This area also included medical offices, the law library, and education facilities, as well as the chapel

I went to the chapel door and knocked. Some of the Men in Blue, who were inmates, saw me, and they called the chaplain. He unlocked the door. He had me sit in the office and observe what was gomgon.

He also showed me the worship center, which could seat approximately a hundred people. It had wooden chairs, not pews. There were about sixty chairs.

The clerk's office was a small office of about five feet by ten feet. There was another larger room that served as the library. In that area, he had all of the books that were available for distribution.

He also had a lending library for people on A Yard. Materials for other yards were put in boxes to be distributed by volunteers to the other yard chapels.

There was also a Level I yard, where all of the inmates who worked outside the walls were housed. It also had a chapel. It was outside the regular prison fences.

The chaplain introduced me to the clerks. Only one clerk was paid; the others were unpaid volunteers. They worked forty hours a week.

I had an opportunity to talk with these men on an individual basis. They discussed with me something of what their work was. We discussed how they benefited by working in the chapel.

They also advised me about how I must behave in order to not be exploited and taken advantage of. Because I'd already had some previous experience through the Men's Group with the Catholic chaplain, I was able to absorb what they had to say. After about thirty or forty minutes of sitting in the chapel, the chaplain told me that he had to go out and make a couple of calls. He asked me to go along with him.

We left the chapel, and he went over to one of the housing units.

The housing unit ended up being cells. It was actually part of the prison reception center. Prisoners were sent to High Desert and then were assigned to other institutions in Northern California.

He took me with him to a cell and talked to a man about his problem.

He told me that when I talked through the door, I should be careful not to put my ear up to the opening, because if I did, some of the inmates might have urine in a bottle or in a can, and they'd throw it at me.

He said I needed to be careful that I didn't make myself vulnerable to something that they might do for or to me. After that short visit, we turned around and went back to the chapel. He told me to come back the next day.

Second Day of Orientation

When I came to the chapel, the chaplain said he had to give a religious speech at the reception center. We met in the area where inmates socialize. The cells were along the wall. There were lower-level and upper level cells. The meeting was in the TV area, where there were wooden benches. It seated about thirty people.

We sang a couple of old gospel songs. "Amazing Grace," which is the national anthem for inmates, was one of them. After we sang, he gave me a moment to talk. I shared a couple of minutes about being a volunteer, that [wanted to serve and help, and that I had come there to do that. I indicated I hoped to have an opportunity to meet some of them in the future.

When I finished, the chaplain gave a short gospel talk. He spoke for about twelve minutes. He was a very articulate and engaging speaker. He talked for a little while and then we signed off.

He went over and talked to a couple officers in his Southern drawl. Several custody officers were located in that area. They had desks in the middle of the room. After the meeting, we returned to the office. We talked some more about chapel procedures. He showed me how to use the copy machine and how to make a list of inmates authorized to attend a daily program.

A list contained the complete names, their CDC number, and their housing location. These lists had to be turned in at least twenty-four hours ahead of the event.

Copies of these forms were then used by custody to let the people come to the meeting. He showed me how to do that and told me that he would expect me to do it on my own and submit it to the appropriate office. He said he didn't have clerks who were able to do it.

When we completed this discussion, he told me to come back the next day, as he wanted to get me started as a volunteer.

Visiting C and D Yards

On my next visit1 there were two other volunteers there. They were dressed in motorcycle garb. It turned out they were Christian motorcycle members who were coming from Redding to volunteer at the prison. They were a little crusty-looking.

Obviously1 their appearance seemed to indicate that they had lived the kind of life that would help them identify with pnsoners.

We talked a bit and I got the feeling that because I was wearing a clergy collar they thought I was a little uppity. We talked and shared our impressions about prison ministry. They went to visit different areas in the housing cell blocks. While there they distributed Christian literature. They also counseled with inmates who might want to talk with them.

The chaplain told me that he wanted to take me down to C and D Chapels. It was about a half a mile walk from the AB Chapels to the CD Chapels. When we got inside the walls, he took me to the sergeant's office and introduced me to the custody staff.

I was impressed with the large, walled patio that separated the area from the lower and upper yards, which were not visible from the patio. The officers in the two towers could survey the yards as well as the patio. C Yard housed some of the toughest and most dangerous inmates at High Desert.

He took me to C Chapel. It was approximately the same size as A Chapel. It was plain and austere, with a communion table, organ, large TV, and wooden chairs.

He said that would be the chapel I would serve, because he didn't have anyone to do it on this scheduled basis.

365

He said D Yard had a volunteer, a postal employee who volunteered on D Yard on Saturday or Sunday for the worship services. Since C Yard didn't have somebody that would do it consistently every week, he wanted me to do it.It was certainly something to which I would be open.

After we left C Yard, we went over to D Yard, which had a lower yard. The upper yard was administrative segregation area. He showed me the chapel. The Catholic volunteer, who had an office there, was not there.

Then we went to the Administrative Segregation Building. We signed in and visited several inmates. They were all in their cells. They only got out for showers and exercise. We went from cell to cell and he talked and sometimes prayed with an inmate.

We walked back to the administrative area and went to the snack bar and had lunch. Thafs the way that day ended.

More Training

For the next two or three weeks, we followed this same ritual, three days a week. I'd walk around with him and observe him. One time, we went to C Yard gymnasmm.

They had made the gyms into housing units. The inmates, who lived in them, were sleeping in bunk beds. They were Level III inmates or 11Men in Blue." Many of them were lifers.

How they lived in these primitive, overcrowded conditions is beyond me. I was surprised that they didn't have more incidents in these circumstances.

When we went into the gym, we met custody and a multitude of Men in Blue (MIBs). We distributed literature to those interested. We followed this routine for about three or four more weeks. It was a good lesson.

I got a little irritated, since I wanted something to happen. But in the long run, it was the best thing that could have ever happened. I learned by example.

Learning by examp[e, I think, is one very great way to learn. It was the method Jesus used.

Obviously, we all learn that way as children, but I sometimes think that it would be well if we had that kind of orientation with every new experience, especially when we become a new employee. I gained a lot of information and inspiration from him.

He asked me to come on Sunday. He conducted a worship service at A Chapel. After he spoke in A Chapel, we went down to C Chapel, and he shared with about forty inmates. Following the service, we went to the snack bar for lunch.

After lunch we went to E Yard. E Yard is a Level I yard. The chaplain had appointed an inmate chaplain, who was also the clerk. He kept the chapel open about forty hours a week. Inmates had free access to come and go to the chapel. Most of them were working during the day.

His worship service at E Chapel had the most participation of service that day. The inmate playing the organ was excellent, and there was spirited singing, and the chaplain gave a truly inspirational talk.

It was a wonderful experience for me to feel and discover the spiritual energy that came in those circumstances.

He told me to come back the next week for more training. He also asked me to cover C Chapel the following Sunday. I agreed. He told me again how to get the inmates signed up. He also informed me that they didn't have any music, other than what I could provide.

I felt I was back fifty years ago in Korea, when, as a young army chaplain, I had to conduct services for several months without any music other than what I could provide. Since I didn't have anybody to accompany me, I hoped the men would not be too disappointed.

My First Sunday at C Chapel

The Sunday morning service was scheduled for nine o'clock. I left the house early, about 7:00a.m., to go over and make sure everything was okay at the chapel. I went to the Main, ate, and they checked my belongings and my Bible, and cleared me.

I went through the gate and walked about a quarter of a mile to C and D Yards. After showing my identification, I got the keys for the chapel. After being cleared by the tower, I went into the patio.

I opened the chapel and checked that everything was clear. I reported to the Custody Office to inform them that I was present for the worship service at nine o'clock. I went to the Volunteer Office and opened the locked cabinet, where the worship center's cross and candlesticks were stored. These items provided a center for the worship on the communion table.

I did some other chores in preparation for the service and then proceeded to inform custody that I was ready for the service.

While there, I met the primary custody officer who would open the gate and pat down the inmates for chapel. He checked the list and authorized them to proceed to the chapel. He would come back at closing time and clear them to go back to their housing.

Upon release to their yard, inmates were expected to go back to the house. Often, they would come to chapel for the primary reason that when they left the chapel, they would get lost on the yard and be out of bounds. There was activity on the yard, and many of them joined that activity, even though they were supposed to be back in their cell block.

That was one of the problems connected with people coming to the chapel.

Later on, I began to keep them in chapel until after the yard was closed.

Sometimes they would meet their buddies from another yard in the chapel. This created additional strain and talking in the chapel, as I tried to control these people who were not there for any reason other than for their own joy or their wanting something.

I suppose that's not too different from the rest of us. Too often, we go to church with the idea of what we're going to get out of it. That isn't what I think God meant when he started the program of worship. He wanted us to go primarily to address ourselves to him.

Shortly after nine o'clock, the inmates arrived. As I recall, approximately fifty came for the program. Three or four of them were from Men's Circle.

As we got ready to sing, I asked for songs that they might like to sing. Of course we sang "Amazing Grace," and 11A Friend of Jesus" and some other gospel songs.

One of the Hispanic brothers asked to sing a Spanish song. He led us in the song. It was a rousing number, and the three or four Hispanics who were there sang lustily, and the rest of us listened.

I shared something about who I was and I talked about my passion for helping inmates find a way to reduce recidivism, so that they wouldn't fall back into their previous behavior.

Recidivism doesn't only work for people when they get out of prison, but it also is something that any inmate or any human being can have when they take advantage of not doing some of foolish things that they've been doing.

If an inmate decides, even though he is a lifer, that he's not going to follow the same procedure that he's followed before-that he is going to act differently toward his inmate brothers and toward the custody and others-he begins to change his behavior, and that is the beginning of the recidivism process,

True recidivism is about those people who never have to come back to prison when they get out. Anyway, I talked about my dream to help people do that.

We read some Scripture and prayed, as is normal in a worship service. After that, I talked about Zacchaeus, a little man who was a sinner, a person who needed help. He was alone. He had exploited his brothers and sisters. He had exploited the system.

He was a user. But he heard about Jesus's coming, so he got up in a tree because he couldn't see Jesus.

The Scripture says it was because he was short, but sometimes I wonder if the short one was Jesus, and maybe Zacchaeus was the tall one. He couldn't see Jesus because he was in the back of the crowd, so he climbed the tree. That was a real gesture on his part, that he would do something like climbing a tree, because that was not adult behavior, yet he did it.

When he got up in the tree, Jesus looked at him and said, 11Hey, son of Abraham, come down." He did not call him sinner, but he called him to his positive nature. That is what God always does for us. He calls us to us to our positive nature.

At 10:00, the education custody officer came and opened the door to the chapel, and the inmates went home. I spent a few moments talking to him about my experience.I went through the gates to my car and drove to the Methodist church to worship with my wife.

Worship Service for Protective Custody Unit

The following Friday, when I arrived at the Protestant chaplain's office, he told me that the motorcycle crew was not going to be there that day. He indicated one of their responsibilities was to have a service at the Administrative Segregation Building for inmates who were in protective custody.

Protective custody was a group of men who had issues with other men on the yard. It may be that was a personal grudge, a gang issue, or somebody was vulnerable to being mistreated. It could be that there was a sexual issue or some kind of crime or implication of sexuality that created the issues. Individuals such as these are placed in protective custody.

At High Desert, if they're in protective custody, it's only a temporary stay for them. They will be transferred to another prison, which has a protective custody housing unit. The men who will be at the service are waiting for a transfer.

I walked down to D Yard to the Administrative Segregation Building, which was divided by a fence from the regular yard. I went in and told custody that I was to have a worship service for the protective custody inmates. Their recreation time was at the same time I was scheduled for the service. These inmates got one hour a day for recreation outside their cells. The rest of the time they were in their cells.

I was taken to the area where they were doing their exercises. I was told that I could have a service on one side of the room. Six or seven inmates who came to the service. Since there were so few and a traditional service didn't seem appropriate, I decided to do a small group exercise.

The format I used was called the ((Four Quaker Questions." The Four Quaker Questions is a way of getting people to know each other and to come

373

to grips with some of the emotional or spiritual issues in their lives.

The questions are:

1. "Where did you live between the ages of seven and twelve, and how many brothers and sisters did you have at that time?" (Everybody then goes around the circle and shares. If somebody prefers not to share, he asks to pass, and he's allowed to pass.)

2. "How did you heat your home at that time, or was there a time when you were extremely cold and getting warm was important to you?" (Then we share that experience.)

3. "Who in your home provided the sense of human warmth, or where in your home was there a place of human warmth?" (Maybe one of your parents provided that warmth. Maybe it was a sibling that did it. It might have been a grandparent. It cowd be any number of people. But probably somebody provided some sense of personal human warmth and told you that you mattered to somebody.)

   There was a second option to that question: "If you didn't have some one who provided that sense of worth, then maybe you had a place where you felt secure." It might have been up in a tree house. It could be in the garage somewhere. It could be in their bedroom in their bed. But there was someplace where they felt a sense of being secure of-being safe.

4. "When, if ever, did God become more than a word to you?" (The group shares this story, because it is important to know if someone has had an experience with his understanding of God. No one is told how to find God. The premise of this approach is that we need to know where a person is in his faith walk. What does his individual"island" look like?)

Then it may be possible to find a place to land on his island or touch his deepest spirit. We need to recognize that there's a place where every human being can be landed on or touched. We are all is lands, and there is a place where somebody can land on our island and get to know us.

374

It could be any number of experiences that provide us with a sense of God. It could be when a pet died during our childhood.

That was a time when we had a sense that there was something bigger than us and something bigger in store for us, bigger for him, and something bigger for us. It could have been that we learned something in church or Sunday school or some classroom. It could be that somebody significant in our lives shared something personal with us.

Most people have an early experience in life when they had a sense that God was more than a word. If someone cannot recall such an experience, it provides information about what we need to do to begin to share with that person in a realistic way.

It was a very meaningful time. It took about forty minutes for us to share. Unfortunately, I never had an opportunity to go back to that particular facility, since it was another volunteer's responsibility.

I was only a substitute. However, it was a rich time for me to be able to share those questions. Since I have shared these questions many times with groups on the outside, it was a joy to share them on the inside.

Worship at E Yard

The following Sunday when I went to the chapel, I was calledl by the Protestant chaplain, and he told me he wanted me to go over toE Yard when I finished at C Chapel.

He suggested that I have lunch, and at one o'clock, he wanted me to go to E Chapel to cover the worship service. About five or ten minutes to one o'clock, I drove over to E Yard.

E Yard is where inmate workers who work outside the walls are housed.

They work in administrative offices and custodial and outside yard crews. Some are skilled laborers and work with free staff in plumbing, construction, and electrical programs.

E Yard has one fence, because it's a Level I yard. The MIBs are housed in dormitory settings. I was admitted to the yard through the visiting room. After checking my credentials, the officer opened the gate and let me go into the yard to the chapel.

We had a terrific service. The service was meaningful because of the electronic organ and skilled musician who played. Because of his beautiful playing, the inmates sang lustily. Then I shared what

I had shared that morning at C Yard. It was a wonderful experience. If only I had a chance to do this other times during my tenure as a volunteer at High Desert.

Leading Worship on D Yard

A few months after I'd started giving services at C Chapel, I got a call one Saturday morning from the volunteer who was responsible for the D Chapel program. He was a postal employee in the local post office. He was going to be absent that weekend, and he asked if I would cover the 10:30 service.

I went to the D Yard on Sunday, introduced myself to the officers in the Custody Office. The sergeant and the lieutenant were there, and I had the opportunity to meet them. I had already picked up a key for the chapel, and I went to the chapel. It was a replica of C Chapel. I went into the chapel with the inmate clerk from the Custody Office.

The Custody Office clerk was the inmate who also supported the chapel. He had been in prison for more than twenty years and had become a Christian early in his incarceration. He was trusted by custody because of his faithfulness and honesty.

He oriented me about what was normally done for worship services.

We had a great service. I felt privileged to have a chance to meet with him and the other brothers who were part of that program. They were much more focused on the program than C Yard. On C Yard, participants have another agenda than worship.

Approximately forty inmates were present. I judged that most of them had some kind of religiosity, and some were experiencing a primary religious experience. It was a powerful day for me, and I felt privileged to have been able to experience it.

Providing Music for Worship

After plugging along for several weeks without any way of supporting the singing, I decided that I would donate cassette tape players to C and D Chapels. A and B Chapels already had them.

I prepared a donation form, indicating that the players would be would be purchased with private money. This form was signed by the chaplain and then submitted to the community partnership manager, who is responsible for the chapel programs. He forwarded it to the correctional captain, who checked to make sure there were no security issues. It was then signed by the chief deputy warden and the warden. After their approval, it could be purchased and donated to the chapels. The approval finally was returned to the chaplain after three weeks.

The players were purchased, along with some cassettes of sing-along Christian music. Transparencies of the words were prepared so they could be shown on an overhead projector, which was borrowed from the education area. The transparencies were projected on the chapel wall. They were stored in a locked cabinet inside the Volunteers Office. These players were also used by the Muslim chaplain, the Catholic chaplain, and the Jehovah's Witness volunteers.

This investment paid off; by upgrading the music, the worship services were more meaningful. It also encouraged more inmates to come to the chapel since music is such a large part of Protestant worship.

Several weeks after obtaining the cassette players, I was talking to a Susanville church choir director, and he told me about a digital player that had more than 2,500 hymns on it. The hymns were used in the Catholic, Baptist, Episcopalian, United Methodist, and Presbyterian hymnals

This machine would play these hymns in several styles and sounds of music- pipe organ, electronic organ, with orchestration, a choral version. Hymns could be chosen according to the hymnal that was in the chapel. The hymnal in the chapel was one of the hymnals in the digital player.

After reviewing the literature of the player, I decided to make the purchase. It cost $1,200. A donation form was submitted, indicating I would be bringing

380

it with me to each program I conducted.

After reviewing my request, the correctional captain turned it down. He decided that it was an electronic communication device. He was correct, but it was a closed system. It could not be used for any other purpose than to play hymns.

I appealed the decision through channels. After a few weeks, it was finally approved. Each week, hymns would be playing as the inmates came into the chapel. In the summer, when the door was open to the chapel prior to the service, music could be heard in the patio.

After this, the atmosphere in the chapel was more meditative and gave one a sense of spiritual belonging. It was a marvelous tool. Worship services were greatly enhanced, and I was grateful that I had been willing to make the sacrificial gift that it took to acquire it.

This instrument cou]d be used in all prison chapels. More often than not, there was little music support unless one had a tool like this digital hymn player. It would be especially useful in Level IV chapels, as musical instruments were difficult to bring to the chapel.

One time, I tried to bring a guitar into the chapel. It was not allowed because it had strings, which inmates might steal and use a garrote.

This was true for me at High Desert. No doubt a mouth organ might have been acceptable, but few people knew how to play one well enough to accompany music. The digital hymnal was a powerful device, and it served me extensively while I was at High Desert.

To help other volunteers who didn't have a digital hymnal, several cassettes of music were stored permanently inC and D Chapels as a library of music for Protestant chapel programs.

Distribution of Christian Literature to Cell Blocks

One of the most time-consuming yet important chores for tihe chaplain is the distribution of literature. The task is getting the literature in a place where it is accessible to inmates.

If it comes in the mail, he has go to the warehouse to pick it up. He needs a vehicle to obtain it, using either his own vehicle or getting someone with a state vehicle to bring it to Main Gate. It is more than a mile from the Patio Gate.

To go the warehouse, I either would get a state vehicle or take my own vehicle and go about a mile to where the warehouse was located. Then I could pick up the literature and bring it back to the Patio Gate, where they rechecked it for contraband.

After it was checked, I'd have to move it to A Chapel, which was slightly more than one-quarter mile from the gate. A two wheeled hand truck required significant energy and effort to accomplish this task.

The inmate librarians sorted it for each of the six chapels. After the material was divided into its appropriate divisions, it had to be taken to the individual chapels.

Without the volunteers assisting the chaplain, this would have been about all the chaplain would be able to do. Again, a hand truck would be pushed up to one half mile. It took hours to take it to the local chapel. There, it was locked up. As volunteers visited a cell block, they would distribute the materials to the individual cells. It was a time-consuming task.

When inmates took the literature, I could have the occasion to give them some counsel. It was difficult, since I had to do it through the cell door. It was not private counseling, as voices resonated throughout the cell block. Neighbors on both sides would know the inmate's business.

Sometimes I could determine that further talk was required and would make an appointment with custody to come back at another time to talk. If it seemed urgent, I could request that custody bring the individual inmate to the open area, where we could sit at one of the tables and have a private conservation.

Unfortunately, custody was reluctant to expend the energy that this required. Sometimes I felt like it was intimidation for me as a volunteer to ask custody to do it. It was a full-time job to take care of the four major cell blocks that were part of C Yard. It was a tiresome task to do it.

When I distributed literature to the cell blocks, I used a carrying case that I threw over my shoulder.

Guidepost magazine was a primary magazine that inmates enjoyed. Another was a newspaper called Inside_the_Walls. Almost everyone in the cell blocks would accept it. There were some Christian stories in it. It also had a section that dealt with the most recent court cases and law changes that had an impact on inmates.

Very seldom did anyone refuse it. Muslims, Odinists, and 11Skinheads" ordinarily didn't have anything to do with literature related to the Christian faith, but they accepted this newspaper because it had information that was important to them. It was the most popular piece ofliterature available to inmates.

A few months before I left High Desert, it was discontinued. It was truly a tragedy to have that happen.

Another popular piece of literature was the *Our Daily_Bread* devotional. Hundreds of inmates would request it every month. Everybody wanted to have one of those. It was used in their cells.

Unfortunately, no more than five hundred copies of each issue were sent to a prison. Five hundred copies didn't go very far when there were five thousand inmates in High Desert.

Distribution of Bibles

Gideons International distributed Bibles to a prison, if someone paid for the shipping. The New Testament they distributed was printed on the same paper used for smoking tobacco. Since tobacco was no longer permitted in prisons, the paper became more valuable-tobacco came in underground without paper. So the New Testaments were invaluable.

A couple of lifers told me they could remove the cardboard in the covers and make the Bible soft-covered-this was to prevent inmates from using the cardboard to forge lethal weapons.

Unfortunately, removing the cardboard was tedious. It took twenty minutes for an experienced person to remove the cardboard. If the cardboard was taken out, glue then was used to glue the inside and outside sheets together. After this, the Bibles could be distributed. This required approximately fifteen minutes per Bible to get them from a hard-cover bible to a soft cover Bible.

The only place that it could have been done was in the A Chapel library because no one can have a weapon of any kind. A knife or screwdriver or anything like that is considered a weapon.

That limited the numbers that we would have to distribute. If we remembered that there were five thousand inmates in High Desert, and say, only 10 percent of them, every six months, wanted a Bible, that was a thousand Bibles, minimum, which would be a thousand dollars. That was a very difficult task for the chaplain to figure out a way to cover those for cost.

Prison Fellowship Angel Tree Christmas Distribution

Angel Tree is a Christmas gift program for inmates' children. An inmate can list his children on the form, and the form will be sent to the National Office of Prison Fellowship. Prison Fellowship takes these requests and distributes them geographically to individuals and organizations that put together the requested gift. A catalog is provided to an inmate with the gift options available for different aged children.

The chaplain is responsible for distributing and returning the completed forms to Prison Fellowship with a prepaid mailing envelope. Materials are received in early August and must be returned by the end of September to Prison Fellowship. The early timeline is required in order to place the request with the donors.

I have not had any personal experiences with inmates' children. However, inmates have told me many times about the value of this program for them. For many of them, this was the first time in many years that a gift was sent to their child from them.

Too often in the past, they did not care, but now that they were locked down and in their right mind, it mattered to them that they could remember their child at Christmas. At least on one Christmas, there would be a gift under the tree that came from them. Someone else sent it, but they were responsible for getting the process started.

It's difficult to imagine how much it must mean to children to know that their fathers had remembered them. Suddenly, absentee fathers were alive and knew that they existed.

I would like to commend Prison Fellowship for developing this caring program for children. It's a very costly venture, but having to participate and see firsthand the response of the inmates will be an honor I will always remember.

Distribution of Christmas Cards on C Yard

One November, the Catholic chaplain was able to get his Catholic diocese to provide Christmas cards for the High Desert inmates. Each inmate would get two cards.

He asked if I would distribute them on C Yard. It was exciting to go from cell to cell and offer the inmates two free Christmas cards, courtesy of the Catholic chaplain. The indigent inmates could use the state prison mailing system for the postage. The cards could be sent to whomever they wished.

It was one of the truly joyous times I had as a High Desert religious volunteer. It took about six hours to distribute all the cards. I know the inmates appreciated the sacrificial effort the Catholic community made to High Desert inmates on that particular Christmas.

Working with the Susanville Adventist Pastor at B Chapel

When I talked about the Men's Circle that the Catholic chaplain sponsored, I mentioned a Seventh Day Adventist inmate who was a part of that group.

After I had been with the Circle group for a couple of years, the inmate was transferred from C Yard to BYard, since BYard, although Level N was not as intense as C Yard.

His points went down, and he was able to move to BYard. When he got to BYard, he wanted to contact the Seventh-Day Adventist minister in town and have him conduct services.

The Seventh-Day Adventist minister came to visit that inmate. After several visits, he agreed to conduct a Bible study on a Saturday afternoon program on BYard.

The minister was a terrific guy. He was not hung up on any of the specifics of his faith. He was concerned about people understanding the larger picture of what God came to do through Jesus and the kingdom. High Desert was very fortunate to have him, because he provided a worship tradition that was not provided often.

Sometimes he could not attend on Saturdays because of conflicts in his schedule, so I substituted for him. Often, there were more than fifty inmates present. The Bible studies and service were provided by inmates. I did not need to do anything but be present so they could have a service. I was pleased to support this unique way of sharing the Christian faith.

Prerelease Teaching at High Desert

One day I was going in to C Chapel when a teacher from the education facility next door said hello, and we introduced ourselves. He told me that he was a teacher for the prerelease program for High

Desert. He was responsible for all four yards inside the walls, as well as the Level IE Yard. As we talked, I shared with him my experiences at California Correctional Center in their prerelease program.

As we talked, he suggested that I should share with his students, since they did not often have special speakers. I was scheduled to speak the next week at C Yard.

I shared some of the ideas that I had used at California Correctional Center.

My First Contact with Odinists

One day when I was at C Chapel, one of the clerks from Medical came to talk to me. It turned out that he was an Odinist. The Odinists are typically white supremacists.

Odin, the Viking god, is leader and god. They want to push a white supremacy agenda. They are a security issue, although they are recognized as a religious group. Thus, they have the privilege of meeting together.

The clerk proposed an Odinist meeting. It wasn't something that I particularly wanted to do, but one of the responsibilities of the chaplain is to be concerned about all the religious groups in his area. We discussed what kind of meeting he desired and how would it be scheduled.

It was interesting to talk to him, because as we talked, I found out that he knew the Christian faith and all the principles of the Christian faith better than anybody that I had talked to in some time. But for some reason, he had gotten a jaundiced perception of the faith. Thus, he had decided that he was going to be a part of a group that would be divisive, one that would keep inmates from working together. We agreed to talk again.

Thankfully, I discovered before that meeting that the administration had decided to move him to another prison. I was grateful that I did not have to do more for this group of inmates, because they would be divisive.

Music Theory Class in C Chapel

One day in one of the cell blocks on C Yard, I was visiting the individual cells and talking to inmates. One of the inmates told me he had an idea that he wanted to talk to me privately.

Custody brought him to the open area of the cell block. We sat at a fixed table and talked. He told me that he had a great deal of music education and wanted to teach a class in music theory. He would like to have a music theory class for inmates on C Yard. This was a unique idea, and I was intrigued by it.

I went to the chaplain and talked to him about what I would have to do to get this started. He told me to write a proposal, and he would submit it to his superiors. If they signed off, the program could proceed. After about three weeks, it came back approved. Arrangements were made to begin the class in the middle of the week.

I was excited because I knew it would help a lot of inmates to learn and appreciate music more effectively. It is important for all of us to find ways to appreciate music. Understanding music theory might help us to understand how to live life more effectively. About twelve men enrolled for four weeks.

We were having a very successful class when a yard incident shut down the whole yard. The inmate who was teaching got caught up in it, and he was sent to administrative segregation. Ultimately, he was transferred to another prison, so we were not able to continue to run the program.

This experience tauglht me that inmates can conduct innovative programs, and it is effective for inmates to teach each other. When peers teach each other, everyone learns better. Sometimes it is a lot better to have a peer teaching in-mates than to have somebody who is above them-in a hierarchal way-wanting to teach them.

It was a lesson I had learned before, but it was a lesson that was well worth relearning- that we must remember that everybody has a gift, and everybody can be a teacher.

Keyboard-Educated Inmate

From the time I started volunteering at C Chapel, I had been looking for somebody who could play the keyboard at the worship service. Someone told me about an inmate who worked in the laundry who was a concert pianist. His parents were university professors, and he had studied the keyboard at Juilliard School. He was incarcerated for life for his crime. He had never been to chapel.

I went to see him about playing for the chapel. I talked to him about his gift on the keyboard and wondered if he would help me by accompanying the songs in the chapel. He didn't want to do it, so I attempted to entice him by offering him practice time during the week in exchange for playing for worship. I volunteered that he could have two hours practice time three days a week. I didn't believe he would refuse it, but he did.

It's hard for me to understand how somebody who has a gift and is offered time to do it would refuse.

It may be that if we have a gift to use, and we don't use it, then we become so wounded by that experience that we don't step up and go through the pain that it would require for us begin to reassert our gift.

I wonder if that's also true for people like me. Do I have some gifts I am not using, but it would take too much work for me to learn how to use them more effectively, because I have neglected and failed to use them? This is an awesome concept to learn. If we have a gift, we'd better figure out a way to use it, not lose it.

Improving the C and D Yard

Chapel Worship Since I was responsible for worship services on C Yard, I decided that I would build an order of worship for clarity. I developed a list of the activities for each Sunday, with Scripture and the words of songs.

We began with a call of worship and singing. Following the singing, we shared what was called "Words from the World," which were stories or ideas that had special meaning. Often, they were humorous but had moral lessons to teach.

One of my primary source was *One Minute Wisdom* by Anthony De Mello. De Mello was a Catholic priest who was a missionary to India. He collected these stories from the different cultures he experienced throughout India.

I also used the book *Jokes that Priests Can Tell*. The author was a Catholic priest. These jokes were the kind someone could tell in church. This was followed by the Scripture lesson and prayer. The sermon was about fifteen minutes long.

There were twenty-four inmates on the first Sunday. Each Sunday, the attendance grew. Initially, I thought it was my remarkable preaching, but I discovered later it wasn't my preaching that increased the numbers but because it was a way for the inmates to get in touch with their buddies or gang members from the lower or upper yard.

It was difficult to control the talking, since they were there to talk with their buddies. In order to solve this problem, I made a covenant with them. The agreement was that I would give them five minutes at the beginning of the program when they could talk with their friends. At the end of the service, they would also have five minutes to visit. In return for this, they agreed to listen to me without talking.

The agreement worked very well. We continued this practice during my time as a volunteer at C Yard.

Volunteering at D Chapel

Every couple of months, I would get a call from the D Chapel volunteer, asking me to cover for him, as he was going out of town.

I was always able to do it. It was convenient since his service followed directly behind the service I had on C Yard.

Since it occurred on Sunday, however, I couldn't go to church with my wife.

Occasionally, I would conduct a service onE Yard if the chaplain wasn't able to do it. That service was at 1:00 p.m. It was an inspiring service at E Chapel because of the mUSIC.

The men sang well, and there was an excellent musician on the keyboard. He would belt out the music, Southern style. My message was always well received and appreciated, much more so than C Chapel inmates displayed.

I have always wondered what made the difference and have concluded that inmates onE Yard were not quite as closed emotionally. They were not so defensive.

If someone is in prison and never is going to get out, that sets the way he thinks. It can keep him on the down side. That's called depression. It can also give him a bad attitude.

Obviously, many of inmates were shut down emotionally and spiritually. It took grace and unbelievable strength to overcome the depressive nature of the Level IV and Level III prisons.

One day I got a call from the volunteer on D Yard. He told me that he was going to retire in about a month and that he wouldn't be able to come anymore1 as he was moving to another area of northern California. He wanted to know if I would cover for him. So I talked to the chaplain, and he asked me to do it.

I discovered that the office clerk was also a volunteer clerk for the chapel. He was a lifer. He had been in prison for approximately twenty years. After his imprisonment, he had found the faith and was an awesome, awesome Christian.

We worked together to enhance the worship service. He found songs that inmates could sing easily. We also used the digital hymn player. In addition, there was the cassette tape player to support other facets of the music. One of the clerks' favorite songs was 11Surely the Presence of the Lord Is in this Place." He suggested we play it before the prayer time.

So that song became the song I used to introduce the Prayer Time during the rest of my prison worship services. It was easy to sing, and it had a meditative quality to it that helped to focus thinking as we prepared to pray. It wasn't as easy to use in C Chapel, since the singers were not as good.

I am eternally grateful for this inmate Christian for introducing me to "Surely the Presence."

The Bag We Drag Behind Us

One of the talks was about *"the_bag we_drag_behind_us."* Everybody has a bag they drag behind them. In that bag, they put their memories, their failures, their successes, their fears, their anger, their illness. Whatever it is, it all goes in the bag. Ideally we should probably not carry any of those things in the bag.

Most of all, we need to rid ourselves of carrying things in our bag. This is especially true of the ugly side of our human nature. Unfortunately, most of us continue to carry those failures inside the bag. We leave them in the bag and drag it around with us.

This is especially true of many inmates. Inmates have had great failures. Those great failures have jaundiced them. It has made them look bad. They feel bad about themselves.

Not only that} many grew up in families that were extremely dysfunctional. Because of the dysfunction} they were made to feel like they were worthless. They were told they were worthless many} many times. They drag those things behind them.

One of the things that the Christian faith can do is help us to clean up our bag} to get rid of all that garbage we are dragging behind us.

Obviously} this bag affects inmates inside or outside the walls. It affects all humanity. We all have bags that we are dragging behind us.

It is high time we get rid of the stuff that's in them so that the bag won1t be so heavy. Maybe we won1t have to drag it; we could carry it or allow God to help us carry it.

Observing an Od.inist Service at "A!" Chapel

My first introduction to the Odinists was at A Chapel. That's where the Protestant chapel served Level III inmates.

396

These inmates could be involved in evening programming.. In a Level IV chapel, inmates could only program during the daytime or work during working hours.

I had come to see the chaplain, and he told me it was the time for the Odinist to have a meeting. There were fewer than ten of them inside the chapel.

His office had a big window that looked out on the chapel so he could observe what was going on. He have a screen on it that could be opened or closed. It was a one way screen so he could see the chapel but participants could not observe him.

The chaplain recommended I observe the service. All the participants were white. They had a ram's horn and two other objects important in the Nordic tradition. During the service} the inmates took turns crawling on the altar. A chant was then offered over each of them. They were stripped down to their skivvies; I suspect they would have been naked under other circumstances.

It was difficult for me to understand why there wasn't direct supervision for the service. Christians were required to have supervision for all of their programs. Supervision was critical, it seems to me, to these kinds of programs.

However in this particular circumstance, they were allowed to have a program without direct supervision. They were on their own. Whatever they wanted to say, they could do it because it was their worship service.

However, since this was one of the primary white supremacy movements in prison, more direct supervision could be required.

Loss of Chairs on "C" Chapel

The seating in C Yard Chapel was wooden chairs. These chairs were produced by the prison system. There were about seventy chairs, and they had kneelers on the back of them.

Over time, pieces of the chair began to loosen, and the inmates would steal

397

the wood from the chairs, take the wood back to their cells, and make weapons. I don't know how they got the material through the search process, but they did.

It was becoming more and more of a problem, even though I would check the chairs before the service and after it. Other groups were not so diligent.

Custody got extremely upset about the vulnerability of possible weapons being made from parts of the chairs. Eventually, it became such an issue for them that they just picked up the chairs and left nothing in the chapel.

One Sunday, I came to a chapel without chairs. When the inmates came in, they had to either sit on the floor or stand up in the back of the chapel. Unfortunately, it was cold in the wintertime, and they didn't want to sit on the floor, so they would attempt to stand around the back wall.

As attendance grew, it became more and more of a problem-so much so that they would be standing up in several rows; only a few inmates would actually sit in the front row on the floor.

Another reason inmates did not want sit on the floor was that it made them vulnerable. Some of them were so defensive that they didn't want to find themselves in a position where somebody might attack them. They wanted to be able to defend themselves so they wanted to stand up. I did not make an issue of it, because I wanted the chapel program to continue.

Unfortunately, as the chapel attendance grew, it became a crowded chapel. They would be standing six deep around the back of the room, and I could not see what was going on. The guys in the back would talk with each other and interfere with the service.

Being as inexperienced as I was, I just walked right back through the group to confront individuals who were talking. I told them they could not do this.

It was risky on my part to do this, but I wasn't smart enough to know the risk I was taking. Nobody ever did anything to me. They were all very respectful. When I look back on it, I recognize it was a pretty naive thing to do. I was making myself more vulnerable than I realized.

It is important to point out that among inmates, chapels are safe havens. Inmates are not going to fight each other in the chapel.

In more than three decades at High Desert and California Correctional Center, there was only one fight, because of this unwritten rule that they would not use the chapel to create fights. For this reason, I never had any problem, although sometimes I was in some face rather hard.

One time things got far out of hand, so I told the inmates who did not stop talking that I was going to push my alarm. They still didn't stop talking, so I pushed my alarm. Of course, custody officers came rushing into the building. They were concerned about my being a hostage. When they came into the building, the inmates settled down.

They told me to go into the Volunteers Office. They called a nurse to check me out, since I might have been hyperventilating. The nurse quickly recognized that I wasn't in trouble.

Custody took the inmates out to the patio one at a time and striped them naked. I was embarrassed, because I had pushed the alarm that caused it.

Custody told me they planned to have the strip-down on this particular Sunday because they were concerned that contraband was being exchanged between the two yards. This was a very traumatic experience for me. I think it was also traumatic for many of the inmates. It did, however, teach them to be more responsive tome.

Learning to Read Your Bible

While I was volunteering for the prerelease program at California Correctional Center, I learned that they had a program at the main patio for literacy.

It was part of what is called the self-help groups. Self-help groups were groups that could be formed by inmates. After receiving approval for a program, a free staff volunteer became a sponsor.

At California Correctional Center, they had a literacy program with about fifty inmates, both inmate instructors and students who were learning to read. It was a very powerful program.

When I went back to High Desert to work with C Yard, I thought about the literacy program, and I hoped that we could have such a program, although Level IV prisons seldom had self-help groups. It was difficult to schedule them. as classes could not be offered in the evenings.

I discovered there was a high incidence of illiteracy among inmates. In most prisons, there was more than a 50 percent illiteracy rate. It was even higher among Level IV prisons. I discovered that High Desert did not have a literacy program.

As I conducted worship services, I discovered many of the inmates who were coming to church couldn't read. They were not able to read the Scripture.

I decided to find a way for literacy instruction. I checked with the prison educational officer, who informed me that although he was responsible for the literacy program, he would not authorize me to begin a program at C Chapel.

I discovered that like most bureaucracies the Educational Department have a very parochial as to the range of their responsibilities. They wanted to control all their programs. Although they did not have a literacy program, they were not willing to give it to somebody else.

I decided that a proposal would be submitted to teach inmates how to read Scripture. After about two months, it came back approved.

In the meantime, I decided that I would see what I could learn about literacy. I asked a teacher, who taught the class in the past, to let me have some of his literature, but he didn't want to give it to me.

I discovered there was a literacy program offered by Lassen County Library. I talked to the director and volunteered to teach and do some literacy reading instruction.

I was assigned a sixty-five-year-old lady who couldn't read. I spent about four months working with her to encourage her and help her to learn to read. I didn't do a great job, but she did improve, and she was able to read a simple kind of material with some fluency.

It was a very important experience for me, because I learned the importance of reading and how difficult it is to do it.

The Lassen County director gave me some literature to copy for High Desert.

She included a video used to teach reading. It was a three-week program for teaching inmates to be instructors and how to work one-on-one with other people. I copied it, as well as a hard copy of the workbook. She gave me handbooks and workbooks that I copied.

The materials were stored in a cabinet in the chapel. I discovered materials were being taken. I complained about it to one of the old lifer inmates. He said, "Let me show you what the problem is, Jack." He went to the locked cabinet. He took his ID, and he slipped it just inside the door and unlocked the cabinet. I moved the materials into the volunteer chaplain's closet.

I announced the program at the Sunday worship service.

After the service, an inmate, who was new to the chapel, had an interest in learning to read. He had emigrated from Armenia and got involved in crime activity in the United States. He had lived in New Jersey. While he was in New Jersey, he learned how to read English. He was fluent in spoken English, and he could read. He was excited that some of his "homeys" would be able to learn how to read. He was housed in upper C Yard. He located nine inmates in his cell block who were illiterate.

One of the problems with illiteracy is that individuals are ashamed of it, and they don't want to do anything to let anybody know they can't read.

However, since this inmate had learned to read, he was able to enlist three or four from the lower yard. I had a class of twelve who were all potential instructors. The class was scheduled on Tuesday and Thursday from 9:00a.m. untilll:OO. We taught this class using overheads and the TV.

After seven weeks of teacher preparation, the class was launched. For the first and second week, we didnt have anybody.

When I talked to the inmates, I discovered that it was because custody would not release the inmates to the chapel. They ignored the class schedule and wouldn't let them out.

This went on for four or five weeks, and the inmates got discouraged, and the program on the upper yard was canceled.

It was canceled because custody would not honor their responsibility to let people come to the program. We continued the class on the lower side1 and we had a fair success.

Laubach Literacy International had an equipment grant program. I wrote a proposal, submitted it and dreamed that we would get the funding. With the funding} we would have been able to offer a first-class program. After six months} it was denied.

We continued to use the Lassen County Library materials as well as what I could scrounge from the Education Building.

Saturday Morning Bible Study at C Chapel

I started a Bible study at C Chapel on Saturday mornings from 9:00 to 11:00.

Inmates were released to the chapel prior to the yard release, and they returned to their houses after the yard had been recalled. Thus, there was no mingling of chapel participants with inmates on the yard, which sometimes caused problems.

We used a Bible study method that Richard, of the Redding motorcycle group, had shared with me.

At the end of a study, a new chapter in the Bible would be chosen for the next week's study. During the week, everybody would study that chapter. They outlined the chapter as best they could. They would determine the theme or primary idea of the chapter, choose their favorite verse, and identify the verse, which was a difficult verse for them to understand. Finally, they developed questions that they had as a result of the study.

The next week, they went around the circle, and each inmate had the opportunity to share what he had discovered. The discussions and questions that followed were profound. It was an effective interactive program.

I found this method of sharing the Bible enabled people to learn on their own and not be spoon-fed by a Bible expert.

Discovery-Rick Warren's Programs

One day I read an advertisement for a DVD titled *What in the World Are You Here For?* by Rick Warren. I later discovered it was a part of his book 40 Days of Purpose.

I decided to use it in place of the Saturday morning Bible study.

It was a seven-session study. When we met, I divided the inmates into small groups. It was a powerful study. We had completed five lessons when I became involved in the faith-based programming at California Correctional Center, and I had to discontinue this study.

High Desert Protestant Chaplain's Job Opening

In June 2004, the Protestant chaplain at High Desert retired, and the job came open. A number of volunteers applied for the position.

I wasn't going to apply, but after learning of some of the applicants, I decided I didn't want them in the position. I recognized that it would be a detriment, at least in my opinion, for some of them to have the position.

I decided to apply. I placed my application and waited patiently for the opportunity to have an interview.

About three weeks before scheduled interviews, it was reported that a chaplain had been hired. He was a former prison chaplain who had returned to a parish. After three years in the parish, he requested reinstatement as a chaplain, and High Desert had employed him. I continued to volunteer, since I was seeing growth among inmates through the material from Rick Warren.

Learning about the Muslim and Sikh Faiths

While Chaplain Green was at High Desert, he invited me to go with him to the Reno Muslim mosque. He had been invited to a potluck meal, and he wanted me to share the experience with him. The mosque was in a modern store building. There was a fellowship hall adjacent to the mosque.

We discovered that 90 percent of those present, were involved in the University of Nevada at Reno. They were either faculty, staff, or graduate students. We had great fellowship. The food was exquisite. The dishes were from the various national food favorites. After the meal, the chaplain spoke, and the meeting was closed after a few more minutes of fellowship. I went with him three other times.

One time I went to the Muslim chaplain's presentation during Religious Emphasis Week at the University of Nevada at Reno. He lectured about the primary principles of the Islamic faith. I went to celebrate and support him in his endeavor, but I also learned much.

The chaplain was very articulate. He came from North Africa and spoke flawless English with a slight accent. His speech was well designed as he spoke about the primary principles that make up the Muslim faith.

When I hear those principles, I could begin to understand what made this faith so powerful. Unfortunately, as in many faith groups, the radicals have taken over and have interpreted the biblical narrative and the Koran in ways that are not appropriate.

As a result of this meeting, I had a clearer understanding of the Muslim faith. Anytime Chaplain Green discovered an inmate from an Eastern or other faith group, he endeavored to know him. He found three Sikh inmates on A Yard. He spent a great deal of time with them. As a result of knowing them, he studied the Sikh faith.

One of the inmate's parents, who lived in the greater Oakland area, invited him to come and visit the Sikh temple, which was located on top of a hill. It is visible for miles.

He invited me to go with him. We went to the parents' home for dinner. They served their favorite foods. We had a very gracious social time together. After dinner, the man of the house took us to the Sikh temple, where we were given a personal tour.

It was truly an educational experience. Again, as with the Muslims, I began to appreciate the differences in worship and why certain religions had attraction, especially if they came from someone's national background.

I will always be grateful to the chaplain for exposing me to these two faith groups. It gave me a new appreciation of what it means to be the melting pot, where America has all kinds of people and religions. I honor and want to support that concept as long as I can.

One Man's Journey through the Prison Recidivism Desert

April14, 2010

Happy Birthday, Chappy,

I am excited to let you know I am three months from going home on July 24, four days before Charlie. I hope this finds you strengthened and in good health. I often think about the growth I've experienced these past six years. And it all began there in Susanville, when I let go of my self centeredness and strived to be Christ centered. I am forever grateful to your belief in me and your dedication to the prison ministry that helped provide me with encouragement and a learning environment of Christ's example and love.

I received some information from Charlie on the CROP Foundation, and I am thrilled to hear he is considering using his God given gifts to go into ministry and enable other inmates to get control of their lives and hopefully increase Christ in their daily lives. I can't believe we are getting out at the same time. I wocld appreciate your informing Charlie that I would like to learn more about CROP and how I could be used, once we parole. I'm under the assumption that it will be a few years before we can enter a prison as a volunteer/sponsor.

My plan is to camp in Lake Tahoe my first weekend, then fly home to Pittsburgh on Monday night. I will be living with my parents and have been offered a good job as an assistant project manager for an architectural woodworking company.

The owner is a member of our church and has been a friend/mentor for me the past three years. I'm still searching for sports management jobs but have not had any success with my resume and letters to date. Since I last saw you all, my sister and I have been encouraging one another to get in shape and compete in a sprint mini-triathlon when I get home. I've been training hard and have lost forty pounds in two years, and my sister over seventy pounds. I just completed eight miles in seventy minutes, and I'm in the best shape of my life, I believe physically, mentally, and most important, spiritually.

Please pass along my love and encouragement to all the Christian brothers at Susanville. Tim from Follow-Up Ministries was in Folsom Prison yesterday and is still grabbing the Men in Blue's attention with his energetic real-life walk and talk. I believe I met him in '07 in the Oasis Chapel. Anyhow, I hope I can assist Charles and the CROP Foundation from Pittsburgh as at least a volunteer and allow the Lord to direct my path. I still plan to return to Susanville in five years to share my testimony, and by God, it will be great!I love you guys.

God Bless!

Matthew

Go Penguins!

Monda June21,2010

Dear Jack,

Congratulations on your retirement! Though unfortunate about your back, it was obviously going to take something along those lines to consider slowing down. I bet your wife was happy. I'm just only too sure that the old saying, "be careful what we ask for; we may just get it," will be echoing in her mind shortly. Nevertheless, kick your feet up for the time being and get healthy. You may need to concede a knitting class or dance lessons soon to make up for all the hours at the chapel away from your wife, so be a trooper and participate.

I received word that you will try to make a trip to Pittsburgh to visit your daughter and celebrate the wonderful transformation I've encountered. Obviously, your entire family is also invited, and I really look forward to hopefully seeing you on the outside of these walls. It will prove to be a wonderful day!I also received word from my parents that the PA parole agent made a surprise visit last week. He appeared to be a Christian and has approved my parole transfer, and I think he has also been invited to the celebration. (God is good.)

I can only smile and give thanks for the path I've found myself on and the people like you that I've encountered along the way. Life is good! I'll keep your surgery and surgeons in my prayers, along with a speedy recovery. And I'll see you next month! (That sounds awesome!)

God Bless!

Matthew

Happy New Year!

As promised, I wanted to update you this holiday season with how the Lord has provided and blessed me in these past five months back in Pittsburgh. The Scriptures have prepared me to expect wonderful things because we serve a big, awesome, and mighty God, though it is still incredible to stand by and witness the sometimes tiny intricate ways the Lord brings a situation to fruition. The promise that the Lord uses all things together to work for good for those that love the Lord continues to come true and put a smile on my face and joy in my heart. I am thankful, but not surprised, how everyone in this community has embraced me with affectionate hugs and personal interest. It is good to be home! Each one of you has been a precious gift to me.

The blessings have come in many different forms, spiritually, materially, and emotionally. Spiritually, I have had the opportunity to share my testimony at various men's groups, student groups, and church services, totaling approximately 1,800 people. I wouldn't claim to be a seasoned public speaker, going completely blank on at least two occasions, though the story I've been given stands on its own. Regardless of the words I've shared, it has been apparent tihe Lord has shaped them to be received as needed individually. The responses have been flattering) as well as constructive) to help shape future opportunities. I remain encouraged by my increasing fellowship opportunities within the church and beyond that) the Lord is remaining front and center in my life and shaping me continually.

Materially, the blessings have come in all different sizes. Living at my parents' home has certainly afforded me an opportunity to be surrounded by love, security) and the ability to not rush critical decisions. I've been gifted a car) clothes) cash and a road bicycle for my triathlon training. Granted) these are all just things; however another clear sign that the Lord is providing what I would not be in position to purchase and affords me both mobility and comfort to plan for my immediate future.

Emotionally, I am overwhelmed. I did not deserve to spend six years in prison. I don't deserve the car, bike, or clothing that was so generously given to me. I certainly don't deserve applause for accepting the love of Christ in my life. I turned my back on him for as long as I can remember, and yet he makes me feel as if I'm the apple of his eye. My interests are of him, my activities are full of him, and my relationships are based in him. For years, I lived my life, seeking to fulfill every area with happiness, only to continually find emptiness in what I thought was important. I still struggle but only minimally in comparison. The joy that apparently is overflowing from me can only be explained through my Savior. I just can't remember why I didn't recognize this truth from the beginning, but thankfully, it's living in me now.

12/29/2010

I'm also thankful I can chuckle at the reality of a prison sentence. The words I've previously shared are the only way to make sense of it all. I believe the Lord has a plan for each of us and apparently a sense of humor. We must simply embrace it.

I'm glad I'm not where I used to be before prison, and if you are feeling like you're in a personal prison of your own, take your thoughts to him and listen. Listen to the whisper of God. Our God is a loving God, faithful and just, and only asks of us to give him reverence while he shows himself to us in all of life. Recognize his desire to fill your heart with his love, receive his gift, and hang on as he lifts you up as if you're on angel's wings.

Lastly, I accepted a job with TEC Benefits here in Wexford. We are an employee health benefits consulting firm for small businesses. I am excited about this opportunity as my future career. The partners are experts in this industry, so I am positioned to learn all I can from them. Last week, I successfully passed my insurance licensing exam and now await the insurance commissioner's decision on issuing me a license, with my felony conviction surely being considered. I would request prayer in this area that the commissioner uses discretion, and acknowledges I've served my time, and allows me to continue in this work. All your prayers have been answered to date, so thank you from the bottom of my heart!It's pretty cool, ,everything that has happened and that which continues to unfold.

June 4th, I plan to compete in an Olympic distance triathlon in Edinboro, PA, which is twice the distance of the sprint tri I did this summer. I will look forward to sharing with you again at this time, which will mark my one-year anniversary since paroling. If you'd like to hear more about my professional career and/or have advice, I would greatly appreciate your interest. Here's to "Community" and an excellent 2011 for all. It's shaping up to be a doozy!

With love,

Matthew

To Whom It May Concern:

For six years, from 2004 through 2010, our son was incarcerated in three separate facilities of the California State Prison System. As a pastor, I was well aware of uprison ministries," but my initial attempts to make a helpful connection were frustrated for one reason or another, until I finally made contact with Jack achappy" Carmichael.

It would not be an overstatement to say that 11Chappy" became our lifeline to the prison system and the strategic human catalyst God used in our son's spiritual transformation. Not only did he become a personal mentor and encourager to our son, but the programs he put in place were instrumental in helping him deal with personal challenges, as well as developing leadership skills.

What I appreciated most was that Jack created an "empowerment model" that allowed inmates to take on real responsibility, develop life skills, and provide experiences that would translate into successful life after prison. I know

411

many consider prison to be 11Wasted years," with no real rehabilitation value, but in the case of our son, they proved to be redemptive in the truest sense of the word. I attribute our son's remarkable success and transition to civilian life, in large part, to the faith-based rehabilitation program that Jack pioneered at California Correctional Center.

Hollis Haff

Senior Pastor Emeritus

New Community Church

Chapter 1

I walked out of the courtroom in shock. My thirty-year-old son had just been sentenced to six years in a California state prison for a crime we were convinced he did not commit. As friends expressed their heartfelt sympathy, the sentencing judge walked through the crowd outside the courtroom. I had the strongest urge to approach him and express my outrage, but I was numb, paralyzed, and unable to speak.

My wife and I returned to our hotel room, hardly saying a word. When we arrived, the pent-up emotion of two years -waiting for his case to come to trial exploded in a torrent of tears and anguish that I had never experienced before. As we held each other and sobbed uncontrollably, I remember thinking, *We need to pray.*

Not that some miracle would overturn the verdict but that God would help us to trust him in the darkness of that moment. I knew what the Bible taught. "God causes all things to work together for good for those who love God, who have been called according to his purpose" (Romans 8:28).

As a pastor and Bible teacher, I knew that passage well. I had preached it from the pulpit and used it in counseling sessions, but this was the litmus test. Did I *really* believe it? I knew that verse wasn't teaching that "all things are good." Injustice is not good; giving false testimony in court is not good; prison is not good; having six years of your life taken away is not good. But that's not what the passage is teaching. It's not that "all things are good"-they're not. Rather, it is that God works all things *together* for good. He takes the injustice, the dishonest, the prison experience, the seemingly wasted years, and he brings good out of it.

I've often used the recipe for Toll House cookies to illustrate the point. The recipe calls for various ingredients-flour} shortening} sugar1 salt1 raw eggs,

413

chocolate chips. Apart from the chocolate chips nothing else tastes good by itself. You wouldn't sit down and eat a bowl of sugar or salt or flour or raw eggs and say, "That's good." But when you work the various ingredients *together*, something really good comes out of it. That's what God promises! He can take all the broken pieces, the evil the injustice and bring something, good out of it. That is precisely what God did in our son's life and in the life of our family.

Chapter 2

In the early days of our son's incarceration, I remember reading of another pastor's anguish. Gerry Sittser had been hit by a drunk driver on a California highway and instantaneously lost three generations of women in his life- his wife, his mother in-law, and his little girl. He shared with brutal honesty his anger with God over the seeming randomness of the accident and his struggle to see how any good could possibly come from such tragedy. But he said something that helped me greatly in the aftermath of our own confusion. He said, "The closer you are in proximity to the event, the more you have to affirm in faith that God can bring good even out of evil.As more and more time elapses from the event, the easier it will become to see the good that God can bring."

Nothing could erase the pain of his loss or change the real evil of the tragedy he experienced, but God did begin to bring some good out of it. He wrote a book about his experience, A *Grace Disguised*, that helped to put our own family's tragedy in perspective and provide us with helpful guidance in how to navigate through our own dark night of the soul.

One of the first signs that God could bring some good out of this was my contact with the prison chaplain. While our son, Matt, had not been pursuing spiritual goals through his twenties, tlhe prison sentence was potentially a wake-up call. I hoped it might be a catalyst for spiritual openness. So I called the prison and asked to speak with the Protestant chaplain. I had a brief but promising talk with Chaplain Ray Davis, explaining my son's background and why I thought he might be receptive to a personal contact. I called back a couple of weeks later, only to discover that Chaplain Ray was in the hospital. I prayed for him, I prayed for my son, and I waited. When I finally called back, I was informed that Chaplain Ray had died. Back to square one! (I would later learn that Ray Davis had been the lead guitar player for the '70s rock group, Three Dog Night. He had himself been imprisoned on a drug charge, converted to Christ in prison, and later would return to prison to minister to inmates.)

The chaplain who followed Ray Davis was Jack Carmichael, or "Chappy," as we came to know him. He had spent time as a paratrooper chaplain in the military and a second career as an administrator in the California University system and had spent time on a volunteer basis at California Correction Center. After Ray Davis's untimely death and at an age when most men were long retired, Jack Carmichael launched his third career.

My first contact with "Chappy" was on the phone, close to a year into my son's sentence. I could feel his guardedness and sensed that he was overwhelmed by the bureaucracy and administrative load of his position. I tried to empathize with his dilemma and shared with him our hope that he could reach out to our son. On our first "family visit" to the prison (we live on the other side of the country, so visits were only an annual event), we scheduled an evening dinner to get to know Chappy and get some insight on how Matt was handling the ordeal and where he was spiritually. It's hard to overemphasize the importance of those annual visits that always included a dinner with Chappy. He was our lifeline and represented an independent voice of hope that we desperately needed.

On our first such visit we checked in around 8:30a.m. on a Friday. Soon after Matt was delivered to our small efficiency apartment on the prison grounds but segregated from the prison population. There we would spend three uninterrupted days} talking} eating} and watching playoff football games. The first day, we didn1t watch anything; we simply talked from 9:00a.m. to 11:00 p.m.!fd never talked so long to any of my kids for such a sustained length of time. At one point Matt got up to get something in the other room. My wife simply looked at me and said, "Who is that and what have they done with our son?"

It was obvious that something was happening (something good) at a spiritual level. Having Christ-centered conversations with Matt had always been like pulling teeth, but now our son was talking openly and enthusiastically about such things. He clearly had a special fondness for Chappy and talked excitedly about his involvement in chapel and Bible studies.

At one point, Matt was explaining the phenomena of 11prison Christians/' a term used to describe those inmates who get religion in prison but end up after release getting busted for the same offense that landed them in prison the first time. After his colorful explanation, Matt looked at me and said, "I think I was a prison Christian before coming to prison!" I knew exactly what he meant. We all have the tendency to use God when we need him to accomplish our agenda, instead of letting God use us to further his agenda. It's the difference between biblical Christianity and American folk religion. When I heard my son utter those words I knew it was the real deal.

Our dinners with Chappy only reinforced and confirmed our suspicion that God was at work. We joked that our meetings with Chappy were something akin to parent/teacher conferences} an annual opportunity to find out how your child is doing from an objective third party. At one of those memorable dinners, Chappy said, "Mr. Haff there are maybe five men in this institution, from the warden to the inmates} that I trust} and your son is one of them.That was the clincher- God was keeping his promise to work good in the midst of this nightmare.

Looking back on the situation now Matt has been out just over one year- the best thing we did was to make a personal connection with the chaplain. He was not only a mentor to our son but an understanding friend to us, who helped us more than he will ever know.

Chapter 3

In his best-selling book, *The Me I Want to Be,* John Ortberg begins chapter 21 with a question: "Imagine you have a child, and you are handed a script of his entire life laid out before you; better yet, you are given an eraser and five minutes to edit out whatever you want."

I'm sure my wife and I would have taken the eraser and gladly 11Wiped out" the accident in which our son was involved in 2003 and the unjust felony conviction that sent him to prison for six years. But could that have been a mistake? Looking back at what transpired over those years, I'd have to say yes.

As Ortberg goes on to point out in that chapter, suffering can be a catalyst for growth. We're all familiar with the term post-traumatic stress disorder, which someone can experience after returning from a war zone. But researchers have recently coined another term:"post traumatic growth." It underscores the reality that some people not only endure their suffering but grow through it.

That was certainly the case with Matt. By his own admission, the first year of his imprisonment, he struggled with anger and bitterness. He was angry at God, angry at the judge, angry at the DA, and the anger could have consumed him. But as he looked around at the wasted lives and chaotic stories that were all around him, he knew he had to start making positive choices.

"The temptation is to lie down and die. But when you don't-when you show up, when you offer the best you have something good is happening *inside* you that far outweighs whatever is happening *outside* you." (Ortberg)

Matt started showing up. He got involved in the mill and cabinet shop, developing some new woodworking skills, and discovered he had an aptitude for it. Better yet, it filled up his schedule and kept him productively engaged for a good part of the day. He got involved in the prison chapel program and even provided leadership for programs like the Purpose-Driven Life. He started working out and got in the best shape of his life.

As we began to observe the way Matt was dealing with adversity and see the transformation that was taking place, I was reminded of Solzhenitsyn's words: uBless you prison for being in my life." Just like the biblical story of Joseph, "You intended to harm me, but God intended it for good to accomplish what is now being done" (Gen. 50:2).

Chapter 4

One of the more subtle and surprising outcomes of our son's incarceration was what it did in the life of our church congregation. When we returned from the sentencing, we were met at the airport by the other pastors and their wives. They simply sat with us, listened to us as we processed the event, and became Christ's loving presence in the midst of our pain.

While we had shared the unfolding story with close friends, staff, and elders, there were many in the congregation and community who were totally unaware of the drama we had been living with for over two years as this came to trial. It was awkward to determine who to tell or when. We didn't want people to feel sorry for us, and we already had an emotional support system in place. Even though our friends and confidants had been incredibly guarded with our family situation, the public nature of my position almost guaranteed that the story would get out. After a number of months and some discussion with friends, we thought it was time to share our story with the congregation. I was in the midst of a series titled "God's Way to Emotional Wholeness." As I began to wrap up the fourth and final message of the series, I said, "If it sounds like I've had some intimate experience with emotions like anger, fear, and guilt, it's because I have!" I then pulled up a stool, sat down, and said, "Let me tell you what our family has been living with."

Not only was that therapeutic in my own healing, but the expression of support and encouragement from the congregation was overwhelming. People who didn't even know our son starting writing him in prison. My wife started an e-mail network to update a growing prayer list of well over a hundred, and many of them forwarded it to their friends. We would include excerpts from Matt's letters that reflected his deepening maturity in Christ, and it had a profound ministry impact on those who were following the story. People thought, "If he can have such faith and joy in his situation, then maybe I can too." It was

421

not unusual to show up at church on a Sunday and have a half dozen people say, "Hey, I got a letter from Matt this week." The impact on Matt was significant as well. The wealth of correspondence he received caused one cellmate to ask, "What are you, some sort of celebrity?"

Our son experienced, in a very tangible way, the truth that the church is the family of God that 11bears one another's burdens" (Gal. 6:2). As I reflect upon the profound spiritual transformation that took place in Matt, I can't help but think that the collective prayers of God's people were central to the outcome.

Matt returned home in July 2010, and two weeks after his arrival, we held a homecoming party for all the folks in the church and community who had supported us. We wanted to say thanks for all they had done for us. In expressing our gratitude on behalf of the whole family, I likened the experience to trying to do a full squat with a lot more weight than I could ever handle. And just as your knees begin to buckle, a couple of spotters come to your rescue and help you shoulder the weight. It's still a load, but at least it's manageable.

Jack Carmichael
PO Box 759
Janesville, CA 96114

May 30,2010

Matt. Every time I went into the Oasis Chapel sanctuary in the last three years, I blessed you for your building the beautiful storage cabinet. The way you used the pew wood and the functional nature of the beautiful piece would be something that your dad would treasure in his church. Thank you for using your talent to bless many generations of Men in Blue (MIBs) into the unforeseen future. Visitors were continually commenting about your exquisite work.

Fortunately, you also left your impact on the faith-based rehabilitation program as well. Thanks for structuring the 40 Days of a Purpose-Driven Life program in such a way that we continued to use it until I retired. Many MIBs have discovered their purpose through what you developed.

I know the inmates will continue the program, if the new chaplain decides it fits his priorities.

For me personally, your letters since leaving Oasis Chapel helped me see my Lord better. I marvel at the way you have allowed adversity to grow you. I felt like I was getting a letter from the apostle Paul when you graced me with a letter. Please continue to use your writing gift to help others grow.

As I think of your spiritual journey the last few years, I recall a story that Rachel Remen, a San Francisco psychiatrist, told in her book, *Kitchen Table Wisdom*. She told that when she was four years old, her grandfather would bring special gifts to her. They were not what others gave her. One day, he brought her a Styrofoam cup filled with dirt. He had her promise that she would water it every day. If she did, an unexpected happening would occur. She promised. She watered it for a week. Nothing happened. She did it a second week. Nothing happened. When he came to visit her, she asked him to take the cup she didn't want to do it anymore. He told her she had promised. Late in the third week, a miracle happened. Green shoots were coming out of the dirt. She was so excited to show it to her grandfather.

When he came, she told him that the water was what made the miracle. He said to her, "No, it was your faithfulness."

That's how I see your spiritual growth and journey. Of course, the Lord was involved, but it was your faithfulness the created your miracle. Keep it up.

I hope we will stay in touch.

Shalom,

Jack Carmichael

Another Man's Journey through the Desert

Hello, my name is Jonathan. I'm doing my best to compose a little bit about myself without going into a whole lot of boring detail. My primary objective is to explain my behaviors and actions that ultimately led to my going to prison.

I won't make any excuses for my actions, because other people may make them for me. If I make excuses, some people won't believe them.

The things that I remember the most about my childhood would be my relationship with my father. My dad always took the time to spend with me and my sister, who is one year younger than I am.

I remember going fishing with him and catching my first fish on his fishing pole. I was ready to give up, but I wanted to please my father. He asked me to hold his fishing pole while he did something really quick, and no sooner had he handed it to me than a fish hit the line. It scared me, and I jumped and almost dropped the fishing pole. My dad coached me through what I needed to do to reel in this little feller, and I also remember getting to eat it.

When I was very young, I was involved in a car accident. I believe I was riding in a 1969 Volkswagen bug. My dad was driving a '50s model pick up truck with many moon wheels. I used to like to look at my distorted figure in these rims, as it made my face look funny.

My dad was driving ahead of us, and my mother was driving this little car following my dad, probably because she didn't know exactly where we were going. I'm not sure where we were going either; I just remember the trip.

I can also remember years ago, having nightmares about an accident that I don't really distinctly remember. Let me explain myself. I think I was fighting with my sister or infringing on her space, because that's something that we used to do a lot. I would get worked up because her hand was on my side of the seat. It was a territorial issue, something fight about with my sister. Her pet peeve was if I touched her or poked her; therefore, I did that as often as I could.

My mother turned around to see what was going on in the backseat. When she did, the vehicle slightly drifted into the other lane. My mother was a very skittish type person, easily spooked. That's why when the oncoming semi-truck honked the horn, she jerked the wheel, causing the suspension to collapse in the front, and the car rolled.

I was two years old, and my sister was one. I don't know my mother's age, but she was quite young too. We were all ejected from the vehicle and somersaulted down the side of the freeway. I believe that I was found next to the freeway, and I know that truck drivers stopped. I can only give a secondhand telling of the story, since I obviously don't remember it.

What I do remember was the ambulance ride. I remember thinking, even at that young age, that there should be a lot of fun. I thought these square boxy vehicles with flashing lights were really cool. They drove by really fast with no regard to the speed limit because they cottld get away with it. And to be able to ride in one, obviously that's every kid's dream. I can't describe the way that I was feeling that made it not such a cool ride, but it wasn't pain.

I'm also aware that I had injuries to my head. Both of my ears were cut almost completely off. I was scraped up pretty good, yet today I don't really have any scars to show for this.

My mother's scars, in my belief, are what finally killed her. She developed cancer later on and without going into scientific reasoning, it just has always been a belief of mine that that accident reduced the number of years that were allowed for her to live. Both of her lungs were punctured. They didn't think that she would live through the night.

I remember being in the emergency room at some hospital, yet I don't know what the hospital was. I remember going in for an X-ray and being afraid. I wasn't so afraid after I realized that there weren't any syringes and needles in this room. It has always been a fear of mine to get poked with a needle.

I was tired, and my back was sore. I requested a pillow, and I remember being given something that resembled a rock. It had soft velvety stuff on it, but when I laid my head on it, was very uncomfortable. Not exactly the type of pillow that I wanted. I also remember being thirsty and not being able to drink anything, because the doctors didn't want to upset any of their tests or pictures that they were taking with the X-ray machine.

Ultimately, when I break it down for myself, I believe that I was just incredibly bored, and I really didn't want to be there. After everything was taken care of at the emergency room, I was then released. It didn't take very long for the nightmares to start happening. I don,t remember what any of them were, but I remember waking up in tears, and my dad would come in to soothe me. When my mother was well enough, I remember her coming in and talking to me, and I remember it being a preference of mine for her to come in and soothe me. She had a softer touch than my father. I should note here, of course, that for all other purposes that life may have requested of me, I always preferred my father. Even though he had a harder exterior, he had the soft, kind, gentle gesture of a father, and every year around Father's Day, I always try to write him a message, sharing with him a different memory than the year before. There's more than enough of them to be able to do this.

As I grew up, I always like to see how much I could get away with. I guess this is normal for most children, but I think I pushed the limits a little bit too far. I learned my lesson with Grandma and Grandpa, though. If I ever thought that my mother and father were strict disciplinarians, Grandma and Grandpa made them look like brownies.

The discipline was just different with Grandma and Grandpa, and most of the time it seemed almost psychological. I was never in any kind of abusive situation in any way, shape, or form. My mother's way of disciplining me, for example, was to tell my father. If dad wasn't going to be home for a while, I could usually get what I wanted from my mother by just continuously asking her. If she said no, it usually meant that I could get what I wanted in just a few minutes if I was persistent.

If I asked my dad for something and he said no, sometimes I would get another no. After this, however, it was usually the belt.

As far as corporal punishment was concerned, it is a part of my background. I purposefully caused damage to a brand new refrigerator that was being stored in the old house on my grandfather's property. I was caught doing this by my father, and he took me into the house. My dad never hit me out of anger and would always explain exactly what was going on and why, before and usually after the discipline was administered. I never had hard feelings toward him or my mother after discipline was administered, and I never felt that it was unfair.

When I got older, probably around the age of eleven or twelve, things started to smooth out a little bit for me. I started to realize what I had in my parents. I was really afraid I might lose my father, because he was having heart issues, or at least that's how I see the information as I would hear it when he would talk to my mother about what he was feeling. We were living in Shingle Town at the time, and there's a portion of the road that has hills on it like a roller coaster. My dad likes to drive fast anyway, so he would drive fast over these hills, and when he would hit a certain one, my stomach would usually float up. It was a strange sensation. For some reason, I developed a fear that I would lose my dad. I even remember having a conversation with my sister that was quite odd, perhaps. We were discussing which one of our parents we would rather lose, if we didn't have a choice. Of course, when this question came up, I said neither one. When she insisted that I had to choose one, I said that if I was to lose one, that it was my dad. My reasoning for this, of course, was that Mom was easier to manipulate, and I didn't know what it would be like to lose any of my family at this point.

In 1989, my mother's death hit me pretty hard. I wasn't expecting her to be the one to go first. She started having problems, and we found out she had cancer that we believe to have started in her uterus. The doctors were going to perform a standard hysterectomy, which is pretty common. There was nothing to fear in this procedure; in fact, it was such a small thing that other "more important" surgeries would take precedence over hers over the course of some time.

When my mother finally passed away, a deep emptiness settled over me. It wasn't too long after this that my dad remarried. He remarried somebody that was much like him, in that she was a strict disciplinarian. Not only did she administer the discipline just as well as my dad, but she would also tell him that I would do it again. I have much respect for her, but there were some issues too.

She had two boys of her own. I had only ever had a sister, and I was quite excited to finally have some brothers. The problem with this was that they were raised quite a bit differently than I was. One example: they listened to a different style of music than I did.

They listened to thrash metal and secular bands that centered on death being cool and Satan and all that. I was listening to the Oak Ridge Boys and the Heritage Singers. I liked that kind of music, but I was interested in what they were listening to also. It seemed like there was a double standard; they were allowed to do things that I wasn't allowed to do.

In hindsight, this makes sense, and the reason I say that is because it would've been fair for them to all of a sudden not been able to do what they had always been allowed to do. On the other hand, I was expected to do what I had always been expected to do. At the time, I didn't have the intellect to be able to see this.

I begin to do things that were quite foolish. I would sneak off with my brother David, the younger of Mom's two boys, because I got along with him better. The older of her sons was Daniel. Daniel was quite a bit older than me and not as interested in doing the same types of things. I'm not sure the type of relationship that David and Daniel had, but I think I got into more mischief with David, and I didn't with Daniel.

I used to ride behind a house where we lived on Riviera Street. There were all kinds of trails back there at the time, but today I believe it's all subdivision. We would go to stores that seem to have security that wasn't as efficient and would steal cigarettes. The first cigarette that I ever smoked was a Misty.

David had this girl that he really liked, and her name was Misty. We would stay up late at night playing with the Ouija board, asking questions to see if David was going to "score." For some reason, the Oracle always went up to the yes side of the Ouija board. I may have influenced that slightly, but it was fun just the same, even though it wasn't the kind of fun that we should've been having. That's my belief anyway.

Slowly but surely, I developed a smoking habit. I would come home after eating some kind of mints or a tube of toothpaste or something to take the smell out of my breath. At least I thought it would take the smell off my breath. I forgot that the smoke was in my clothes, and as I began to smoke, I wouldn't realize this.. My dad would ask me if I'd been smoking, and I would tell him no. There were times when he would catch me doing stuff, and I would still deny it.

This started to develop problems between him and me, and we began to fight like we'd never done before. I blamed these fights on my stepmom, Lenita.

I began to rebel quite a bit more than I had been. This became abnormal. My dad thought that maybe I needed to get away for a while, and he got me into a great school program at Weimar Institute. This was a boarding school, and my brother David wasn't there. The trouble I got into there was definitely on my own. I'd steal a pack of cigarettes and would sneak off to smoke them.

There was a small area where I could go to smoke, because it was an area in the compound that wasn't used anymore. This facility was a Seventh-Day Adventist facility, and they were very big on a health message. This was a problem for the school when they found out that I was smoking. The way they found out, of course, was that my roommate told on me. I was proud of what I was doing, and I missed my brother. I wanted somebody else to get in trouble with, because trouble is so much more fun when you're sharing it with somebody else. My roommate, however, wasn't interested in the same types of trouble that I was. He wanted to get into trouble by staying up too late, studying his books to get good grades.

So the school board finally called a meeting and my dad was there. He drove down to Sacramento, where the institution was, in order to have this conference. I had a very simple choice in front of me. At the time, I didn't think it was very simple at all. The choice I had to make was whether or not to be honest and tell the truth. I continued to deny that those cigarettes were mine; I said that they belonged to somebody else. In my mind, that made sense because somebody else could have possibly had cigarettes in the school, and that would've meant that I wasn't the first one.

The problem on the dean's side of the story was that he'd never run into this issue before. It was very unlikely that those cigarettes had been there for a very long time. He played with them for a while and told me that if I was honest with him, he wouldn't take me out of the school. He really wanted me to stay in the school, because when I was in school, I was doing what I was supposed to. My trouble was only caused when I was not in the classroom and when it was on my own time.

I guess what I'm trying to say is that I was never very good with managing my freedom, and that started at an early age. Either way I look at it, it was a very fair request that I just tell the truth. My dad encouraged me to tell the truth and told me that if I couldn't tell the truth here, that I wwould be placed somewhere for help, because I had a problem with lying. The place that he was referring to was Redding Specialty Hospital. This hospital was designed for people that were going through DTs, and it was designed for people like me, and also for people like me that have wanted to hurt themselves, because they thought that life was unfair, and they didn't want to live anymore.

Needless to say, I ended up going to Redding Specialty Hospital. I continued my lies, and the team ihad no choice but to release me to my father. My dad was very disappointed and tried to reason with me, but that wasn't possible for him at the time, because I wasn't receptive.

As frustrating as this was for him, he never lost patience with me. I'll never forget that.

As time went on, my issues began to get a little bit worse. I eventually went

431

to stay with my grandfather, and he was very understanding. I was able to persuade him that my dad was the one that was having problems. Because Grandpa knew that my mother had passed away, that she had died, he suspected that my father's parenting may be the result of some of my issues. I want to quickly say here that that's not the case. It was just a belief at the time, because I would go over to Grandpa's house and cry, but I never let my feelings be known, and I would never share my sorrow in the presence of my father. To this day, I can't tell why that is; it just is what it is.

My behavior began to get a little bit more erratic, and eventually my grandfather started to see the truth. The Bible says that the truth will find you out; in this case for sure, that was the truth!

It didn't take very long for me to steal from my grandfather. He kicked me out of the house because I was refusing to abide by his rules, and he began to see that my dad was telling the truth about how my behavior had changed. Quickly, my grandfather began to believe that it was the loss of my mother that was causing a radical behavior, not the loss of my dad's wife that was causing his erratic behavior. It was definitely erratic behavior on my part, the son's part, not the father's.

I would make sure that there was a way to get into the house every time I would go in, either by leaving the window open or halfway setting the lock so it would be easier to force open. I never broke anything in coming into the house. I would wait until my grandpa went to work. He was a carpenter, and I knew about what time he would leave and when he would come home. It was fairly easy to do this.

Eventually, all I wanted was to get on with it, though, and be able to do things on my own, without having to do this every day forever. I knew it wouldn't last, and I knew Grandpa would eventually catch on. What I didn't know at that time is that Grandpa had already caught on.

I took one of his checks, which had big bold print on it, indicating that the check would not be valid if written for under two hundred dollars. This was a business account associated with his construction business. I thought I was being pretty slick when I took a large flashlight and used it as a table to place another check and signed his signature. The other check was written for $1,100, so I copied that part too. When I took it to the bank, the bank knew that this wasn't right, because they had been doing business with Richard Rabun for so long, and they knew I wasn't him.

I ended up going to jail, in which case I served sixty-seven days. I was released after that on what was referred to as the three-year joint suspended probation. This meant that I was supposed to go to prison for those three years-that's the deal that the district attorney made-but that I didn't have to go right now. That's what the suspended part meant. What I had to do in order to not go was to follow a list of rules; that's common to most parolees and probationers today.

I began to drink, and I regret it, and use grass or marijuana. One time I was called in to test, and I always had been able to regulate myself so that I was clean. I never used anything to get clean, I would only use a small amount, and I was just always clean when I went in to test. It was, however, my suspicion that my probation officer was not testing me for marijuana. I came to believe this because most of my friends told me that the test was incredibly expensive and that there was no way that they would test me for that unless I was arrested for possession or really high on marijuana when I was arrested. I chose to adopt this logic, because it allowed me to do something that I wanted to do. Alcohol was only in my system for a short time; therefore, it seems pretty rational to drink, and the next day it would not be in your system anymore.

The problem with this line of thinking is that it always leads to more and more and more. What I mean by that is, I eventually began to drink and drive. Around this time, as my behavior was getting more erratic, I was called into the Probation Department, and my probation officer requested a test. I was actually honest with her, and I told her that I would be dirty for THC area. I don't know why I was inspired to tell her this, but it just seemed like it was the right thing to do. I had also most recently smoked marijuana, and she was very big on telling me to be honest with her or else. She was a fairly nice person, and her name is Judy Eichelberger.

433

Judy told me that she wasn't a going to violate me, but that I needed to knock it off, because I could go back to prison for testing dirty. I told her okay, I would do so, even though I didn't plan on knocking it off immediately. I was already dirty, and I just acquired what was referred to as "an eighth."

I finished off the eighth and told my friends that I would have to knock it off. In all honesty, that was the last time that I smoked marijuana for a very long time.

By very long time, I'm referring to at least twelve if not fifteen years. I was simply afraid of getting caught and didn't think that I could get away with it any longer, because I'd already been caught once. That was my thinking. It wasn't very repentant, but it's the way that I thought at the time.

I did, however, continue to drink. As I said previously, I would also drive. My first going to prison was as a result of getting drunk driving. This was also my third violation. My first violation was getting caught with alcohol, and it was just dumped out and thrown away. I didn't know that I'd been violated until I received my paperwork and learned what a COP was. That meant ({continue on parole."

My second violation was the THC dirty test, and the third one was driving under the influence of alcohol. This was escalated, of course, and ended up becoming a prison violation. They reduced it to a reckless driving. After going to court, I still had to do sixteen months, but they gave me something called "halftime." After going to prison for the first time, I realized it wasn't so bad.

I had arrived at my reception center, and I would be lying to you if I told you that I wasn't scared. I was everything that scared was. I have never been so afraid in my life. The ride up wasn't so bad; it was quiet, and it didn't seem like there was a lot of tension. Most of the guys that were in the prison-bound van, or bus, were sleeping, because it was peaceful and there was music playing. Once arriving at the prison, the compound was huge. I looked at High Desert State Prison, which was my reception center, and was beside myself. When we pulled up to the gate, I couldn't believe that I was going to be staying here for a period of time. For the first time in my life, I honestly wanted to die. I didn't

434

want to kill myself; I just didn't want to be there. Dying seemed to be the only way out.

I was admitted into the cell block in Building A. I got along pretty good with my cellmate, and we told stories and passed the time. Everything just seemed to get very boring, as we were waiting for a counselor to figure out what kind of a risk we were to the prison system. Once this was figured out, a point system was issued. You got certain points, and certain points were deducted, depending on whether you'd ever been to prison before, whether you were married, had children, and also depending on whether you were a life sentence, and also depending on how much time you had to do. The nature of the crime also was looked at, and points were issued or deducted based on this.

The idea was to go see the counselor and get a low score, so that you could go to a low-level security prison area. The lowest level is a Level I, in which case there are no gun towers and very few officers to patrol the block. The inmate population is pretty laid-back, and it's not a very dangerous environment. You are allowed to have things that you're not allowed to have on the higher levels. In fact, you are allowed to go into town to work on the sides of highways.

If a Level IV inmate was allowed to work on the side of a highway, picking up trash, he might use his rake as a weapon, try to escape, hijack a car, and go to what he considers safety. Like the safety of a bank he's robbing?

A Level II facility is identical to a Level I. The difference is that a Level II facility is inside of a secure perimeter. There are usually gun towers, or there may be an electric fence. You are not allowed to go outside of the fence without supervision. and the number of officers to patrol the area is quite a bit higher. In this facility, you suddenly have a new concept called "the rule of twenty-five." This means that you have to have one armed officer for every twenty-five inmates.

A Level III facility is a watered-down Level IV. The facilities run pretty much the same, but there are differences. In a Level III facility, you have the rule of ten, which is to say one officer for every ten inmates. On a Level IV facility, this is called a "max" or a maximum security facility. When an officer

435

approaches you, before he is fifty feet away, you have to turn, place your arms behind your back as if you're cuffed, and rest your forehead against the wall. You are not allowed to go into a library without having some kind of an armed escort. It's one at a time, and the supervision is much more critical. On a Level IV facility, it's a rule of five-one armed officer for every five guards.

I was a Level I inmate my first term, and my second term I was convicted of nonsufficient funds, multiple checks. This particular crime carries a sentence of sixteen months, two years, or three years. Since I had been to prison before, that meant that I could have a one-year enhancement. If I was sentenced to sixteen months, I could then get sixteen months plus one year. The two-year term would become three, and the three would become four.

I got two years with halftime, and a plea bargain with the district attorney was to drop the enhancement.

I can't refer to the author, partly because I don't know who it is, and I'm not sure how their copyright rules work, but there is a book that deals with what's known as "the show of evil." What this means is, when you stand before the court and before the judge, or even before the jury, your story is told by two professionals. At your jury trial, your attorney is trying to get you off the hook. The prosecutor is trying to pin you to the wall.

The funny thing with this is, if I'm supposed to be treatedl as innocent until proven guilty, and we suddenly run into a contradiction in terms, I wouldn't be cuffed and placed in jail if I was being treated as innocent. Then again, this statement makes sense, because I'm not in prison, which is the final penal institution, and have not received a sentence yet.

Depending on who is better at defending whom-my attorney defending me, or the district defending the district-a verdict is reached. Sometimes the guilty party goes free, because the guilty party had a better representation in the courtroom area. Is this justice? What if it's the other way around? What if the party that's not guilty gets convicted? Now I'm not trying to say anything here, because I was never not guilty, and I never went to jury trial because I always took the plea bargain.

The system was still fairly new to me, but I knew how to work it. Over time, I ended up getting convicted of arson.

The arson story is one of true tragedy. My best friends were residing in a trailer that belonged to me. There were staying at a location known as the Barge Hole. This is an area along the Sacramento River where people owning four-wheel-drive vehicles and boats can launch their boats directly into the Sacramento River. The current is very calm, and there is a lot of beautiful landscape around this area. There's not a lot of traffic, and there's definitely not a lot of homes. What you do have a lot of, however, is a lot of transients and people who are homeless. If you saw this location, you would question why there are homeless people out there, because most of them have cars and most of them have jobs. If they didn't have jobs or vehicles, they would have a hard time living out there, because there is absolutely nowhere to panhandle, there is no help facilities like the mission, and you would have to walk almost twenty miles just to go get food or alcohol or whatever.

My friends were residing in this facility in a camp trailer. I and three of my friends became very intoxicated and decided to start my car and drive into town. During the course of turning the vehicle around, I backed into the trailer and knocked it off its blocks. A small candle was in a wall sconce, held up to the thin walls via thumbtack. It fell directly next to the door and landed in some freshly laundered clothes that we just brought back from town. The fire started and quickly began to spread. A small can of white gas had been stowed underneath the table, which was at this time folded down into a bed, and it hit the corner of the stove barbecue pit that was in the trailer for safekeeping so that no one would steal it. The can of white gas vented and aided the flame.

I remained at the scene for almost forty five minutes, trying to put the fire out. There were several witnesses to this fact, but when I realized the fire wasn't going to go out, I knew that eventually somebody in town, eighteen miles away or so, would see the smoke and call the fire department, and eventually there would be attention out in this area. I got in the vehicle and proceeded to leave. I was so intoxicated, I didn't know which way to go. When I reached Jelly Ferry Road, I took a right hand turn instead of a left-hand turn and was headed toward Cottonwood instead of headed toward Anderson, which is the direction I wanted to go.

A vehicle came up on me pretty fast, and at first I was worried that it might be law enforcement. I thought about speeding up, not about turning around, and decided to just slow down a little bit. The car passed me, and it definitely was not an official vehicle. Another vehicle was headed toward me, and I began to worry that it might be law enforcement.

I want to make it clear here that I was not worried about law enforcement having anything to say about the fire. I was more interested in them pulling me over and getting another DUI. The thought of arson never entered my mind, because it wasn't an intentional act to burn the trailer. It was, however, not an accident that I was driving under the influence of alcohol-again.

Once the vehicle that was heading toward me got close enough that I knew it wasn't law enforcement, I turned around and chased after it. They were going pretty fast, but my vehicle was fast also, and I passed this little car at over 100 mph. I slowed down with the intention of keeping this vehicle behind me, so that I would know who was back there. On my way out, close to Anderson, a fire truck came flying around the corner, just as my vehicle slid into his path. It was a near miss, and the fact that I didn't get killed that very instant is a testimony of the God I serve first and foremost, and also a testimony of the good driving skills of the person behind the wheel of that fire truck.

I now definitely looked very guilty. I was driving erratically, and if somebody didn't know that I was intoxicated, it would look like I was driving recklessly with something else on my mind. If it's not alcohol, maybe it's guilt.

The fire truck operator radioed in an APB for the vehicle in question. They said it was a suspicious vehicle, and they gave a description of it. I made it all the way up to the Dersch Road and continue to drive erratically, with the intention of parking my vehicle somewhere out of the way and reporting it stolen. I also planned on calling in sick for work, or calling in and telling my boss that I wouldn't be able to make it to work, because I didn't have a car. I then planned on drinking large quantities of alcohol at my house.

Driving erratically, I ended up going through the intersection of Dersch and Victor. The road turns into Churn Creek, and it wasn't very much further down this road that I ended up crashing and burning

The car came to rest upside down and still running. It was stuck in gear and the rear wheel was spinning very fast. There was no rubber left on the rim, and sparks were flying everywhere. Some guys from just down the street had witnessed the accident and had actually witnessed my erratic driving before the accident occurred. They had flashlights and ran out to help us. I wasn't able to find my rear-seat passenger. He'd been ejected, even though he was wearing a seatbelt. All of us were wearing seatbelts, and I found the girl in the front seat still belted in. She was unable to orient herself as to where she was. I got the seatbelt offher and got her out of the car. We checked the perimeter around the car to make sure that if we pushed it back onto its wheels that my rear-seat passenger would not get crushed. The only way we were able to get the car to stop running was to push it back onto its wheels with all three of us. I had intentions in my head of getting in the vehicle, starting it up, and taking off. The car was beat up pretty bad, and obviously this wouldn't have been possible, but my thinking was still irrational, and I was still under the influence of alcohol.

The real fun began to start when law enforcement arrived. I knew that this was going to happen, and when I walked up to talk to one of the officers, I was pushed away. I was told that there was a crime scene and to make room. I attempted to talk to three professional officials and received the same statement each time.

I decided not to push my luck by telling them that I was the driver of the vehicle, and instead, I took their advice and left the scene. I wasn't charged with this crime later, because the officers said that they had told me to leave.

I walked the short distance across the Sacramento River to a pay phone in front of a 7-Eleven store. I made a call to my stepmom, and she came and picked me up. I was taken to the hospital, where my dad recommended that I be seen by the emergency room. I refused this, as I didn't think it was necessary and just wanted to get on my way. I was very grief-stricken, and I couldn't believe what had just happened.

I didn't know where the girl and my backseat passenger were. I didn't know what hospital he had been taken to. My dad told me that I should face the music and be responsible. He told me he would not call law enforcement, telling them where I was, unless I gave him permission to do so.

I did give my dad permission to call law enforcement. They showed up and did a sobriety test out in front of the hospital.

I passed the simple field examinations, as several hours had gone by since these situations that occurred. It wasn't very long after the situations occurred, however, that other officials arrived, questioning about the fire.

Things proceeded pretty painlessly, and eventually I was released. I proceeded home and slept very good that night.

I woke up in the morning needing a cigarette. I didn't have any tobacco in my little house, so I went out to my car, only to realize very quickly that I didn't have a car anymore. All of my tobacco was in that car. I felt like I had just lost everything, and the weight of the situation from the previous night, in my newfound sobriety, which was only minutes old, came down on me like a ton of bricks.

I didn't know what to do, so I picked up my phone and began making some calls. I finally was able to locate my front-seat passenger, the girl. She told me what was going on with her and what happened moments after the accident. She asked if I was okay, and I told her that I was. She was too. I was glad to hear this, because she was pregnant.

The rear-seat passenger was still in the hospital with a compound fracture to his arm. He was the only one that was really hurt, and I guess it had something to do with the way the car rolled over and then flipped. The backseat sat over a fuel cell and had panels that removed and ironically, the seatbelt was connected to these panels. This was a Toyota manufacturing error for the year of 1984 and especially in this vehicle. The rear seat was designed to seat children or people of a much lesser weight capacity. The vehicle in question, a 1984 Toyota Celica Supra.

The girl asked me if I would be willing to show up, to meet her at the Walmart in Redding. I agreed, and I knew she was scared. I explained to her that if law enforcement was questioning her, the chances of me going back to prison that very day were very highly possible. As it turned out, that's exactly what happened. I was expecting to get charged with a wreck, with reckless driving, or a number of other things that came to mind. One thing that was for sure; I was definitely in violation of my parole. This really bummed me out, because I was supposed to discharge my parole in only nineteen days! I continue to ask myself why I couldn't just have waited the party just nineteen days!

I thought that my life was ending. I arrived at the Walmart and was taken into custody. The whole purpose of asking the girl to show up was because they knew I would also show up with her. They never gave me the opportunity to turn myself in but instead tackled me by checkout station number eight. It was embarrassing, but I kind of saw it coming. As a matter of fact,

I put together a prison package for myself and had it ready to go before I went to meet the girl.

It was a long stay, those two months in the county, and an even longer stay in the reception center. I was introduced to a whole new mind-set when I realized that I would be residing in the system a lot longer than I ever had. Most of the other times I spent in custody, I was able to find a way to just relax, read books, do Bible studies of some type, and then just go to church when convenient, which only seemed to be happening in the system, certainly not on the streets.

I didn't immediately just jump to it when the church bell rang this time, because just like many times before I really did want to do something different. I really wanted to be someone different, but I truly didn't know how. My father believed that after my mother passed away, the signs of a personality disorder began to show more and more.

The disorder was called schizoid personality, and was discovered by Eugen Bleuler. I believed that this was a pile of horse feathers and didn't want to hear all that nonsense. I refused to take the pills and just rebelled against the idea

441

that there was anything wrong with me, and I was hurt to be told that it was a "personality" disorder-something that was wrong with my person?

No one else seemed to notice all these personality disorder things, and I was relieved to find a few friends that could accept me for who I was. It didn't take long, though, for those that really knew me to discover that whatever my issue was, personality disorder or not, I was interacting with the wrong crowd. We were getting drunk all the time and just living the party lifestyle to the limit, and this is what had been putting me high and mighty into the recidivism stats.

For the first time in my life, I found myselflooking at what seemed like an end to my life, and I truly didn't want to live anymore. I was too much of a chicken to do anything about it, of course, but I knew that I was going to have to make some kinds of changes if I wanted things to be different.

I was introduced to a program in Susanville CCC, which appealed to me. It was called Freedom from Addiction and was taught by Reverend Wayne McKibbin. McKibbin was a professional guitar player and had played lead guitar in many roles, including house bands and pro studio contracting. He also has credits in many albums, including several Three Dog Night records.

The program was fun because of the music, and getting to go to church was fun since it felt like a rock band concert. This, of course, was short lived for me, an amateur keyboardist that got into the band for a few months and was blessed. Reverend McKibbin got sick and when he did, we all prayed. He shared his passion with us, and I felt that I had known McKibbin forever. I remember one Sunday, he stood in front of the congregation and all of us men were sitting there, waiting for the reverend to speak.

He waited, and everyone was patiently waiting to hear what he would say. He presented what I believed to be personal business about his planned recovery in faith and then some of the options that were in front of him. None of this was any of our business but rather something that I could see him talking to his wife or mentor about. It was amazing that he was so open to sharing with us, and for the first time in my life, I really felt that I was in a church where the clergy cared. And why not?

There was no offering plate to go around or any activities requiring anything more than us just sitting there listening to the Word.

When McKibbin died, the entire community pulled together, and we all grieved. My experience was only just beginning, as I had a lot of time left to do, and now I was really discouraged, because the one and only person that I felt cared for me (at this time) had just passed away, the same as my mother, grandmother, and grandfather.

I decided to just get off the yard for a while and relax in the cool quarters of the church. I knew that we were right back to regular old church, where we sit like baby birds and then just open wide and let daddy bird puke his theology all over us. Boy, was I wrong, because the person that we saw coming into the prison chapel day by day had seemed to share a love similar to that of McKibbin but so very different too. It was the Santos family, and they worshiped our Lord with us every Thursday.

I was hoping that someone like him would be with us on a regular basis, and that I would be able to find a way to grow. I was really hoping that the Freedom from Addiction program would resume as well, because that is what I felt I needed. I already knew Christ as my Lord and Savior and had no reason to need to hear that message reiterated a billion different ways. I wanted to actually learn something that I could apply.

This prayer was answered through a man I came to know as Jack Carmichaell who did nothing but what I would have expected from anyone in the chapel business. I worked with him closely for over three years having resided in the system in Susanville for five years and I watched this man supervise the growth of a church unlike anything I have ever seen before or since.

He called us the Men in Blue} because of our prison "blues." He treated us like we were humans and then started putting virtually everything he was making at this job right back into the church. He was tithing more than 90 percent of his income and spending more than 70 percent of his time with us there atthe chapel. He liked doing this, and he practiced what he preached, unlike most of the people I have been around in the church sphere. He didn't micromanage the growth of the church but rather was a moving part of it, and boy, did the teaching commence.

We were expected to bring our gifts to the table and help the program grow and run. We were the clergy, the pastors, the innovators, and the congregation, all in one! I was first introduced to a program called 40 days of Purpose- Driven Life. Pastor Rick Warren gave a powerful sermon with his life experience and testimony, and then he shared how he started his congregation. We used this church setting as a template for our congregation, since we had to pick something, and I watched it work and then became a part of this family myself.

As a result of this, I feel that I was given the opportunity to grow and learn something that was really new to me, and that was how to recover, how to deal with failure, and how to reach out to others. I learned that the only reason anyone should ever stand over another human being is when they have their hands out to help raise someone up or are helping them up.

I was moved more by the sermons I saw than the ones I heard. I witnessed rival gang members sitting and talking and being humane to each other, looking for a new lifestyle too.

Celebrate Recovery came next, and I was given more responsibility. At this time I had only known Dr.Jack Carmichael for about three or four months, on and off, as he would volunteer his services at High Desert and CCC, and now the program was really starting to take off.

There was one particular day that I will remember above all others. I should have possibly mentioned it before, but it didn't seem very relevant until now. This is the day that I arrived at the Susanville prison that they call the California Conservation Center. When I arrived at this prison, the van pulled up to Receiving and Release, and the door opened, and a younger sergeant who was pretty well built stepped up to the open door and gave the specific instructions: do not move out of our seats until he gave us the word. Everybody seemed to understand this, and then the first name was called. I don't remember the man's name, but he was in his sixties or maybe early seventies, and the sergeant grabbed him and shoved him hard enough into the side of the van to leave a mark on both the van and this man. He yelled at the top of his lungs that this is what happens when people don't comply with what he said, and the whole time I'm sitting here, thinking that this man did comply with exactly what he was told to do. I was confused.

This was my first introduction to the mentality of this prison. Having been to multiple different prisons, I understood that different places operated on different sets of rules and had different personalities.Some inmates prefer going certain prisons because of the way that the officers behaved in those parts better than other prisons. Likewise, the inmate population also behaves differently too.

This prison was one of the toughest ones to get along with the officers that I have ever been in. It was incredibly frustrating and scary at the same time. Once I had been there for a certain duration of time, it seemed like the officers were just a bunch of hard-nosed cops that had to act big because their brains were small. Of course, it's not very nice of me to say this, but that is what I was thinking.

The reason I bring this stuff up is because at this part of my testimony, I remember that the stuff started hitting the fan. The program was great. There were more inmates coming to the church on Monday, and that meant that the officers had to work harder in order to process through security. The sign on the gate stated that security was never convenient, and they definitely worked very hard to make it as inconvenient as possible. If an inmate did not shave the morning of his service and he had a little bit of stubble, the officers would tell him that he didn't look like his ID. This had nothing to do with the rules, because we were all within compliance and grooming standards. In some cases, the men would get turned away because they were wearing faded clothes, and these were the very clothes that were issued to these men by the linen room.

On one occasion, I set out in front of the door to the chapel on my day off, in excess of six hours, because it was requested that I do so, even though this was my day off, and I was volunteering my time. I don't make this statement to glorify anything that I did, but rather to show the type of motivation that was inspired in all of us by the programs that were being brought to our chapel.

There are so many experiences that I could share that if I'm not careful, I will end up composing a book of my own. The experiences that I shared with the men and women who volunteered were priceless.

I will conclude my testimony by stating that there is a huge diamond field right here at home in America, in California, and this is a mission field, ripe for the harvest.

I ask myself why we spent so much time, effort, and money trying to send people to witness the Third World countries when we could be doing the same witnessing here in our own country.

In the five years that I was incarcerated, I wrote over five thousand letters to various places, requesting literature. Thirty-seven hundred of those letters were written to my home church that I was raised in, and that is the Seventh-Day Adventist Church.

As I was participating in the Catholic study, I would ask questions and receive answers from virtually anybody within this chapel- from my chaplain and volunteer chaplains and even from the Catholic priest.As a result of this effort on their part I was introduced to a course study known as apologetics. This helped me to complete my life mission or at least start it, and as a result, I finally felt like I had direction. I can also put that in the present tense and tell you that I feel that I have direction now.

I can't thank John Baker enough for creating the syllabus known as Celebrate Recovery. I can't thank Pastor Rick Warren enough for offering the syllabus to his program known as 40 Days of Purpose Driven Life. But none of those things would amount to the thanks that I owe to Dr.Jack Carmichael for coming to a place that I thought of as a hellhole, putting up with all of the tension thrown at him by the guards, attitudes that were directed at him by the inmates, including me, and continuing to keep on doing what he knew was the right thing to do. This unwavering respect toward us as men showed me a sermon more powerful than you will ever hear in any church from any pulpit.

APPENDIX II
ATTA-BOY LETTERS FROM
INMATES ABOUT PROGRAM

The value of any map is how it helps those who use it. In the case of the CCC faith based rehabilitation} it is the inmates who are the true test of its worth and success. The following letters from participants in the program will help you determine if was worthwhile.

A Salute to the "Freedom from Addiction" Program

Having been incarcerated for over seventeen and a half years, I have been involved with many programs, some of which I fail to see the benefit of,and others, I am amazed to have experienced the impact they have made in my life. Two of these programs I will speak of here.

One such program was dubbed "Freedom from Addiction." This program was put together by Chaplain Wayne McKibbin, who had built this program based upon the things that he had encountered in his life and how God had helped him to overcome them.

One of the principles of this program was about not letting the distractions we find so common to lead us away from the true focus of our lives, and it utilized a practice of meditation to enable and develop this awareness, coupled with developing a sense of personal responsibility and accountability for this awareness. This program was addressed toward those who have dependency issues, but even as one who did not fall into that category, I found it to be life-changing in more ways than I could have ever imagined.

It is so easy for those who are incarcerated to fall into this mind-set that tells them they hold no worth, no value to society, and this perpetuates the cycle that leads them to undesirable behaviors for which they find themselves incarcerated at a later date.

If I only know to do that which I do, how can I ever change? Freedom from Addiction enabled me to become aware of and observe this cycle, which is literally one of the reasons that I find myself now having been successfully on parole for over a year now, even after such a long incarceration.

Chaplain McKibbin had a way of presenting everything he did like an onion-sometimes sweet, sometimes it made you cry, but it always h.ad more

451

than one layer to it.

It is with joyous sadness that I must relate that Chaplain McKibbin is no longer with us but has accomplished his mission here on earth and has since been promoted to be with the Lord of all creation.

The impact of his life and teaching continues to live on in those of us whom he invested in, and the Freedom from Addiction program is no longer in

Another program that I can safely say is one of the most effective programs ever developed is called the Alternatives to Violence Project (AVP). This program was developed by the Quakers in conjunction with and at the request of some inmates incarcerated in Greenlhaven Prison New York State and has since grown and become a worldwide movement of nonviolence.

At the heart of AVP is the concept of "transforming power," which enables one to deal with conflicts in a nonviolent manner.

This program emphasizes communication and community} both of which are instrumental in creating a safe environment where one can participate in introspective reflection and make sound decisions} something that was almost unheard of with the California Department of Corrections and Rehabilitation during my stay within its confines.

While other programs have made a significant impact upon my life during my incarceration, it is these two that stand out the most.

Both of these programs run in the similar vein of doing more than the status quo and making a serious investment in individuals and their mental, physical, and emotional development.

The definition of insanity within addiction circles is 1 1to do the same thing over and over again yet expect different results." This saying reveals more and more wisdom as time goes by.

-Michael J.

My second day at CCC, I got a pass to go talk to 11Chappy" Carmichael about a job as an inmate clerk. When I met with the man, he interviewed me, prayed with me, and told me, 11If you're serious about being a clerk, then start attending service, and we'll go from there." That I did, and it is the best decision I have made in my life!I say this, because I now walk with the Lord in my life. The choices and decisions I now make are rooted from what I learned while attending the faith-bas•ed rehabilitation programs that 11Chappy" facilitated at CCC.

I can say with absolute certainty that my life is forever changed.... I never got the job as a clerk, but I did get the job as a steward of God's Word and agape love and to share this with everyone I can.

-Michael H.

The chapel programs at CCC, Susanville, changed lives. I felt privileged and blessed by God to be there and a part of it. Perhaps the most significant change I experienced was through leading some of the small group programs that Pastor Carmichael set up and ran for us. I remember that the turnout for Crown Financial Ministries "God's Way of Handling Money" was never large, but it gave me a new understanding of being a steward of the money that God provides us. What a fortunate chance to have students becoming disciples of Christ and turning away from the easy money of drug dealing to the much more difficult task of planning to earn an honest living with hard work and proper money management. Only by building a true foundation of faith, rock solid, could this become a new way of living. This is the true meaning of repentance-that is, turning around our thinking and way of living.

-Acke

My name is Mel Novak, and I have been in prison ministry over twenty-eight years, ministering in prisons all over the country. I have minist,ered at CCC three times while Chaplain Jack was there. He was called "Chappy" by us all. He led the most excellent faith-based rehabilitation program. One of the main reasons this program was successful was because of Chappy's leadership. The inmates trusted and loved him.

I observed the inmates who would embrace this program with zest. They were all encouraged to do what they learned when released. This was crucial because of the high percentage of those who return. Those in other prisons and penitentiaries without programs return... over 80 percent. Those who made a commitment to the Lord and did this faith-based program, well, about 11 percent returned. This is an incredible drop in returning. The only other program that was like Chappy's was the MERIT program in the LA County Jail system.

It was dedication and faith by Chappy, whose faith was instrumental in leading the inmates not only to come but to bring others. I have ministered in twelve other states, mostly hardcore and every Level III and Level IV prison in California. If this program could be implemented in prisons around the country, the population and returnees would be drastically reduced.

It is always choice, and that is what I saw the three times I was there-choice to get better, healed, and delivered from being incarcerated. God is a God of the second chance and builds on ruins. I personally saw this through Chappy's faith-based rehabilitation program. I pray other prisons would allow it in their facilities.

Blessings,
Mel Novak

Dear Chappy,

Thank you for the opportunity to tell you how much we appreciated the work you did at CCC. We have attached a letter, and you are more than welcome to use it or edit it however you see fit. Good luck with the book. We will want to buy a copy when you get them ready to go.

Yours in Christ,

Gary and Helen Crane

The times we were privileged to come alongside the work Chaplain Jack Carmichael did at the California Correctional Center inSusanville were eye-opening experiences. Not only did his faith-based programs prepare the men to re-enter life outside the walls, but they were trained on how to take leadership roles so they could impact the new lives that awaited them upon their release.

There was one time the men allowed us to sit in on one of their small group sessions. These were sessions where the inmates took leadership roles and discussed common problems and how to manage them. Because of the faith-based programs, they were profoundly aware of the behavior that had landed them in prison and their need to approach life with a different mind-set.

"Chappy," as the men called him, gave the men the greatest gift one person can give to another and that was the gift of knowing how to live a Christ-centered life. Because of the programs they participated in, they knew Jesus Christ was the answer and how to apply the principles laid out in the Bible. In our opinion, these faith-based rehabilitation programs are essential if we are going to break the recidivism problem. If men leave the prison system with the same thinking they came in with, they are destined to return.

-Gary and Helen Crane

As a pastor and as a Christian, I believe in change-change for the better. It is fundamental to the Gospel of Jesus Christ.

Change for the better is what moves one forward. Change for the better is how we leave our past in the past. Change for the better, lasting change for the better, must be rooted in something greater than our own good intentions. Such is the work and ministry of Jack Carmichael at the California Correction Center, Susanville.

This faith-based rehabilitation goes far beyond behavior modification. It could be called "Creator" modification. You see, at the heart of this rehab is an intimate relationship with the God of heaven. It is steeped in and based on God's amazing love for his creation, each of us created in his image.

Lasting change for the better is not someone gritting his teeth in order make something happen. It comes from a sense of trust in one greater than self. A faith that is confident in and cognizant of God's desire for me to live an extravagant life. A life free from addiction, dysfunction, abuse, self-loathing, and loneliness. This is faith-based rehabilitation; something we cannot do for ourselves.

Jack Carmichael is adamant about rehabilitation, and he doesn't mince words or waste time. There's a way to better oneself, and Jack helped many, many inmates get to that place. Engaging state officials, the administration, or correctional officers, anyone or anything that might hinder recovery, became an obstacle for Jack. He didn't take no for an answer; being put off only angered him and being placated only made him work harder for the good of those he served. And Jack served those under his care well.

The program worked, because God was at its source, and Jack was faithful to his calling. I can say this because I saw these things firsthand, there in the prison itself and in my church. Many of those men came back into the local community, and now I have watched them continue in that better life that came through the programs administered with faithful determination by Jack Carmichael at the California Correctional Center.

His work and ministry there has had lasting effects. Faith-based rehabilitation has God's power behind it, and the statistics to convince even the harshest critics.

- Rick Conrad

This book, *One Barrel at a Time*, is the story of the author's five-year study of the prison that led to the faith-based rehabilitation program at the California Correctional Center inSusanville,

California. It is forthright and well written, reflecting the findings of the author's research. This is not an armchair study but a tried and trusted program that actual works. I have visited prisons on the East Coast, where some of his findings have been implemented with considerable success. This is an excellent work.

It is my hope that this book will be widely read and used in the programs of other prisons throughout the country. I recommend this book without reservation; and send it out with the prayer that God will greatly use it. It has been my joy to have served in the prison ministry with Chaplain Carmichael in prisons throughout California.

He is a scholar, one who studies and shares his knowledge. This book is but one of his excellent works. May God richly bless it and my many read i1t!

-Harold F Green, MA, MEd, ThD
Retired prison chaplain
High Desert State Prison
Susanville, California

Dr. Jack Carmichael was called Chaplain Jack by the Men in Blue (inmate population) and most everyone else that knew him. I was a religious volunteer under Chaplain Jack during his five years at California Correctional Center. I am a retired correctional sergeant with twenty nine years of service, and twenty-one years service at CCC as a religious volunteer.

Chaplain Jack, in my opinion, was an excellent chaplain. He was fair, firm, and consistent. The Men in Blue knew he cared for them. He lived and demonstrated loving unconditionally, with balance and exhibiting the Christian life he taught. Chaplain Jack was very dedicated to training, developing, and equipping men to succeed.

His heart was to reach out to the religious Men in Blue in a nonsectarian fashion. He also evangelized the Men in Blue that represented the church to and among the general population of both staff and inmates. He promoted and used programs like Purpose-Driven Life and the support programs like Celebrate Recovery. He organized Alcoholics Anonymous and Narcotics Anonymous, Second Base, and lots of leadership training and development through hands-on expen0ence.

Chaplain Jack pioneered a 501c3 program called Lassen Sierra Prison Ministries (LSPM). Its purpose was to purchase and donate specified supplies for chaplains assigned to county, state, and federal facilities. LSPM collects funds donated from people wanting to support the programs; then at the direction of the board, the chaplain facilitates the purchase and donation of supplies, such as Bibles, books, training material, music equipment, projectors, etc., that support religious programs to a designated facility.

Chaplain Jack, through donations from other churches, replaced the pews in the Protestant chapel with 2 50 chairs, to facilitate small groups better.

The efforts put forth by Jack Carmichael are still used in the Protestant chapel, still guaranteeing the success of those men who truly desire to change their lives.

-Len Santos

In the years I have been involved in prison ministry, the most success I'm aware of is the men whose lives changed because of Jesus Christ. These changes came from the inside. I find the men fall into three categories-those who have never been inside a church, those who at least attended Sunday school as a child, and those who were regular church attendees. What they all have in common is they are ready for a permanent change in their lives.

There are second and third generations of inmates, following in their parents' footsteps of being career criminals, illiterate, drug abusers, alcoholics, welfare recipients, and in general, slaves to their "normal." And when asked, two-thirds, on an average, are fatherless. Through Christian faith-based programs, these men learn a different way to do life, a new "normal." They find freedom from anger, addiction, and self-hatred. They learn how to be gainfully employed and, the most important, in my opinion, is finding their value and worth and how much they are actually loved by their heavenly Father.

I know they are successful because of the number of former inmates who stay in contact, happy in their changed life outside of the prison walls.

-Phillis Santos

I'm writing this letter on behalf of Chaplain Jack Carmichael, to give my opinion and assessment of the four rehab programs that I was involved in at the California Correctional Center in Susanville, California. The programs were

The Purpose Driven Life, The Purpose Driven Church, the Around the Bases series, and Celebrate Recovery.

I was the first inmate to graduate all four programs, which entitled me to be what's called a camp facilitator. Being a camp facilitator allowed me to teach these programs at one of the sixteen northern fire camps.

Chaplain Carmichael gave us inmates who chose to participate in these programs in a leadership position hands on experience by actually allowing us to perform in that capacity- with ongoing leadership meetings with him and the other leaders for guidance, advice, and constant assessment of our thoughts and concerns of those inmates we were servmg.

By getting on-the-job training (for lack of a better word), I was able to do and learn at the same time. Not to mention I had to complete eighty hours of course work, which included reading books, watching DVDs, and taking notes on certain pastors/ preachers, such as Joyce Meyer (The Battlefield of the Mind series), Cloud/ Townsend on Christian counseling and leadership, Pastor Rick Warren *(Purpose Driven Life book)*, and Bishop T. D. Jakes and Bishop Noel Jones, to name a few.

Having Chaplain Carmichael's mentorship and ongoing advice and guidance gave us inmate leaders invaluable experience and tuition that has only helped to improve my Christian walk and to be a more successful person in private and public life.

-Dion K. Bethune

My Reflections of the Chaplain's Rehab Program at CDC Susanville

It was a delight for me to work as a volunteer in this program. The program was well administered with the chaplain kept a great team of volunteers well informed and organized. It was obvious to allthat the chaplain had training and personal skills and experience in administration. We were given lots of encouragement and were well informed on expectations and results for our contributions to the program. The program was very ambitious, with wonderful courses being an essential part of the whole. The inmates were excited, and hundreds of men's lives were touched weekly. There was a rhythm and rhyme in the program that organized the participation of the inmates in a learning flow. Morale among the inmates and volunteers was high. Continuity of programs and volunteers was evident.

It was a continual challenge to get the necessary support from the guards, but the administration at the prison was most supportive.

A strength of the program was the participation required of the inmates. We were required by the chaplain to make our contributions in an interactive environment with the inmates. Participation in the actual elements of the program by the attendees was good. There was a great rapport between the chaplain and his recipients, and this flowed over to the volunteer staff. I have always held that a ministry that is conducted in love with good content and fine organization will bear good fruit. Chaplain's program was such a ministry, and I enjoyed and learned from my participation in it.

-Pastor Bernard Van Ee, a prison volunteer for twenty years in Montana and California

June 25, 2013

Thanks, Jack, for opportunity on your new book. The program was number one for the years I worked with you at the prison, and the impact that I saw that you were having on the systems was positive to inmates.

The impact you had on the inmate lives was exceptional for prison chapel programs. Your work aimed to promote and assist the disadvantaged into an evolving new life. Your goal was to prepare them to be good-quality citizens and live the good life in a stable society.

Shalom,
Elbert Herring

Dear Jack,

Just a brief outline of my observance of your years leading the faith-based rehabilitation.

As chairman and CEO of an international company, in which I had an opportunity in my position to meet and work with heads of state, world dignitaries, and business leaders. I have had a chance to critique and observe your faith-based rehabilitation program, in which you provided faith, strength, hope, and comfort to those who encountered emotional and psychological pain and suffering. You provided means or solutions to combat such despair and guided them to become immune to failure and defeat.

Each of us may one day be cast into a great drama, in which we may be following an uncertain script, and therefore, it's up to each one of us to write the final scene in the script

In closing, I would like to add that that your faith-based rehabilitation is very inspirational and motivational.

Your friend,

Richard B.

My Experience with the Oasis Chapel

I was one of Chaplain Jack's inmate clerks for the faith-based rehabilitation program mentioned in this book. Prior to this job, I had also been actively involved with the Oasis Chapel. This was one of the most significant and defining moments of my life, for not only had I been undergoing a profound personal transformation, but also had the good fortune of becoming involved with this program, which encouraged me in my own transformation. I had been involved with other prison chapel programs prior to my time with Oasis Chapel, but I'd never seen a program quite like this one. The sheer number of inmates who were regularly involved with the programs Chaplain Jack had brought to the chapel, such as Rick Warren's *40 Days of the Purpose Driven Life* and Celebrate Recovery, spoke volumes about these life changing programs that challenged the inmates to contemplate their lives and gave them the tools and skills necessary to forge a meaningful life where there was none before. I'd never seen so many inmates involved with any prison chapel program- and CCC and its chapel is a only a small- to medium-size prison, as far as most California prisons go.

It's a rarity for most prison inmates to regularly attend chapel. Sure, there is always a core group of regular attendees, but these usually number very few. But at the Oasis Chapel, *scores* of inmates were not only active and enthusiastic participants but attending nearly every night of the week. There was always something going on at the chapel, and they were eager to go every chance they got.

Why would so many prison inmates be so enthralled with chapel? It is because Chaplain Jack truly cared about them, and *they knew it*. Prison staff (including civilian staff, as well as correctional staff) and inmates are naturally at odds with one another, but in Chaplain Jack, the inmates found a true friend and mentor, someone who accepted them, encouraged them, believed in them, challenged them, and saw them not as criminals, as "undesirables," but as people with potential and talents. He saw them as worthwhile people who could contribute to society and whom society would want. Most of these inmates had never known such things as acceptance and encouragement, and for the first time in their lives, they could see hope. Along with the faith-based programs, Chaplain Jack also facilitated quite an elaborate music program, consisting of a full-scale men's choir and band. During the Christmas holiday, the inmates were able to produce, entirely by themselves, a Christmas play and musical production, replete with multimedia, also produced by inmates. From the initial scripting and conception to the final presentation, these inmates from diverse backgrounds came together, believed in themselves and in each other, laid aside their differences, and created something of beauty. Again, many of these inmates had never produced anything like this in their lives, had never even thought they were capable of such an accomplishment. All it took was someone who cared enough.

My own life has been completely turned around from the ruin it was, and this is largely because of the opportunity and caring I received from Chaplain Jack. I'm honored and enriched because of him.

- KevinJue

To those interested, my name is Buck Steele, and I had bee:n serving as a religious volunteer for thirteen years when Jack Carmichael became chaplain of CCC at Susanville, California. One of the first things I became aware of as a volunteer working with Jack was that I was once again privileged to be working with a man with a vision, not a job. I've worked under people, 11bosses" with jobs, and the job mentality is evident from the time the day starts until it ends. Men or women with jobs punch in and punch out to go do better or more important things. Unfortunately, I've worked under a few religious professionals who saw their call as a job and treated it as such. Jack didn't have a job; he had a passion to see the inmates he was given oversight of grow in their relationship with God. This was evident in the vast amount of overtime Jack put in to get programs like the Purpose-Driven Life and Celebrate Recovery implemented and functioning on as regular a schedule as possible.

Jack was determined to see these men develop into spiritually minded men, men who, with the understanding and skills needed, could learn to walk out their responsibility as men of God. With developed integrity and defined purpose, these men would become equipped to function in their roles as husbands, fathers, and friends. Unfortunately, the way I saw it, anyway, Jack's biggest opposition came from the correctional system itself, a system more designed and operating out of a sense of warehousing and punishing inmates, rather than rehabilitating them. This opposition came more often than not in the form of closing down the religious programs for one excuse after another. I use the term excuse, because very seldom have I seen a real reason to shut down programs. The most often-used excuse was being short of staff. I know that on account of budget cuts and reduction of academy training and so on, there are difficulties in staffing. But when you are told the reason for shutting down the program for the day or weekend is on account of being understaffed, and you walk by the watch sergeant's office and see four to six men standing inside, talking and drinking coffee, it sends a more realistic message, one whose bottom line is rooted in the job verses vision mind-set. When all you have is a job, you tend to not care about anyone but yourself, and so anything that might add anything extra to a so-called job description is often resented and viewed as a burden, rather than an opportunity to serve.

Another form of opposition came from within. By that I mean there were-and always will be-men within the core of professing believers who outwardly appear to be spiritually minded and interested in their spiritual development but who are still holding fast to their will and self-centered desires. These men made

Jack's life and mission difficult on several occasions, primarily on account of the truth that "your sins will find you out." When these men's sins found them out, the hypocrite shock waves would hit and fuel the fire of the already antagonistic mind sets of the Cos, who were already resistant to religious programming. Don't get me wrong here; there are a good number of COs with a heart to see these inmates develop into better men, and they show it by their support.

Despite the perpetual resistance from both the physical and spiritual realms, I saw some great changes occur in the lives of a lot of men on account of God's grace working through a man with a heart to see transformation in the lives of men, who were considered by many to be incorrigible. Jack believed all men could be saved and made better, and he demonstrated it in his love for the inmate.

- Buck Steele

Words of commendation regarding the faith-based program at CCC I was a volunteer at California Correctional Center during the time that Chaplain Carmichael served as the

Protestant chaplain. The respect that the Men in Blue had for 11Chappy," as they called him, was remarkable. Respect and appreciation would best characterize the men's response to their chaplain friend and mentor.

The programming had a consistent thread that recognized and honored the power of God in changing the lives of men who had come to the institution feeling hopeless. Chaplain Carmichael is a man who has a unique understanding and appreciation for tihe life each man is attempting to rebuild.. Years after some were paroled, the men who were especially touched by Chappy and the faith-based rehabilitation program maintain ongoing contact with their friend and model for living a responsible adult life.

Chappy is a man who has consistently demonstrated that God can make a way where there is no way. Jack is to be honored for his commitment to substantive change; God is to be praised for making the change.

-Jeff Anderson

Volunteer at California Correctional

Center

Five years with "Chappy Jack" added a huge dimension to my life and hundreds of others seeking a better life... now. Thirty years of traditional 11Church" had lulled me into a saved and satisfied mentality. Looking back, it's easy to see that most Christians attending services once or twice a week don't connect on a personal level and share their hurts, habits, addictions, or even their everyday successes and setbacks. I had no idea of the behaviors and baggage that I was carrying around. This is the result of many factors, and result is separation from your family, neighbors, and God. Probably the vast majority of churchgoers are just spectators and are reluctant to become part of the team/body of Christ.

Faith-based rehab opens avenues of growth and provides the average person with tools to overcome barriers in our physical life and our spiritual counterpart. We discovered that everybody is in denial about some behavior. Most of our negative behaviors are legal, but the results are the same as the illegal ones. We had all tried to change our issues with little permanent success.

When we experienced 40 Days of *Purpose Driven Life*, the truths of the Bible, we got an astounding look at his divine plan. It was with a sigh of relief when we learned that each day of our journey has great purpose. I didn't know what had happened until looking back, I knew what I have is that ({freedom" from bondage that God promised. Praise him!

Then the group therapy of Celebrate Recovery was and is the crowning revelation of what I am, who I am, and what I can be today. The kingdom of heaven is at hand.

We believe because we have tasted, and it is good. No words can describe the rest that we have entered.

-Frank Katanic

Little Country Church

Pastor Bryan Blank

Where restoration through Christ can be found (Luke4: 18, 19).

My wife and I have been doing in-prison events for the past twenty-eight years. And that is the very thing that caused us to come in contact with Jack Carmichael. It was 2006, and he was the new chaplain at the California Correctional Center in Susanville. From the first time we met Jack, we knew that there was an energy and zeal for the Men in Blue that is rare today. He came on board with a passion for teaching men to be real men.

Jack put programs together to take the new believer and usher him into full maturity, as well as taking the mature believer and giving him a vision for the future man God intended him to be. He started Celebrate Recovery, and Purpose Driven Life, and Passport to Purpose. He brought as many ministry teams as time would allow into the chapel to enhance what he already had going on. He taught the men to function as a team and look beyond the prison games and politics. He was, in every sense of the word, a father to the men at the correctional center. He never made distinctions between races or creeds. He once told me that Jesus came to save all men, not just the ones we thought deserved it.

All the while, he was lobbying the community to support the chapel program, not only at CCC but also at High Desert State Prison in Susanville and Herlong Federal Prison. He looked for support for programs, books, Bibles, and other materials for all three chapel programs. He looked for and got someone to donate chairs to the chapel, so that the old pews could be taken out, thus making it more user-friendly for large classes and small-group interaction.

Jack Carmichael always took a no nonsense approach to everything he did. And because of that, the men knew that they could trust and rely on him, never having to wonder if he was for real. Every service that was held in the chapel was full to overflowing, and every man who spent any time at all in the chapel loved and respected him.

Jack Carmichael is one of the most interesting people I have ever met. Not only is he brilliant, but he is also very humble and kind. And I, for one, miss his quick smile and kind word when I am privileged to be at the chapel.

-Roger Ralston

Little Country Church

My letter to Jack Carmichael, for all that I learned from an amazing man:

First off, Jack gave me more than my words will ever describe, but I will try. When I was sent to prison, I knew it would be life-changing, but never thought it would be to change my life for the better. Jack gave me a job as his clerk to run the attendance programs for all the different religious groups, but it turned out to be a whole more than that. My first group that I attended with Jack was a select group of inmates he chose to attend a round circle group of ten men. He brought out a piece of paper with a shield on it and told everyone to write four different thoughts at four different times in their lives, which we all did. One was, "Tell me about the worst time you had from the age of ten to fourteen." We started to all explain this time in our lives, when Jack had to leave to attend to prison inmate count. As he left, he instructed me to keep the group talking but try to keep answers to ten minutes. When he left and came back, the same young man was talking. He looked at me as if to say, uwhat happened? Can't keep track of time?" It had been about thirty minutes. Then he heard the young man talk about being molested and raped by his father for years, and Jack knew why we were all quiet and why he was still talking. This was the start of Jack's stretching me to become a real Christian-that it was always about the other person. This is what I would call Jack's personal life's reflection; it was always about everyone else. There was God and his son, Jesus, then everyone else, and then himself.Jack didn't just teach; he made teachers of everyone else.

He allowed anyone and everyone to have a time to talk, a time to teach, and a time to love. The programs he established made life-changing differences in people's lives. He didn't rely on simple emotional games that would last minutes; he gave you real life useable programs, from financial to spiritual.

The programs that we used could teach whatever you were in need of besides a broken spirit. Real-life applications, along with a mended spirit, was what you left with when you left Jack. He changed my life in so many ways, not just from years of bad religious teaching but also from so many bad habits of life in general. I came away not just refreshed from being in prison, but from life in general. I apply every day what I learned from Jack and the wonderful place he made within one of the worst places to be. Only a very special person could have accomplished this, and this is why that place will never be the same without him. Jack is an inspiration to mankind. If we could learn one thing from him it is that this world is about others, not ourselves. Imagine what this world would be like if we could just think that way for a few moments in a day.

Thank you, Jack Carmichael, with all my love,

-Todd

On November 18, 2004, I was found guilty as charged on several counts.

There is a quote that says, "It's always darkest before God's greatest miracles." I knew this was the consequence of my actions, but I knew nothing about sin. Despite the verdict, I had surrendered it all to God, and I knew I had to continue to fully trust in Him. "For I know the plans I have for you," says the Lord. "They are plans for good and not for disaster, to give you a future and a hope."

In a courtroom nightmare that my words don't nearly capture, the judge showed no mercy as he hammered the gavel down.

I stared ten years of incarceration down the barrel that day and walked out of the courtroom in handcuffs on my way to pnson.

At some point, I knew I had to start believing in miracles.

There was a moment of complete silence as my kids had to witness their dad being sentenced, humiliated, and deeply embraced, but it was only a brief moment. I wish I could tell you that I walked out of that courtroom and felt God's embrace, but my recovery didn't end with a courtroom miracle. Within hours, the verdict and sentence became public knowledge and was highly publicized.

Fear of the unknown replaced the joy and freedom I longed for with Christ.

I was battling with depression, shame, and low self-esteem all over again. Uncertain as to where I would end up or what prison they'd put me in, I lived in a state of fear for months, awaiting and hoping for a miracle.

Mter all, God does miracles, right?

Ironically, a place that once plagued me with fear was about to change my life.

I had the unique opportunity to be sent to a CDC fire camp facility. Being that I was a first-timer and serving a half-time sentence, I was told by my appointed prison counselor thatI would get out earlier now, due to becoming a fire fighter -this would reduce my sentence by a third.

The constant blows seemed crushing, as life simply appeared to be a cruel, vicious, and emotional roller-coaster ride that I created and that I brought upon myself. Even while evaluating my past relationships and trying to make amends, all of my efforts were met with less than favorable responses that I would simply rather not repeat.

I can honestly tell you that I cried more in prison in one week over my past actions than I had in my entire childhood, often curled up on my bunk, trying hard to trust in the words I still display in my bedroom, "Be thankful; be patient."

I still don't know why God spared me, but I do know that his Word teaches me that with much given, much is now expected.

I was introduced into the Oasis Chapel by a man named Ken Ackerman, as he was the working clerk for the chaplain.

Ken seemed to be content working at the chapel and always was happy-go-lucky.

He invited me to be a part of the church, and I took part in some of the programs, such as Celebrate Recovery.

I signed up immediately and joined in on the Celebrate Recovery groups:

During that time, I held tight to the biblical principles of recovery and worked the steps in my step study by openly examining and confessing my inventory of past wrongs and voluntarily submitting to the changes God wanted to make in my life. Those principles not only allowed God to heal large wounds in my life, but they also laid a solid foundation on which to grow.

By mid-November, I was asked to lead a group, but almost right away, things became more and more difficult. Some of the facilitators/group leaders started manipulating many facets of the program by spreading bad rumors and arguing within the many groups.

To add even more insult to injury, many men quit and/or dropped out.

In fact, I stood up at the altar and argued why I should walk out.

As I stepped down with my tail between my legs, something amazing happened.

While locked inside my dorm, several men were asking for me.

"Don't quit!" At least twenty men I'd never met begged me to stay!

The next morning, I found myself before the chaplain (Jack Carmichael).

In his own way, he tore into me. "Never do that again!"

At first I was taken back. *Doesn't he know who I am?* I was hurt, and I felt betrayed.

I learned many times, the hard way, that my personal feelings rubbed Chaplain Jack (Chappy) the wrong way.

Finally, my big day was approaching. I was going to fire camp. When I arrived for my interview, I was denied, flat out. At the same time, I was humiliated by the acting associate warden, regardless of my counselor assuring me that I would be accepted. Later, he told me that the associate warden was drunk and belligerent.

He even argued that just before I entered the room for the interview, I was already approved and would be going to fire camp.

What I didn't know/understand at the time would prove that God was at work in my life.

Oddly enough, I never flinched or got the least bit angry over the issue. Actually, I could have filed a 602 (argued my case). My counselor kept at me, but I never did. Many people felt I should have, especially for the sake of my kids.

A stranger CO prison guard asked me, "What do you anchor yourself to?" I didn't think much about it at the time, but later that night, I searched my heart for an answer. What he said was true, about anchoring yourself to people who will break promises and even unknowingly hurt you. About being anchored to this life, to hopes and dreams that may never see the light of day. All my life I've prayed. I've always felt that there must be something more than this world. Something always reminds me that I cannot do this on my own.At times, I've felt very close to God - a comfort that held all the pieces of this life for me in place. Other times, though, I've felt entirely abandoned and lost- an anchor too light to grab hold of anything substantial enough to keep me from drifting aimlessly, from running aground and wrecking.

My life is not perfect. I still go through the normal stresses of life, but I thank the Lord for the outpouring of peace that I have now. God's guidance of mercy leads me to discover all his promises.

I now believe Jeremiah 29:11: "For I know the plans I have for you, declares the Lord, plans to prosper you and not to harm you, plans to give you hope and a future."

I have found my purpose in life. I have begun to acknowledge my strengths , and with courage am taking on life in an assertive way. Despite losing many years with my kids

I am hopeful we will grow closer. In the meantime I am blessed and content to live life as God has planned it to be. After all God knows best.

Things would have been easier if I could have felt a miraculous force of the divine Spirit come upon me and change my apprehensive way of thinking and living. But if that had happened, then what would have been the point of my afflictions and struggles? The death of my best friend and losing everything was not in vain. If I had never gone through these tribulations and adversities know now.

I wouldn't have the privileges I My passion in life now is to give back to others all the blessings I have experienced - to assist or inspire anyone who is struggling with hardships inlife, to offer them hope in themselves and hope in God.

These days I feel like my anchor is a bit heavier. I've been tried and tested countless times, and my faith, fragile though it may be at times, remains a lighthouse to illuminate my darkest corners. I do anchor myself in God and undoubtedly believe that he has had to remind me in the most radical of ways that, although I may be the captain, he is the owner of this ship.

I'm far from being where I need to be spiritually, and even farther from understanding even the smallest part of his plans. Was my life saved, and was I pulled from the wreckage of crushed metal and iron to spend the rest of it behind steel doors and brick walls? Will the tragic mistakes I've made and the undeserving hearts I've scarred leave me forever in seclusion at the bottom of this sea? I don't know. Some days I see a great light again and have this beautiful feeling of surfacing ...and then I wake. And in the wake of my dreams, I wonder what this world wants of me. If only to peek inside my soul and see the truth in all its conquering reverie, maybe then some days I'll be free.

In the voices and written words of the people in my life, I hear of such emptiness. The world outside has taken such a toll, and the people they've trusted have only disappointed. I hear of the great struggle of survival and the problems with money, work, and lovers. I know of the cages people build around themselves. I do see glimpses of happiness that breaks through the hardness but not enough to remind them of their true fortunes.

When everything you cherish is taken from you, and almost everyone you held dear is gone, you begin to reassess the value of everything. When your very freedom has vanished and all you have left is yourself, then you must look deep within yourself and contend with your heart and mind's profusions. When all the wind has disappeared from your sails, you drift ... or you anchor yourself to the one thing that will never forsake you and never break a promise made to you and will always be there when you fall from hopes so high.

479

Today, I'm living again (perhaps for the first time in my life) with many dreams and goals on my mind. My life seems to be one miracle after another. I speak openly about sexual purity, have a great job (unbelievably) back in the tree business, more true friends than I can ever recall in my life-ones with whom I can discuss real struggles with openly without fear of rejection-and I now know in my heart that everyone I know gets the "real me," the man God intended me to be.

I could go on and on and share many more examples of God"s grace and mercy in my life, but there is really only one thing I'm excited to share. When I originally wrote and shared this testimony, it was that I had fallen asleep with my pregnant wife in my arms, unsupervised, for the first time in years.

But today, what I'm excited to share most is simply my life-the highs, the lows, the frustrations and the joys-a living testimony of God's greatness. Today, I cherish the simple blessings of praying with my children, loving on them, listening to them, and simply being with them-knowing that they now get a "real" dad, the dad God intended me to be.

Today, I'm free from the crippling bondage of alcohol, manipulating others, money, adulterous behaviors, and inappropriate actions, to name a few. My sins are what I did, not who I am. I learned that from Chaplain Jack.

Thanks to so many recovery programs like Angry Heart, Under Cover, Life Connections, and many more I have experienced.

My sufferings and hardships at the Oasis Chapel set up one of the greatest blessings in my life-my personal and intimate relationship with Jesus Christ. I've learned through the step-study recovery process at Celebrate Recovery to trust in God completely. It hasn't always been easy, and I still struggle with various things today, but I've learned that God wants to work miracles in my life, and it only requires my faith. Today, I tithe, fast, pray, and worship but not because it might look good to the outside world.

Today, when no one is watching and no one is there, I talk to Christ, and that has completely changed my life.

Second Corinthians 5:17 says, "Therefore if anyone is in Christ, he is a new creature; the old things passed away; behold, new things have come." The miracle in my life is a changed heart. It's a different look at life and a better understanding of life's purpose-a hope to smile again, a hope to laugh again, and a hope to finally live again through Jesus Christ.

Thanks for letting me share and celebrate with you.

-Charlie T.

About the Author

This is the personal account and experience of an army airborne chaplain who volunteered at two California state prisons as a volunteer chaplain and as a Protestant chaplain at the California Correctional Center in Susanville. Mr. Carmichael is eminently qualified to share his prison experiences and observations. After fifty years as an ordained minister with army airborne chaplain's experience, administrator in private and public colleges for twenty years, and local church pastoral experience of thirty years, he discovered prison ministry. It was the highlight of all his life experience. Mr. Carmichael lives in the Honey Lake/ Susanville area of Northern California and relishes the majestic view and outside living available at his home.

About the Book

In April 2005, two days after my seventy sixth birthday, I became the Protestant chaplain at California Correctional Center in Susanville, California. The warden hired me for the job of creating a faith-based rehabilitation program, taught by inmates, supported by unpaid outside volunteers.

It was anticipated that it could be a reha bilitation program for the twenty-six state prisons in California, as well a challenge for the myriad jails and prisons through out the United States.

To overcome the warehousing model of incarcerating and housing inmates in pris ons throughout most prison systems, it is imperative that inexpensive programs be developed to counteract the chilling effect of sparse and ineffective free-time support for the inmate population.

California recidivism rates in state prisons exceed 80 percent. It is expected that it's much the same across the United States. Something needs to be done to counteract this, and the CCC model is one attempt to do it. Included in this book are anecdotal examples and testimonies that point to this possibility.

The challenges, or 11barrels,11 related in this attempt to change the recidivism rate at one institution tell us it won't be easy. New ideas are hard to come by in prison; "the old, and tried and failed" to often have the upper hand in the operation of state pris ons in California.

As you follow my story, you will see how and who are the advocates and foes of change in the way prisons are operated.

The story told here can benefit the families of the more than one million inmates in the prisons and jails in America. It can provide insights into the prison life for the students in the correctional curriculums in the colleges and

485

universities of America. If the book were read by the personnel in the administration of state prisons, they might be challenged to work to change the climate in their jails and prisons.